Bribery and Extortion
in World Business

BRIBERY AND EXTORTION IN WORLD BUSINESS

A Study of
Corporate Political Payments Abroad

Neil H. Jacoby
Peter Nehemkis
Richard Eells

Studies of the Modern Corporation
Graduate School of Business
Columbia University

MACMILLAN PUBLISHING CO., INC.
NEW YORK

Collier Macmillan Publishers
LONDON

Macmillan Publishing Co., Inc.
866 Third Avenue, New York, N.Y. 10022

Collier Macmillan Canada, Ltd.

Library of Congress Catalog Card Number: 77–6942

Printed in the United States of America

printing number

1 2 3 4 5 6 7 8 9 10

Library of Congress Cataloging in Publication Data

Jacoby, Neil Herman
   Bribery and extortion in world business.

   Includes index.
     1. Corporations--Corrupt practice. 2. Bribery.
3. International business enterprises. I. Nehemkis,
Peter Raymond, joint author. II. Eells, Richard Sedric
Fox   joint author. III. Title.
HV6768.J3   364.1'32   77-6942
ISBN 0-02-916000-6

The authors acknowledge with thanks the use (in chapter 1) of material originally presented in "Business Payoffs Abroad: Rhetoric and Reality," by Peter Nehemkis, © 1975 by the Regents of the University of California. Reprinted from *California Management Review*, vol. XVIII, no. 2, pp. 5–20, by permission of the Regents.

Contents

Contents

Contents

Contents

Preface

For some years prior to the recent revelations about corporate bribery and government corruption, each of the authors had had an interest in the problem presented to corporate officers by the demands of foreign political figures for payoffs from American businesses. A meaningful study of these payments and the conditions under which they had been made, however, only became possible with the publication of a wide spectrum of information about them in 1975 and 1976.

The original idea of publishing a book on foreign political payments by U.S. corporations was Professor Eells's, and the first study papers for a book were prepared by him. The initial versions of chapters 3, 4, and 8 were drafted by Professor Jacoby; of chapters 1, 2, 5, and 7 by Professor Nehemkis; and of the introduction and chapter 6 by Professor Eells. All three authors participated in the writing and integration of the book, so that it is completely the joint product of all three.

The authors are indebted to many people who have contributed to the research for, as well as the writing and production of, this book. We are particularly happy to express our appreciation to the many scholarly colleagues and business executives who attended conferences at which many of the ideas in this book were discussed and clarified.

The authors gratefully acknowledge the perceptive research, writing, and editing of Chauncey G. Olinger, Jr., who worked with them throughout the writing and production of the book. They also wish to acknowledge the scholarly work of Dr. Douglas B. Ball and Paul Levinson on a number of special research projects for the book.

Appreciation is also due to Pamela G. Constable, Carla R. Dragan, and Caroline E. Gaynor, who assisted with the editing of the book. The authors are especially appreciative of the dedicated work of Adelyn Hickman and Marilyn McElroy, who conscientiously typed several versions of the manuscript, and of Solomon Jones, who assisted in the production of the manuscript.

Finally, for any errors or omissions that remain, the authors are, of course, solely responsible.

Neil H. Jacoby
Peter Nehemkis
Richard Eells

Los Angeles and New York City
March 15, 1977

Introduction

In this book we examine an important aspect of international business that has been singularly neglected. One will search in vain among treatises on world business for any discussion of bribery, extortion, and other political payments by business enterprises. Political payments by multinational companies in foreign nations have long been a pervasive practice; but a cultural taboo against discussion of the subject, combined with a lack of public information, has created a vacuum in public understanding. Only recently have events in the United States thrust this subject to the forefront of national attention.

Our purpose here is to examine this phenomenon objectively, to explore its historical roots in national cultures, and to propose actions to reduce political payments in the future. We believe that these payments impede the efficient operation of markets and worsen the allocation of the world's resources, and that the world would be better without them. We seek mainly to understand and explain this behavior, rather than to justify or condemn it. Because conduct judged improper or illegal in one culture may be considered quite proper—even unavoidable—in other cultures, we have been chary of making moral judgments. Thus, we have sought to avoid the twin pitfalls of arrogant ethnocentrism and moral absolutism.

Morality and Reality

Corporate morality is a highly sensitive subject, and, like all discussions of morals and ethics, it can quickly inflame our emotions. It is also a subject of great complexity—much more so than is commonly understood. Viewed broadly and objectively, the subject of political payments in world business raises a number of interrelated issues: How can the conflicting customs and business practices of various nations be harmonized? Are political payments abroad necessary to the successful pursuit of prosperity for the enterprise and a favorable balance of payments for the nation? If American companies operating abroad abandoned the making of political payments, would this confer great benefits on foreign corporations competing with them in host countries? Is bribery (in more or less subtle forms) not inherent in government aid programs to other countries? Is bribery also not an accepted practice in the foreign intelligence activities of governments? And if the last two questions have affirmative answers, is it reasonable to hold multinational corporations to a different standard of morality? In other words, should foreign political payments made by a government in the name of national security be condoned, when similar payments made by a corporation to advance American economic interests overseas are vigorously denounced?

In a recent article, Irving Kristol explored the problem of morality in U.S. foreign policy. After noting the rising public criticism of American foreign policy for its alleged *lack* of moral substance, Kristol observed that these critics lack a mature understanding of the relationship between moral ideals and reality. He wrote:

> Self-righteousness flourishes where personal involvement and personal responsibility are minimal. But ever since . . . our emergence as a great power, we have discovered that "moral idealism" has to make its own way in a world that is not particularly hospitable to it.

... there is no unequivocal "moral" answer to our social and economic problems. These problems are complex, and so the relation between reality and morality will also be complex. Doing the "right" thing cannot be divorced from doing the effective thing. And, to complicate matters even further, doing the "right" thing in one respect always means doing the "wrong" thing in other respects.[1]

These words are peculiarly applicable to the phenomenon of corporate political payments abroad, which are, in a sense, an aspect of American foreign policy, albeit lacking in official status. The self-righteousness with which they have been condemned by critics in Congress and in the media matches the unthinking condemnation of American foreign policy by moral absolutists. In the complex reality of today's world, conflicting moral principles are involved. Which principle should be given top priority, in particular circumstances, often poses a difficult problem to the responsible decision maker, however clear the answer may seem to be to the critic far from the scene of action. Thus the principle that no foreign political payments shall be made often collides with the principles that we should expand international trade and investment, that multinational companies should conform to local business practices, that the United States should avoid extraterritorial application of its laws, or that this country should abjure moral as well as political and economic imperialism. In this connection it is interesting to note that after long condemning foreign political payments by U.S. companies, the *New York Times* concluded in an editorial on February 23, 1977, that ". . . qualified discretion is preferable to unqualified morality. In a volatile world, the need for flexibility is great."[2]

The Watergate Affair and Its Aftermath

As American business burgeoned around the world after World War II, it found itself everywhere required to adjust to local business practices. One of the most troublesome to American businessmen was the intense demand from politicians in many countries for payments to secure and protect business investments, and from minor governmental officials for facilitating payments to induce them to perform their official duties. Because such payments are viewed askance in the United States, accepted accounting practices were often skirted to conceal them. Not until the Watergate affair and the subsequent investigations by the Securities and Exchange Commission did the extent of questionable payments and accounting practices come to the attention of Congress and the public.

The revelation that American companies were making payments to foreign political parties and government officials touched a sensitive nerve in the post-Watergate era. Although most knowledgeable people were aware of the bribery of domestic government officials, they felt more keenly about the payment of millions of dollars to foreign officials. Somehow, it seemed to diminish the image that Americans wished other peoples to have of them, that America played an idealistic role in foreign affairs.

Over the years, waves of public concern about corruption in the business-government relationship have swept over the nation. The most recent wave was involved primarily with the financing of political campaigns. It began to rise in the 1960s and crested in the post-Watergate era of the early 1970s. The financing of political campaigns had been on the nation's agenda of needed reforms for many years. The Corrupt Practices Act—forbidding contributions to political campaigns by corporations and labor unions—had been widely violated for decades. But there was now a rising public demand to put an end to this unsavory condition.

Curiously, the Finance Committee to Re-elect the President during 1972 gave little heed to this new concern. It proceeded to make the most aggressive efforts to extract political contributions from the business community that the country had ever seen, paying scant attention to laws long on the books.

In the spring of 1972 came the notorious Watergate break-in. During the investigation by the Watergate Special Prosecutor, it was discovered that American Airlines had made a $55,000 contribution from corporate funds. When this was announced, Archibald Cox, the Special Prosecutor, called on all corporate officers to disclose voluntarily any illegal political contributions. Then, in the summer of 1973, the Finance Committee to Re-Elect the President was required to reveal the names of companies that had made illegal political contributions.

This led the Securities and Exchange Commission to investigate these companies to determine whether there had been any violations of federal securities laws. Its investigation revealed falsification of records and secret slush funds, used not only for domestic political contributions but also for questionable *foreign* payments. In the year following the spring of 1974, the SEC took injunctive actions against nine companies, leading to consent decrees. More important, it invited all registered U.S. companies to voluntarily disclose any questionable foreign payments or accounting practices. By March 1977, some 360 companies had done so.

The number of companies reporting questionable or illegal foreign payments was small in comparison with the more than 9,000 firms registered with the SEC or the more than 30,000 firms engaged in overseas trade or investment. And the total amount of payments by these 360 companies was negligible in relation to their gross receipts. Still, the fact that major American corporations had been involved in questionable moral behavior indicated to many Americans that the nation confronted a serious problem.

Introduction

The Organization of This Book

The time has come for a careful and objective examination of bribery, extortion, and other political payments in world business. An effort is needed to arrive at a set of judgments that incorporate all of the relevant factors in a complex equation. On the basis of a firm grasp of the sociocultural, political, and economic aspects of political payments, we attempt to provide national governments and multinational companies with guidelines to shape their behavior along lines that will minimize corruption in the future.

In striving to achieve these goals, we begin in Part I by describing the nature of the problem: the social environments around the world in which political payments occur, the investigations that brought them to light, and their many forms, modes of payment, and purposes. In Part II we analyze the phenomenon of political payments from economic, political, and ethical perspectives. These analyses lay the groundwork for Part III of the book, which addresses the question: What should be done? Here we present a critique of various reform proposals that have been made by governmental officials and others. Because we find many of these proposals to be ineffective, we then present our own recommendations for actions by multinational corporations and governments, which could, over time, materially reduce corporate political payments.

In the first two parts of the book, we have endeavored to be descriptive and analytical. In the final part, however, we have made our own values clear. Although they unavoidably reflect our Western cultural origins and affinities, we hope that they also reflect our deep concern to take into account the history, culture, attitudes, and beliefs of other nations. In our steadily shrinking and increasingly interdependent world, there is an imperative need to approach all judgments about international affairs with humility and tolerance.

Introduction

Boundaries of the Study

In focusing attention on the *foreign political* payments made by American enterprises, our study does not attempt to deal with *commercial* bribery—improper transactions between business firms—whether domestic or international. Nor does it comprehend corruption in business relationships with labor unions or institutions other than governments, either in American or foreign societies. These are important fields for ethical investigation, but they lie outside the boundaries of this study.

This book is written from the perspective of American companies doing business in other nations of the world. However, much of what we say is equally applicable to the multinational corporations based in *other countries,* and to the governments of the countries in which they do business.

On Semantics

We have frequently used the term "political payments," or some variant of it, to identify the range of transactions examined in this book. This term has been deliberately chosen in order to avoid semantic ethnocentrism and cover the full range of these payments. "Bribery," "extortion," "kickback," "payoff," and "graft" have pejorative meanings and associations in American usage, denoting and connoting as they do transactions that are, or are considered to be, illegal, immoral, or at least suspect. Indeed, the American media have often lumped all political payments indiscriminately into the one category of "bribes," which is a serious error. More sophisticated observers, seeking to avoid prejudicial terms, have made use of such euphemisms as "questionable" or "sensitive" payments. However, these terms lack descriptive content.

The second reason for our frequent use of "political payments" is that it covers the chosen ground, whereas "bribery" or "extortion," or both combined, do not. For example, a contribution by the Canadian affiliate of an American corporation to a Canadian political party is perfectly lawful, and, if made voluntarily without threat or coercion or promise of favor, is neither a bribe nor an extortion. But it is a political payment, as we have defined it.

Limitations of the Data

A problem confronting anyone dealing with this subject is the lack of systematic factual information about the extent of political payments by multinational companies. Because there are laws in most countries against extortion and bribery, many political payments have been concealed. Nor does any nation publish an "index of corruption" that reveals the trend of such payments over time. We have made an extensive search for evidence of such payments in many countries. Evidence has come from reports in news media and in court records of charges, indictments, and convictions on account of improper business payments to public officials and organizations. Evidence has been found in the reports of domestic and foreign governmental investigations. It has come from the authors' interviews with executives of multinational firms. By the nature of the subject, most of this evidence consists of case studies rather than systematic and complete data. On the other hand, we are satisfied that it has in the aggregate "the ring of truth," and that it fairly presents the state of affairs in the world. Our confidence in this belief is fortified by the personal experience of the authors over many years, variously as directors, advisors, or staff members of multinational business corporations, or as members of the staffs of the SEC or other federal government agencies.

The Global Interest in Resolving the Problem of Political Payments

A solution to the problem of political payments by multinational companies is important to the United States. Indeed, it could make a significant contribution to a prosperous world economy. Multinational corporate business has grown enormously since World War II in response to global demands for the international transmission of capital, management skills, and technology. More than $120 billion has been invested abroad by U.S.-based multinational companies alone during the quarter-century from 1950 to 1975. This investment has probably done more to improve living standards, in the less-developed as well as in the more-developed nations, than the approximately equal amount of U.S. government economic aid extended within the same period of time.

Today, multinational business is under attack by socialist and other critics on a wide spectrum of issues. New charges that multinational firms corrupt the officials of foreign governments have been added to the litany of criticism. Many governments, especially those of the Third World, have taken or threaten to take punitive and restrictive actions against foreign companies. Such measures would impede international investment, slow down economic progress, and damage the economic welfare of all countries concerned. It has become urgent, therefore, to remove this basis of criticism of multinational corporate behavior, and thereby to enhance its potential contribution to the world economy.

Concluding Note

As this book went to the publisher in April of 1977, a bill endorsed by the Carter Administration was pending in the U.S. Congress that would penalize an employee of an American corporation for bribing a foreign government official. For the reasons developed in this book, we believe that such legislation would be unwise and ineffective, and that other measures, which we have proposed here, should be taken to deal with the problem.

PART I

Description of the Problem

1

Political Payments
Around the World

Since 1950, American enterprises have invested in virtually every part of the world. Their annual exports in 1976 were more than $117 billion, and their foreign investments in book value were about $133 billion. This unparalleled international movement of goods, capital, technology, and managerial resources has had both successes and failures, but the former have by far outweighed the latter.

As U.S. companies have crossed national boundaries to trade or invest, they have found themselves operating under complex and unfamiliar sociocultural, economic, political, and legal conditions. Each environment has imposed unique constraints on corporate managers. The successes achieved by U.S. firms have reflected their managerial flexibility and their ability to adapt to varied environments and cultures. Where American companies have experienced failures—apart from faulty business or financial judgments—the reason can often be attributed to American ethnocentrism, to a belief that American customs, attitudes, and values are su-

3

perior to local customs, traditions, and accepted ways of doing business.[1]

The rewards of successful management have accrued to those American executives who have demonstrated psychological and intellectual flexibility in adapting to new situations in foreign environments. But when these managers have displayed these characteristics in accomodating themselves to foreign business practices that are different from those (officially) proclaimed in the United States, they have often received a verbal cat-o'-nine-tails from the media, Congressmen, and the Securities and Exchange Commission.

The Pervasiveness of Political Payments

Political payments are institutionalized facts of international business. In almost every country in which they have ventured as investors or traders, American businessmen have encountered the phenomenon of the payoff—the practice of bribing government officials as a condition of doing business, of government employees extorting money as a condition of the performance of their official duties, of government employees expecting—indeed, demanding—kickbacks on contracts awarded in pursuance of their discretionary power, of politicians extracting campaign contributions for their parties and campaigns, frequently under duress or threats to the security of investments.

Unlike the United States, in which the majority of corporate managers have little direct contact with government and its administrators, the conduct of business overseas involves frequent personal relationships by corporate managers with government officials at all levels. International business would be unable to function without the cooperation of the lower-tier functionaries who provide the governmental services on which business depends. They process goods, ma-

chinery, and raw materials through customs. They issue visas
and work permits for company personnel. They grant permits
to build plants or additions to existing facilities. They issue
authorizations for oil rigs to enter territorial waters and for
their offshore anchorage. They clear the papers that enable
an investor to acquire foreign currency in order to pay an exporter in some other country for an air or sea shipment of raw
materials or manufacturing equipment. They approve the
repatriation of capital and the remittance of dividends and
royalties to a parent company. They can expedite or delay the
release of an investment agreement or of an agreed waiver of
taxes. They can accelerate or retard the receipt of cash
needed for the training of local workers. They can interpret
an ancient law in ways that will cripple the operations of the
business; or, in their discretion, in ways that facilitate operations. They can supply or withhold police or military units for
plant protection in remote parts of a country. They can help
clarify misunderstandings in the application of local labor,
health, or sanitation codes.

And these are just a small sample of the many ways in
which a local bureaucracy can affect an overseas business.
These administrative services ought, from an American perspective, to be made available to foreign businessmen as a
matter of convenience and as a legitimate right. In practice,
however, in most countries they are not forthcoming unless
the local functionary is provided with a "token of appreciation." Few companies doing business abroad can escape this
toll; even the majestic IBM Corporation has been forced to
make a few such payments.[2] Although individual "lubrication" payments may be nominal, their cumulative total over a
period of years can be substantial.

Lubrication payments are not subject to a going rate. They
are usually determined by what the traffic will bear. The
usual way for a governmental official to extract a payment is
by threatening obstruction or delay in carrying out his official

5

duties. The anxiety of the businessman to avoid such delays —which can be very costly—induces a payoff, which, of course, is the objective of the stratagem.

Large political payments are rarely transferred directly by a principal to an upper echelon official; rather, a middleman is used. He may be a professional "fixer" who is himself a low-level government functionary; more often he will be a member of the same family as the high-level recipient. Sometimes the transfer is handled by a trusted local businessman or the local agent of the payer, a native who enjoys the confidence of the recipient. In the Middle East, only a person in the confidence of the recipient will be entrusted with the negotiation of the amount of the political payment and the method of delivery.

Politicians "on the take" generally designate a numbered Swiss bank account as the depository for a payment, although Japanese politicians seem to prefer to be paid in yen and to receive the funds directly. In making a payment to the former Honduran President-General, Oswaldo Lopez Arellano, United Brands deposited $1.25 million in a numbered Swiss bank account. Prince Bernhard's $1.1 million "commission"— he had originally solicited a $4 million payment to facilitate a contract from the Dutch government to Lockheed—was channeled through a Swiss lawyer and deposited in installments during 1960 and 1962 in a numbered Swiss bank account in the name of the husband of the Prince's late mother. The number of the Swiss bank account was supplied by Prince Bernhard to Lockheed's representative.[3]

Such payments are so much a part of nearly every culture that most languages provide a word for them. Some of these terms are:

Brazil	*jeitinho*	Greece	*baksissi*
Egypt	*baksheesh*	Honduras	*pajada*
France	*pot au vin*	Hong Kong	*hatchien*
Germany	*trink gelt*	India	*speed money*

6

Indonesia	*uong sogok*	Pakistan	*roshvat*
Iran	*roshveh*	Peru	*coima*
Italy	*bustarella*	Philippines	*lagay*
Japan	*wairo*	Soviet Union	*vzyatha*
Malaysia	*makan siap*	Thailand	*sin bone*
Mexico	*mordida*	United States	*payoff*
Nigeria	*dash*	Zaire	*tarif de verre*

But the pervasiveness of political payments is best illustrated by looking at the phenomenon in its various manifestations around the world. We begin with the Middle East where so much recent attention concerning this matter has focused.

The Middle East

The political payment is a pervasive feature of Middle Eastern life. Four centuries of Ottoman misrule fastened the habits of corruption on the Islamic world.[4] In consequence, the payment of *baksheesh* in the Arabic- and Turkish-speaking countries and of *roshveh* in Iran is deeply embedded in the social and cultural fabric of these countries.[5]

The prevalence of the political payment in the Middle East also derives from the historical presence of the all-powerful state. Typically, governments have been the major source and owner of capital, usually land, the primary dispenser of contracts, and the arbiter of the rules of trade and investment. State ownership of, and control over, much of the means of production has been an essential part of Middle Eastern economies.[6] Unlike Europe, the Middle East did not produce a politically and economically influential bourgeoisie that could act as a countervailing power to the state and its rulers.[7]

Paradoxically, as the French scholar Fernand Braudel has observed, the political payment was an accepted method by which the tyranny of the ruler and venality of his officials were curbed.[8] Political payments bought for the businessman

7

the protection of person and property that an imperfect or abusive legal system failed to provide. A minority religious or ethnic group (Jews or Christians in the Middle East, the Chinese in Southeast Asia, and the Indians in sub-Saharan Africa), who controlled and dominated trade and commerce, traditionally resorted to political payments to obtain personal security and protection for their capital and investments.

Contemporary governments in many Middle Eastern countries are not only the largest employers but also the largest investors in their economies. Like their counterparts in other Third World nations, Middle Eastern socialist-oriented regimes are inefficient and mismanaged, and they tolerate the use of the political payment by those who must deal with them.[9] And corruption is not a monopoly of government employees of the swollen state bureaucracies; businessmen who have sought contracts or concessions from the royal families that continue to rule nations have encountered the demands from some members of those families.

The Middle East is one of the world's most politically volatile regions. Nationalization of foreign investments is frequent, and taxation is high. National rivalries and the unresolved Israeli-Arab conflict contribute to the investor's political risks. Yet, despite these uncertainties, the Middle East is the fastest-growing market in the world for U.S. goods and technology. These conditions sharply challenge a corporate policy of abstaining from the making of any political payments. U.S. companies that have determined not to make political payments may be cutting themselves off from contracts that will be awarded instead to international competitors whose managements and directors possess a different sense of Middle Eastern realities. For the Middle Eastern official in a position to award a contract, the easiest way to resolve his own doubts over the efficacy of dealing with U.S. firms that must disclose a political payment, or even a payment to an agent, is *not* to deal with them! Thus, whether the determination to avoid making a political payment originates with the U.S. firm, or whether it is spared having to make a decision because a government official wishes to avoid publicity, the American company in the end may be the loser.

The sale of military equipment to Middle Eastern governments by U.S. aerospace companies invoked voluble criticism in the United States. The payment of $450,000 by Northrop to two Saudi Arabian generals, in connection with a multimillion dollar sale of fighter aircraft, focused this criticism on the role of the agent as a conduit for political payments.[10] The governments of Iran and Saudi Arabia, the two largest purchasers of U.S. arms, later instituted arrangements for the procurement of matériel *directly* by their ministries of defense. High-ranking Middle East officials also proclaimed their desire to see the middleman eliminated in arms procurement, thereby reducing the "influence factor" in the selection of military equipment.

In assessing these commendable measures, however, it is necessary to distinguish between reality and expediency. In the Middle East, words do not always mean what they appear to say. Although heads of state and defense ministers have expressed *their* desire to see the middleman eliminated in the procurement of military equipment, this will not per se bring about change. There still will be present in the ministries and departments lower-ranking officials who have influence in the selection of equipment. Frequently, these officials are technicians possessing some degree of weapons expertise. In the armament market, it is this level of official whose decision can often be bought.

Moreover, a distinction should be drawn between what high-ranking Middle Eastern officials say publicly (because they may believe it is a useful gesture to American "public opinion" or to U.S. government officials) and "political-payments-as-usual."[11] In one Middle Eastern country, the Minister of Defense repeatedly declared publicly that no "third party" would be used in the procurement of military supplies for his country's defense modernization program. Nonetheless, the Defense Council of which he was a member approved—indeed, required—that local agents be used for the procurement of military equipment.[12]

Finally, the French, British, West German, and Swedish armament contractors, who sell their wares in the Middle East and who are in direct competition with U.S. suppliers, are not obliged by their governments to disclose any information about fees and commissions paid to local agents, or whether they have used agents as conduits for political payments. Moreover, West European governments actively assist their munitions and aircraft industries in obtaining contracts. In the case of the French, it is the government itself that is frequently the supplier. And the Russians and their East European allies make their equipment available at bargain basement prices to any government willing to play the Soviet game.

Sub-Saharan Africa

Among their many problems, most sub-Saharan countries have two that are paramount and that feed on each other. The African nations that won their independence from the European colonial powers are, for the most part, uneasy confederations of tribes that are traditional enemies. The primary loyalty of their citizens is not to the state, but to the tribe and its chiefs. The political objective of the dominant tribe is to capture the country's economic power base, which is the government, and, once it has been seized, to hold on to it. The second problem of these nations, linked to the first, is political corruption. It has been called "the most destructive of Africa's moral diseases." Although this malaise is found in nearly all societies, it appears to be especially virulent south of the Sahara, except in Rhodesia and South Africa, and in Tanzania and Zambia. A European businessman with extensive African interests says, "I bribe a good deal in Uganda, some in Kenya, but not at all in Tanzania and Zambia"—a tribute to the high personal integrity of Julius Nyerere and Kenneth Kaunda, respectively, presidents of the latter two countries.[13]

Kenya

Some Kenyan politicians—not infrequently members of the government's ministries—extract political payments from foreign businessmen through a shakedown reminiscent of the "protection" rackets employed by gangsters in some of the big U.S. cities and by the Mafia in southern Italy. The solicitations are made in the guise of "contributions" to hospitals, churches, and charities. These demands can reach six figures. In return, smooth sailing in the establishment of a business and its continued unhampered operation is promised. Few businessmen believe their contributions ever reach the designated "worthy cause."

By all accounts, Kenya has one of the most efficient and honest civil services of any African country. But at the ministerial level, the politicians are wheelers and dealers who dabble—it is said, with the president's approval and encouragement—in all kinds of outside businesses. The political side of Kenya's officialdom exemplifies a widespread condition throughout much of sub-Saharan Africa, which Frantz Fanon, the French Martinique-born Negro psychiatrist and Third World ideologue, deplored. Nationalization, he wrote, was being used as a smoke screen for effecting the involuntary transfer of the entrepreneurial system founded by foreigners into the hands of a new black middle class.[14]

The late Dr. Fanon's impeachment of a corrupt black bour-

11

geoisie who engage in larceny is exemplified by Kenya's politicians. An incident involving two Americans—Kenyans refer to it as "the great ruby mine scandal"—epitomizes the situation in that country. In 1974, a ruby mine was staked out in Tsavo National Park by John Saul and Elliot Miller, graduates of the Massachusetts Institute of Technology. Hoping to protect their ownership, they took a number of Kenyan officials as partners in the venture. It soon became apparent that Saul and Miller had discovered what promised to become the world's largest source of rubies. As awareness of this began to grow, the Americans' ownership began steadily to diminish. No longer satisfied with their original 50 percent interest in the mine, the Kenyan "partners" insisted on a transfer to themselves of increasing increments of the ownership. Finally, the two Americans were ordered deported as "prohibited immigrants"—a Kenyan anathema that prohibits Saul and Miller from returning to the country. Now the ruby mine is "owned" by the Kenya Trade and Development Corporation in which Mama Ngina, the wife of President Jomo Kenyatta, is a partner.

The U.S. Department of State has made formal protests against the mistreatment of Saul and Miller, as well as against Kenya's disregard of international law, in confiscating foreign-owned assets without the payment of compensation. The Kenyan government, however, has not taken this protest seriously. Apparently it feels secure in the knowledge that, no matter how outrageous the conduct of its officials and its flouting of the traditional rules of international law, the Kenyan government will not be brought to account. Third World countries like Kenya have taken the measure of the U.S. Department of State. They know that the greatest power in the world is unlikely to take any retaliatory action. The abuse of power by some of Kenya's political leaders, primarily at the expense of American and West European businessmen, has led even Kenyans—at considerable personal risk—to complain openly of a " 'spreading cancer' " of corruption among the country's politicians.[15]

Uganda

From President Idi Amin's Ugandan dictatorship and its atrocities against Ugandan citizens has come additional confirmation of Lord Acton's dictum that "absolute power corrupts absolutely." In the confiscation of the savings and businesses of thousands of Indians and their expulsion from the country, Amin removed the economic backbone of his own country. This was a case of government larceny on a grand scale.

Elsewhere in East Africa, corruption among politicians and civil servants is so rampant that the elite class of government officials has earned the derisive Swahili name, "Wabenzi." (*Wa* is a prefix that means "group of people." *Benzi* is a root word coined from Mercedes-Benz cars, the hallmark of virtually all elite Africans.)

Nigeria

Two kinds of corruption thrive in Nigeria, sub-Saharan Africa's most populous and—thanks to oil revenues—richest country. One has its origin in the traditional "dash" system of West Africa, where functionaries expect or seek a tip, which they call "dash," for services rendered to the public.[16] In Nigeria and other former British West African colonies, the foreign firm that doesn't "dash" the local functionaries will eventually be unable to operate.[17] An editorial in *The Renaissance*, one of Nigeria's leading national papers, commented on the corruption that had engulfed Nigeria: "Of all the ills that have so long befallen this country, lack of fair play, godfatherism, unequal opportunities, barefaced cheating in high places remain the most malignant."[18]

The second type of corruption prevalent in Nigeria involves high officials. Men at the top of government, holding ministerial posts, expect a cut or kickback when they award a lucrative contract to a local or foreign business firm. Most Nigerians believe their government ministers, civil and military, systematically take a rake-off on government contracts.[19]

India

As Gunnar Myrdal has observed, two aspects of business-government relations in Third World countries generate corruption. One is the discretionary power over private business activities vested in officials. The other is the low compensation paid to civil servants.[20] The Indian subcontinent offers a classic illustration of these two root causes of corruption. In India's socialist-oriented economy, civil servants are vested with discretionary power to grant or withhold authorization of almost every activity with which private industry is concerned. At the lower and middle levels of the bureaucracy, wages and salaries are pitifully inadequate. Hence, at every stage of the administrative process there is scope for corruption. "Not a single file can move if the clerk's palm is not greased," a correspondent for the *Hindustan Times* wrote.

India's political democracy was built on political payments. "Speed money," shakedowns, and gaining illegal access to wealth—known as "black money"—occupied much of the time and energy of the Congress Party while it was ruling India. For generations, corruption of government officials by Indian businessmen has bought official tolerance for hoarding, adulterating, smuggling, and black marketing. Payoffs have been an integral part of Indian business-government relations. This must be taken into account *before* the management of a multinational company decides to invest in India; once a U.S. company is established there, it is unrealistic to believe that it can remain outside the mainstream of political payments with which Indians have lived for centuries.

Southeast Asia

Throughout Southeast Asia, political payments are a by-product of the ancient smuggling trade, which today still continues. To be sure, there is a developing market for consumer and industrial products, some of which are manufactured locally, but the bulk of which are imported from Japan, the United States, and Western Europe. But a second market, reaching by far the larger number of people, is served by contraband. In this market, anything moveable can generate a profit, but especially exotic merchandise such as rubies, jade, thousand-year-old antiques from the temples of Angkor Wat (along with yesterday's fakes), and even elephants smuggled out of Burma into Thailand.

Economic behavior in this contraband market is governed by speculative efforts to make a "quick killing"—facilitated by corruption. When a Singapore syndicate ships a cargo of 10,000 automobile tires to Indonesia and "persuades" a director of customs and his inspectors to drop one zero from the assessment of duty, a profitable piece of business results— for the membrs of the syndicate who financed the shipment and gambled on its sale and for a group of Indonesian officials who developd momentary blindness to an erasure on an invoice.

Evasion of tin prices fixed by the International Tin Council offers smugglers and customs officials mutually advantageous benefits. Tin moves by ship from Burma to Thailand to Ma-

15

laysia. No customs duties or other imposts are paid while the cargoes are in transit. Thus, free international trading exists in a price-controlled commodity. Similar "duty-free" markets obtain in rice, rubber, tungsten, and timber. Smuggling as an organized business depends on the connivance of government officials. In an area as vast as Southeast Asia, the involvement of government officials, primarily the customs service, is widespread and the loss of revenue is enormous.

Where the contraband trade has been a way of life for centuries, it would be altogether surprising if the symbiotic relationship between smugglers and officials did not condition the expectations of those officials when they come to deal with legitimate businessmen from the West. When officials along an entire bureaucratic chain have long been paid off to cooperate in the profitable ventures of smuggling, it becomes extremely difficult for the same officials not to expect—and demand—similar treatment by Western businessmen with legitimate transactions.

Burma

Burma's socialized economy has lacked competent and honest management. Since the nation's inception, smuggling and an "underground commerce" have gained in economic importance. It is estimated that, by 1976, perhaps 90 percent of the country's domestic commerce was transacted in the black market, a consequence, as Professor Richard Butwell observed, of the "Burmese way to socialism."[21] Smugglers are said to "import and export" more goods than are involved in the country's legal trade. Although no official figures are available for the illegal Burmese-Thai trade, some estimates place the value of this smuggling at 200 to 300 times the legal international commerce.[22] In Ragoon and Mandalay, according to Barry Kramer of the *Wall Street Journal,* who recently was permitted to visit the country, the shelves of cooperative stores are bare, while vendors in side-street stalls sell Thai silks, Chinese toilet paper, British cigarettes, cooking oil, and countless other items that either have been smuggled into Burma or stolen from state-owned factories.[23]

The "Burmese way to socialism," like the Indian brand, has fostered a climate of corruption. Under-the-table payments are necessary to persuade poorly paid government clerks to process an application, issue a license, or act on any kind of official paper. Licenses reserved for the Burmese are sold to Chinese and Indian merchants, who use the Burmese as fronts to obtain them. Foreign businessmen face long delays in purchasing raw materials, unless they grease the palm of the right official in the government's export corporation. One German teakwood buyer who refused to "grease" saw his teak logs rot on a Rangoon pier for more than a year. When he demanded their release, he was told he would have to pay a new higher price for the logs, a year's storage fee, and a new export fee based on the additional charges. He gave up in disgust.[24]

It is ironic that corruption is more prevalent in Asian socialist regimes than it was in the same countries under colonial rule.[25] The Netherlands Indies was practically free of corruption in colonial times. Yet some decades back, Mohammad Hatta, one of the leaders of Indonesian independence, lamented: "Corruption runs riot through our society."[26] Probably the same indictment can be made of most of sub-Saharan Africa's socialist regimes, under whose rule there is greater corruption than there ever was under British dominion.

Singapore

The Chinese-dominated socialist island city-state of Singapore is a Southeast Asian anomaly. Prime Minister Lee Kuan

Yew, a Cambridge-educated, socialist lawyer and an authentic "Chinese puritan," has created a climate of honesty among the civil servants that is unique to this region. Even the policeman on the block thinks twice before accepting a cigarette from the owner of an illegally parked bicycle. Although Lee and his advisers have ruthlessly extirpated corruption by civil servants, they have tolerated the existence of a different and more critical form of corruption: smuggling. Among the member countries of the ASEAN (Association of South East Asian Nations) organization (consisting, in addition to Singapore, of Malaysia, Thailand, Indonesia, and the Philippines), Singapore is jokingly referred to as a "smuggler's den," which may be a classic example of the pot calling the kettle black. Singapore is an entrepôt for an illicit traffic in contraband merchandise, directed primarily at neighboring Indonesia. Dr. Sumitro Djojohadikusumo, while serving as Indonesia's trade minister, once estimated that his country's foreign trade was largely in the hands of Singaporeans, and as much as 80 percent of his country's exports were smuggled out of the country by Singapore-based syndicates.[27]

Singapore is a veritable Garden of Eden by comparison with another Chinese-dominated community, the British crown colony of Hong Kong. Prior to the recently inaugurated "anti-corruption campaign," virtually the entire Royal Hong Kong Police force was on "retainer" for overlooking petty crimes—and some crimes of major proportions. Even Hong Kong's cynical residents were shocked on learning that Chief Superintendent Peter Fitzroy Godber, second highest-ranking British police officer, had amassed a small fortune in payoffs and had fled the colony just ahead of the constables and inspectors who were on his trail.[28]

At meetings of the ASEAN organization, complaints are voiced over the deleterious effects of smuggling on the economies of the member nations. But little is done to reduce the incidence of smuggling. It is easier to talk about the problem than to institute the draconian measures needed to eradicate it. Considering the immense territory and waterways that would have to be placed under strict surveillance, it is patently beyond the collective resources of the ASEAN organization to police this enormous expanse. Even if the ASEAN organization were disposed to cooperate in a regional effort to curtail smuggling, practical considerations deter any effort to stop it. Not the least of these is that it would step on the toes of too many Thai and Indonesian generals. To do away with smuggling in this part of the world would require an act of political *harakiri:* too many high-ranking politicians have a vested interest in perpetuating their rich rewards from smuggling.

Indonesia

Indonesia dramatizes the dilemmas of the poor countries whose officials are forced to be corrupt. Maladministration reduces the collection of income taxes to provide revenue for the national treasury. Widespread smuggling further deprives the treasury of needed customs revenue. Lack of revenue prevents the payment of adequate salaries to the bureaucracy. This function of government is, then, fulfilled by private payments to underpaid civil servants. Thus, a vicious cycle breeds corruption in business-government relations.

Because the Indonesian government fails to provide a decent wage for its civil servants, virtually the entire Indonesian bureaucracy is obliged to moonlight. Even military personnel moonlight to obtain additional income. The army rents out trucks, imports foreign movies for commercial distribution, operates textile mills, shoe factories, plantations, and banks, and runs trading firms, hotels, a hydrofoil service, and an airline.

The activities of the Indonesian armed forces as entrepreneurs and capitalists have led to large-scale graft and nepotism. Payrolls are loaded with family members and relatives. Government funds are used to establish commercial enterprises, which, in turn, profit on official contracts let by the central government. Military officers line their own pockets through the awarding of development contracts. Officers serve as directors of Indonesian private companies in which there are additional opportunities for aggrandizement. The Indonesian Chinese, the country's greatest reservoir of commercial, managerial, and financial talent, find it expedient to have an Indonesian "house general" as an associate in their own profitable ventures. In return, they are able to receive special favors in the form of government contracts, letters of credit, waivers of discriminatory anti-Sinitic legislation, and relief from onerous regulations.

The pervasive habits of corruption among Indonesian government officials prevent them from distinguishing between legitimate and illegitimate business activities. Thus, military officers and civil servants alike expect to receive gifts, cash, or stock in foreign companies organized and domiciled in Indonesia as the quid pro quo for helping them "adjust" to the Indonesian business climate.

The effrontery with which high-ranking Indonesian military and civilian officials extort political payments from foreign firms seeking to contract for sales to the Indonesian government was graphically depicted in recent revelations. General Telephone and Electronics, seeking to obtain a contract for $330 million of electronic and telephone equipment, was informed by Major General Sohardjono, Director of the Indonesian Department of Posts and Communications, that it would have to pay him $40 million as the price for being declared the successful bidder. The company's representative demurred, and the contract was awarded to a competitor, Hughes Aircraft.[29]

A second payoff in connection with the same transaction was demanded of a representative of General Telephone and Electronics by Udaya Hadibroto, Jr., the civilian director of the communications system operated by Pertamina, the now-bankrupt Indonesian government oil company, which had provided some of the financing of the proposed nationwide satellite system, with which the company's electronic and telephone equipment was to be used. According to senior executives of the company, Hadibroto had demanded a commission of 30 percent of the amount of the contract. " ' "That's the money Pertamina usually gets," ' " he declared.[30]

Pertamina and its deposed former chief executive officer, Major General Ibnu Sutowo, according to a complaint filed by the Securities and Exchange Commission in the U.S. District Court in New York in February 1977, extorted over $1 million from companies and individuals in five countries. (This was the first time that the SEC has moved against the *extortioner* of political payments.) The primary targets of the shakedown, the SEC alleged, were U.S. oil companies and Canadian, Italian, Swiss, and Japanese companies "either doing business with, or negotiating to establish business relations with . . . Pertamina." The objective of the extortion was to obtain subscriptions in the stock of an Indonesian restaurant in New York City, whose corporate ownership was controlled by General Sutowo. The solicitations, the SEC charged, were made on Pertamina's letterhead by General Sutowo "in his capacity as president-director of Pertamina." The "investors" responded to Pertamina's request by subscribing to shares in amounts ranging from $5,000 to $35,000. Among the restaurant's shareholders were: Mobil, Atlantic Richfield, Armco Steel, Continental, Brown & Root, a construction subsidiary of Halliburton, and East Oil Trading of Tokyo. In its complaint, the SEC quoted from General Sutowo's letter, which asserted that the establishment of an Indonesian restaurant in Manhattan would

". . . enhance the Indonesian image in the U.S.A. . . . promote tourism . . . [and] attract the interest of U.S. businessmen in investments in Indonesia. Since the establishment of this restaurant will be of great benefit to Indonesia's economic development, we request all companies which have business relationships with P. N. Pertamina to assist us in this project. . ."[31]

Prospective investors who did not respond to General Sutowo's letter, the SEC stated, received telephone calls from Pertamina employees in which the potential investors were again reminded of Pertamina's "interest" in the restaurant venture. Not all "investors" believed that they had been coerced into buying shares. A spokesman for Atlantic Richfield in Los Angeles, perhaps articulating the views of others who felt they could not afford to ignore a personal request from General Sutowo, declared: "We don't feel we were coerced. We felt it was a good investment as far as our relationships with Indonesia are concerned."[32]

The Overseas Chinese in Southeast Asia

Political payments in Southeast Asia cannot be understood without reference to the Overseas Chinese, who have played an immensely significant role in the development of the region. Although they comprise barely 5 percent of the area's population (around 15 million out of about 300 million inhabitants), the Overseas Chinese control about 60 percent of the region's trade and commerce.[33]

The strong commercial and financial success of the Overseas Chinese in Thailand, Indonesia, Malaysia, and the Philippines—all countries in which another ethnic group is dominant—has earned them the paranoid dislike of the indigenous populations and their political leaders. To overcome their political weakness, to minimize the effect of discriminatory laws and regulations on their capital and investments, and to deter harassments from police and other officials, the Overseas Chinese have endeavored, in all the lands in which they have settled, to buy personal and financial security by means of "protection payments." This method of obtaining security has reached not only the police but every level of government. In addition, the Chinese language associations, their trade organizations, Chambers of Commerce, and the interlocking directorates of their large commercial enterprises have paid off the political and military leaders of their host countries in the same manner as those countries of Southeast Asia were wont in the past to pay tribute to the Middle Kingdom, the ancestral home of the Overseas Chinese. In this reversal of roles, some Southeast Asian intellectuals, who resent the Overseas Chinese, see a fitting application of poetic justice.[34]

Although all the Southeast Asian countries have pursued harsh anti-Sinitic policies—at times some have actually promoted an Asian version of a pogrom—the policies of Thailand and the Philippines are in sharp contrast. As far back as the seventeenth century, Thai kings granted the Chinese titles and appointments to manage the state's trading enterprises and monopolies. The Chinese commercial elite married into the Thai political elite, and today there is a fusion of genes, money, and economic interests, although the balance of political power remains with the Thais. This amelioration in their condition did not, however, relieve the Overseas Chinese of the necessity to make protection payments. The late Thai strongman, Marshall Sarit, was notorious for blackmailing the Overseas Chinese by promoting hostile anti-Sinitic legislation. His immense private fortune was reputedly derived in large measure from having systematically squeezed the Chinese business community.[35]

The Filipinos have enacted the most severe anti-Chinese legislation to be found in Southeast Asia. Whether this discriminatory legislation was designed for the purpose of extorting money from the Overseas Chinese or to drive them out of certain businesses and professions is beside the point; the Filipino politicians were paid off. Political extortion is such a part of Filipino political life that some of its Congressmen have been accused of introducing anti-Sinitic legislation for no other purpose than to squeeze funds out of the Overseas Chinese.

Latin America

With a cultural heritage much different from that of Southeast Asia, Latin America nevertheless shares common cultural characteristics that contribute to corruption in business-government relations. As in the Asian societies, the loyalties of most people in Latin America do not extend very far beyond the family network. Central governments are seen as remote, distant institutions, to be viewed with suspicion and distrust. It is the bosom of the family that shields the individual member who may have incurred the wrath or suffered at the hands of the ruling group. And thus it is the family that must be protected against the depredations of the regime in power.[36]

Government employment is eagerly sought, not for the pay —it is woefully low—but for the prestige, power, and pelf it brings. As in Southeast Asia, the rich and powerful pay little in taxes. Since the Alliance for Progress, however, efforts to collect taxes have begun in a few countries, notably Brazil and Chile, with some success. (It is not without interest that the Spanish word for tax is *tributo* and a taxpayer is a *tributario*.)

History and culture conspired in Latin America to produce an environment that lends itself to political payments. Payments are made because of the need of private business to ensure, on the one hand, flexibility in the application of the discretionary administrative powers vested in civil servants, and, on the other hand, to enable private firms to compete with, and avoid being swallowed by, the heavily subsidized state-owned enterprises. The bureaucracy and private industry are thus bound to each other by a profitable cash nexus: the payoff.

Peru

Professor Charles Goodsell is one of the few American scholars to have studied foreign political payments by American companies. In Peru, through interviews with scores of U.S. executives and others that extended over a period of five years, he concluded that bribery of government officials was more prevalent among Italian-, German-, and Japanese-based enterprises in Peru than among British and American.[37] He reported that his respondents, from university intellectuals to Peruvian businessmen to Fernando Belaunde, the last freely elected President of Peru and reputedly the only one to leave the presidency a poor man, all confirmed the absence of bribery by subsidiaries of U.S. and British companies in Peru.

This difference in behavior on the part of the American and British firms was not a consequence of a superior Anglo-American morality, Professor Goodsell observed. Rather, it flowed from a difference in business management, coupled with a "greater image problem" than obtained among West European and Japanese firms. The political enemies of capitalistic business in Peru are legion. The danger that a payoff by an American-owned company would be revealed was ever present. This hazard, rather than any pronounced differences in management morality, may have been the controlling deterrent. And there may be another explanation for the infrequent corruption of business-government relations by U.S.

25

subsidiaries in Peru. The more recent entrants into the Peruvian market, e.g., Sears, Roebuck and General Motors, are not required, by the nature of their business, to deal much with the Peruvian government. They interact, for the most part, directly with the consumers of their products. In consequence, these companies are not under pressure to make political payments.

In any event, field grade officers of the Peruvian military establishment who man the ministries and departments have shown exemplary rectitude in their relations with foreign businessmen. Moreover, the managements of the more recent arrivals have been greatly concerned with creating a favorable public image for their companies. Hence, there has been a conscious effort to avoid any corrupt entanglements with the bureaucracy. A similar preoccupation with maintaining a good public image, according to Goodsell, was not evidenced by the older U.S. companies in Peru.[38]

Mexico

In the Mexican political system, the incumbent president, through an elaborate ritual, selects his successor, whose election is then a foregone conclusion. (In 1976, there was no opposition candidate to José Lopez Portilla, the new president.) During his six-year term, the president of Mexico is a virtual dictator, whose authority is rarely challenged by the Mexican press or by the rubber-stamp Congress. (That Luis Echeverría Alvarez was challenged in the closing days of his presidency by the Mexican business community was unprecedented.[39]) Those in the presidential circle are likewise virtually immune from any public criticism. To the American press, this state of affairs would be seen as a structure to cover up corruption.

As the entire top layer of government officials changes with the advent of a new president, those "on the take" have only six years in which to line their pockets. Indeed, the average Mexican, holding a profoundly cynical view of the moral rectitude of public officials, believes that the official who doesn't take while he has the opportunity is a fool. Few Mexican officials disabuse him of this conviction.

Businessmen and others who deal with the Latin American bureaucracies say that corruption in business-government relations is pervasive in Mexico. In that country, it seems that the entire structure of officialdom—from the traffic cop to the immigration officer to the law enforcement prosecutor on up to the highest reaches of government—is on the take. Few who are obliged to deal with the Mexican bureaucracy are immune from *mordida* ("the bite").

The Securities and Exchange Commission unwittingly may have lifted the curtain on the venality of certain Mexican officials, when it obtained an injunction in June 1976 against the Firestone Tire & Rubber Company, and in January 1977 against Uniroyal.[40] According to the SEC's complaints, a Mexican trade association was the vehicle for a payoff by the Mexican subsidiaries of the two U.S. companies to a Mexican official or officials. Six tire companies, including Firestone's and Uniroyal's subsidiaries, had been endeavoring to obtain the approval of the Mexican government for a price increase. It cost $420,000, according to the SEC, for the association's members to obtain this approval, which was granted on the same day, July 18, 1974, that the payoff was made.

In Mexico City, D.F., as in Washington, D.C., *who* you know is frequently more important than *what* you know. The political fixers in the Mexican capitol, because of their cunning and craftiness, are known as "coyotes." Their services are brought into play when the time comes to determine how

27

much a government official is to receive or how wide the payment must be spread.

A Mexican agent for a foreign company selling in Mexico may have little choice but to rebate a portion of his principal's selling price, if he expects to do business with some Mexican government agencies. An original bid, containing a list price plus commission, submitted to an agent, is only the first act in an elaborate charade. It will be returned with a 60–100 percent markup over the original quotation. After the shipment has been made, the exporter will retain the amount initially quoted and rebate the markup to his representative to cover payoffs in the bureaucratic chain. A Mexican automotive trade association recently charged the Mexican government with paying two to three times the invoice value for imported Soviet tractors; the inflated markup was used for political payments to government officials.[41]

Colombia

U.S. aircraft suppliers are not the only firms who make payoffs to influence Latin American government procurement decisions. In Colombia, a commission was appointed to investigate charges of payments having been made to Colombian army officers in the late 1960s by French and West German arms suppliers. It was alleged that the West German armaments firm, Keckler & Koch, beat out a Belgian rival for an order for 20,000 rifles by paying $200,000 to a group of army officers. And France's Dassault aircraft company was alleged to have secured an order for eighteen Mirage-5 fighter planes by slipping $300,000 to key officers of the Colombian air force.[42] Corruption was not confined to the armed forces; what the Marxists call "white glove" corruption is said to be widespread in the upper echelons of government as well.

Costa Rica

Robert Vesco, a fugitive from U.S. law enforcement agencies, may have obtained Costa Rican citizenship by buying his way into that country's political power structure. The SEC has charged that Vesco helped bail out a financially ailing company owned by former president José Figueres in order to secure a safe haven in Costa Rica, a charge which Figueres vehemently denied.[43] A New York court-appointed receiver has charged that in 1968, when Mr. Figueres was a candidate for president, he obtained $2 million for his financially sick company from Clovis McAlpin, president of Capital Growth, a mutual fund now based in Costa Rica. In return, it is alleged, McAlpin obtained diplomatic immunity by being appointed to a diplomatic post. Mr. Figueres also denied these charges.

Dominican Republic

Philip Morris, the second largest U.S. cigarette company, disclosed to the SEC on December 15, 1976, that its 43-percent-owned affiliate in the Dominican Republic, E. Leon Jimines, C. Por A. (ELJ), had made political payments to Dominican officials and paid $1,000 a month during 1973 to the president of that Caribbean nation. Actually, the checks were made payable to the "Presidente Partido Reformista," President Joaquín Balaguer's official title as head of his party. In a memorandum dated June 18, 1976, the Philip Morris auditors reported such monthly payments on ELJ company checks, and that: "Several of them even show the official stamp of the central headquarters of the 'Partido Reformista' located in the National Palace of the Dominican Republic," which is also the official office of President Balaguer. According to the *Wall Street Journal*, the Dominican embassy in Washington confirmed what the auditors had reported.[44] As an editorial in *Listin Diario,* the island republic's second largest newspaper, pointed out:

> For some time now it has been known that when a company gives to the Reformist Party, the check is made to the order of the president of the Reformist Party. First of all, the president thereby knows that a contribution has been made and, secondly, to avoid the possibility that the check might be cashed illegally.[45]

In any event, it is both customary and legal for a Dominican corporation to make political contributions.

Eduardo Leon, president of ELJ, informed the Philip Morris auditors during an interview in his office on June 21, 1976, that he expected ELJ would be asked to contribute a "substantial amount" to President Balaguer's current reelection campaign. A special audit of ELJ showed that "contributions to the president's political campaign amounted to $200,000."[46]

The *Wall Street Journal* story of the campaign contributions, published in its edition of December 27, 1976, became something of a cause célèbre in the Dominican Republic President Balaguer denied receiving monthly checks from ELJ, and ordered a government investigation into the "origin and destination" of the checks as well as into the accounting records of the Philip Morris affiliate. Balaguer also threatened that, if ELJ refused to furnish the names of government officials reported to have received payoffs, Philip Morris "should be declared undesirable and should be asked to stop operating in the Dominican Republic."[47]

This presidential wrath was in response to a statement in a memorandum by ELJ that in 1975 it paid $16,000 for a favorable ruling "on laws 'regulating business in the Dominican Republic.'" The recipient of the payoff was identified by the auditors as an "'inspector of the tax authority, Rentas Internas ... who was in charge of tax review for the fiscal year 1975.' "[48] Sr. Leon told the Philip Morris auditors during his interview that such payoffs were necessary for corporate survival and profitability. He recalled an incident a few years ago when ELJ didn't grant what a tax official had demanded. The official thereupon proceeded to disallow, on supposedly rigid technical grounds, a legitimate $700,000 expense for distribution of sample cigarettes. The frequency of such payments underscores what the auditors described in a memorandum entitled " 'E. Leon Jimenes, Special Audit,' " as a " 'way of life in the (Dominican Republic).' "[49]

The auditors also reported that ELJ believed payoffs were essential to obtain the enactment of favorable legislation. About six years ago, Sr. Leon said Philip Morris had helped ELJ cultivate so-called blond, or Virginia, tobacco. ELJ wanted legislation passed that would ensure that its competitor, Compania Anonyma Tobacalera, S.A., which had a 75 percent market share compared with ELJ's 25 percent, would be required to purchase this tobacco from ELJ. To accomplish this objective through legislation necessitated paying various Dominican legislators $120,000.[50]

President Balaguer's sharp reaction to the Philip Morris disclosure that its Dominican affiliate had made campaign contributions may in part have been induced by the inference that he, personally, had pocketed the sum received by his party. This seems highly improbable. Joaquín Balaguer has throughout his adult life lived simply and austerely; his material ambitions have been negligible. The official rejoinder, however, was predictable. Third World chiefs of state—even when they have in fact been the recipients of political payments, as Gabon's president—are obliged to enter strong disclaimers of any official wrongdoing lest they become the objects of ridicule at home and abroad.[51]

The Dominican incident underscores the dilemma of the U.S. international corporation. On the one hand, it is requested to disclose political and other payments on the theory

31

that shareholders have a right to know; on the other hand, the media publicity attendant upon disclosure can jeopardize the company's continued ability to operate in a country in which such payments are traditional.

Western Europe

Except for such notable scandals as that which erupted around Prince Bernhard of The Netherlands for soliciting and accepting $1.1 million in commissions from Lockheed Aircraft, corporate political payments are probably no more prevalent in most of Western Europe than in the United States. West European firms, particularly those connected with the armaments industry, do make political payments to obtain business. West European governments must be aware of the practice and, if not condoning it, they certainly have not interfered with it thus far. Indeed, where state-owned corporations make payoffs, as they have in France, the governments themselves were parties to the practice.

Belgium

The approach taken by Belgium's authorities in dealing with business-government irregularities is exemplified by a case involving the former managing director of Belgium's state telephone system, Germain Baudrin, and the Belgian subsidiary of International Telephone and Telegraph. In 1976, Mr. Baudrin was convicted and sentenced to jail for nine months for receiving gifts from ITT's president and managing director, Frank Pepermans. In a separate case, involving an estimated $100,000, for which Mr. Baudrin was unable to account and of which the sources were not known, he was convicted of corruption and receiving bribes and sentenced to four years in jail.

An investigation of Mr. Pepermans' role disclosed that over seven or eight years he had given Baudrin merchandise with an estimated value of $7,500. Mr. Pepermans, said an ITT spokesman, called them "business gifts within the range of common practice." The gifts, the spokesman said, were all products of the company's Belgian unit and included a color television, two telephone sets, and an " 'obsolete' " mobile radio telephone unit that had been " 'used in a Brussels taxi' " and that was installed by a ITT-Bell technician on Mr. Baudrin's boat in Italy. Mr. Pepermans received a suspended six-months' jail sentence on charges of having bribed Mr. Baudrin. He has appealed the conviction.[52]

United Kingdom

An official investigation of the scandal-ridden Lonrho company is instructive in showing the approach to bribery taken by a British socialist government. The case involved kickbacks and conflicts of interests among the company's board of directors, including the chairman, an émigré German wheeler-dealer, and eminent Conservative Party politicians.

In this chronicle of shabby financial practices and evasions of British law, only a scanty three pages of the official report dealt with "special payments" and the distribution of "substantial sums of money by way of gift or reward or inducement"—the British terminology used to denote overseas political payments. The investigation traced the beneficiaries of $1.6 million of "special payments" to politicians in several African countries. However, the names of the recipients and their countries were discreetly omitted, presumably in defer-

33

ence to the Foreign Office's desire to avoid embarrassment to the Labor government and its African socialist friends.

The official report illuminated the manner in which the titled aristocracy were employed as corporate political agents. Lonrho used Lord Duncan-Sandys, a son-in-law of Sir Winston Churchill and a member of Tory cabinets from 1943 to 1964, to intervene with the South African government to drop fraud and criminal charges against several Lonrho executives. His $390,000 fee was paid in a tax haven country to avoid the deep bite of the British income tax.[53]

By American standards, the British government's investigation of Lonrho would be written off as a whitewash. But the British (and other West European governments) view the problem of business political payments differently. West European governments—even those dominated by socialist parties—do not indulge in wringing of hands and indignant rhetoric over political payments by their corporations. They regard corruption in business-government relations in the Third World as a fact of life; unfortunate and regrettable, to be sure, but something over which they lack effective control. The Dutch parliamentary censure of Prince Bernhard for his involvement in the solicitation and acceptance of political payments from Lockheed Aircraft dealt with the matter sternly and unequivocally, but it did not adopt a moralistic posture.

France

With Gallic realism, French industry makes political payments abroad and is addicted to kickbacks at home. Contrary to the views of anti-business politicians, American businessmen are uncomfortable in such a milieu. William Fowler, a former chief executive officer of a U.S.-owned French subsidiary, exemplified this prevailing American business attitude. He wrote that he was shown "on a very confidential basis" by his own sales department a "schedule of bribes and kickbacks" demanded by buyers of a number of the leading French and European retail chains that distributed his company's appliances.[54] His decision *not* to sanction such payoffs was greeted with consternation by his French sales personnel. His explanation that the U.S. parent, Whirlpool Corporation, in the more than fifty years since its founding had never engaged in political payments or kickbacks was received by his colleagues, Fowler says, as the ravings of an American out of touch with reality. The moral of the story is that Whirlpool's French subsidiary went out of business because it refused to do business as French custom dictated.

The management of a Canadian company may also have found the European environment, which sanctioned kickbacks, distasteful; however, the company—Polymer Corporation—adhered to the European practice. It paid nearly $2 million in kickbacks to European customers by billing them " 'at inflated rates' " and remitting the difference to designated numbered Swiss bank accounts.[55]

Italy

The U.S. corporate subsidiary domiciled in Italy is confronted with two Italys—the Italy of the North and the Italy of the South. Each adheres to different cultural patterns. The manager of a U.S. subsidiary whose plant is located in the Turin-Milan-Genoa industrial triangle—the industrial heartland of Italy—functions in a familiar cultural environment. He encounters a strong work ethic, almost Protestant in its faith in the values of an industrial society, in the importance of enterprise, in efficiency, in punctuality, in risk-taking. Management practices not unlike those followed in the United States are customary. The northern Italian businessman's disdain of the Italian politicians and the Rome government is similar to the U.S. businessman's attitude toward American politicians and the Washington bureaucracy.

Southern Italy—the Mezzogiorno—on the other hand is a predominantly agricultural, preindustrial, and politically corrupt society. For the northern Italian businessman, Rome is the symbol of this society. The northern industrialist dismisses the nation's political capitol with the scornful phrase: "Africa begins at Rome." What he implies is that the southern politician, who dominates Italian politics, has carried into government, the paternalistic, family-client relationships of the Mediterranean.

Northerners focus their resentments on the political fortress of the southern politicians—the Italian bureaucracy centered in Rome. Italy's civil service is among the least efficient, most overstaffed, and corrupt to be found in the industrial nations of the West. In addition to the conventional ministries, there are nearly 60,000 different agencies employing around two million persons. Many appear to exist solely as a means of support for their employees—a kind of Italian welfare system.

The colossal, Byzantine bureaucracy responds to its administrative obligations through *bustarella*. (The word is derived from *busta* meaning envelope.) Only an envelope stuffed with varying amounts of 10,000 lira notes, worth about $12, can overcome the chronic chaos, buck-passing, indecision, and extortionate rulings. *Bustarella* is mandatory for domestic and foreign businessmen, and for the wealthy in Italian society. The labyrinthine bureaucratic system has produced a special class of expediter, the *spicciafaccondi*. These specialists know whom to see for the signing of papers, which official can be bribed and how much it will cost, and the most effective route for speeding the flow of papers to obtain vital decisions.

Luigi Barzini has written that his country's regulatory

structure is a "tropical tangle of statutes, rules, norms, regulations, customs, some hundreds of years old, some voted last week by Parliament and signed this very morning by the President."[56] Within the vast bureaucracy, no one knows for certain which laws are still valid and what some of them really mean.

Italian taxation is especially complex and, for the collectors of *bustarella*, particularly rewarding. Italian officials have wide discretionary power in applying the tax laws and regulations. Hence, a prolific source of corruption is the arbitrary assessment of taxes. Take this hypothetical example: a U.S. manufacturing subsidiary with $5 million in annual sales reports a $100,000 loss and, thus, no tax liability. But in Italy should the tax inspector find that other companies of comparable size were profitable during the same year, he will assume from his experience with Italian companies, who practice tax evasion as an inalienable right, that the U.S. firm is attempting to escape the payment of taxes. He therefore levies a $200,000 tax assessment. Theoretically, an appeal could be taken through the courts—not to the tax inspector's superiors, for that route would merely create additional claimants for *bustarella*. But if American court calendars are years behind in the trial of cases, the Italian courts are decades in arrears. It could take a dozen or more years before a decision could be obtained. And, as Barzini says, only a madman would wish to become involved with Italian judges and courts.

So what does the American plant manager do to avoid the prospect of being shut down by the authorities as a tax evader —to say nothing of finding himself in jail? The same thing the Italians do—pay off the tax inspector and have the assessment cut down to a manageable amount![57]

In Italy, a web of statutory ambiguities, inconsistencies, and contradictions, subject to the interpretations of poorly chosen, wretchedly underpaid, and badly organized bureau-

37

crats, can only be made to function by means of *bustarella*. The political payment enables a chaotic system of government to function.

The Communist World

Communist propagandists have long maintained that capitalism is the breeding ground of corruption. One would, therefore, expect to find in the communist orbit a "new man" who has no appetite for the decadent bourgeois habits of the West. But fact as distinguished from myth reveals that corrupt practices abound in the communist nations. (Not enough is known about these matters in the People's Republic of China to permit of generalizations regarding the eradication of the ancient practices of gift-giving and payoffs.)

Internal corruption grows out of the very nature of the communist economies—chronic shortages of consumer goods, their poor quality, the interminable delays in obtaining service and repairs, a centralized planning system that decides what people should wear or consume, whether they like the product or not. Since a great multitude of Soviet citizens do not like what the *Gosplan* decrees, there has developed what Hedrick Smith, a former *New York Times* Moscow correspondent, calls a "counter-economy." Andrei Sakharov, the dissident physicist and Nobel Prize winner, estimated this counter-economy involved "certainly ten percent or more" of the Soviet gross national product, or, around 50 billion rubles ($66 billion).[58]

The counter-economy, Smith writes, has become "an integral part of the Soviet system, a built-in, permanent feature of Soviet society."

> It encompasses everything from petty bribing, black marketing, wholesale thieving from the state, and underground private manufacturing all the way up to a full-fledged *God-*

father operation which was exposed and led to the downfall of a high Communist Party figure, a candidate member of the Politburo. It operates on an almost oriental scale and with brazen normality that would undoubtedly incense the original Bolshevik revolutionaries. Yet, ordinary people take it for granted as an essential lubricant for the rigidities of the planned economy. What the elite get legally through their special stores and system of privileges, ordinary people are forced to seek illegally in the country's counter-economy.[59]

A Reuters dispatch from Prague in December 1976 reported that pilfering and corruption are part of everyday life in Czechoslovakia as people try to get their hands on the goods and services that are in chronic short supply.[60] The Reuters correspondent noted that to make their lives endurable, the Czechs, like the Russians, utilize a "parallel economic system." It is significant that communist officials revealed that 4,215 "economic crimes"—the official euphemism for internal corruption—had been uncovered during the first half of 1975 in Slovakia alone. The Communist Party newspaper *Rude Pravo* pointedly observed that some Czechs had extended their "parasitic activities" to deals with Western firms. Occasional local newspaper stories, Reuters states, have confirmed this official commentary. Thus, it was reported recently that three foreign trade officials had pocketed nearly $90,000 in "commissions" from Western companies. They were convicted and sentenced to jail terms of ten to thirteen years.

Our primary interest, however, is not with internal corruption but with corruption in communist countries that involves the governments and foreign companies. We have dwelt on the former because of the myth propagated by the communists that theirs is a corruption-free society while capitalism breeds corruption. But the reality is that corruption is widespread in the communist world; indeed, both societies experience the phenomenon. Because internal corruption is endemic to the communist system, it ineluctably conditions a privileged elite to the habits of corruption in their external relations with other communist officials in the Eastern bloc countries and with the Western and Japanese businessmen who negotiate with the state enterprises.

A Soviet–Eastern-bloc arms scandal, involving Red Army officers, factory managers, and intermediaries, and matching capitalist political payments in the sale of armaments, has been reported. In East Germany, Soviet officers are alleged to have sold military vehicles to civilians and charged special tolls on tanks delivered to the East German armed forces. In turn, East German army officers are reputed to have sold repainted military trucks to state farms and factories. The same system of illicit sales of military matériel for cash has been reported in Czechoslovakia. Investigators in these cases have turned up large sums of dollars and Swiss francs in officers' quarters. The hard currency was obtained by trusted emissaries (who received a cut for their efforts) from West Germany and Switzerland. Syria, a current Soviet Middle East client, has also complained that Russian military "advisers" have demanded a rake-off on unloaded military supplies.[61]

Only a few incidents of Soviet officials "on the take" from foreign businesses have filtered through the official censors and the self-censorship that inhibits most Russians from speaking candidly with foreigners about their society. Plainly, the Russians are not eager to advertise to the rest of the world the misconduct of their own high-ranking officials.

As a warning to other Soviet trade officials who deal with Western businessmen—and to foreign businessmen who negotiate with Soviet trade officials—the former head of the import-export corporation trading in furniture was executed by a firing squad for accepting $150,000 from a Swiss supplier.[62] In July 1976, two Japanese businessmen, who had been negotiating a multimillion dollar contract for the design and installation of a natural gas processing plant for western

Siberia, were arrested by Soviet police for bribing a trade official.[63] And in August 1976, according to the Russian newspaper *Izvestia,* a senior official in a foreign trade organization was given a long prison term for divulging "commercial secrets" to two West German businessmen in return for a $2,000 bribe.

Yugoslav officials have extorted money from West European firms and deposited it in Swiss bank accounts.[64] In Bulgaria, bribery and extortion are widespread. And in Poland, payoffs to middle-level officials are common.[65] Western salesmen and service representatives appear to have experienced the greatest pressure for payoffs in Romania. There, political payments are frequent despite President Nicolae Ceauşescu's campaign against "economic crimes." The Romanians may have created an innovation by turning acts of extortion by their officials into demands for "ransom." General Refractories Company of Bala Cynwyd, Pennsylvania, for example, paid $250,000 in 1974 to obtain the release of an Austrian engineer, employed as a sales and service representative by its Austrian subsidiary, who was accused by the Romanians of engaging in " 'industrial espionage.' " The Romanians called the payment for the release of the company's employee a "fine"; but executives of General Refractories described it as a "ransom." They contended that the payment was necessary to enable the company to do business in that country.[66]

The United States

Lest it be presumed that the United States is an oasis of moral purity in a desert of worldwide corruption, Nathan Miller reminds us that:

> ... from Jamestown to Watergate, corruption runs through our history like a scarlet thread. Although we self-righteously

congratulate ourselves on our high moral standards, the graft-
ing politician, corrupt business tycoon, and crooked labor baron
are prominent fixtures in American folklore.[67]

Although corruption is no longer rife in American life, it
can hardly be said that the body politic has been cleansed of
politicians on the take, businessmen who pay off, and labor
leaders who extort. Moreover, even where the more blatant
forms of corruption in business-government relations are no
longer present, more subtle and insidious types prevail. To
believe that corruption can be totally eradicated from the
American political system is perhaps utopian.

The United States is scarcely in a position to chide the
rest of the world over the state of its moral conduct in light of
the corrupt behavior in our own inter-business transactions,
labor-management negotiations, and business-government relations.[68] Norman Jaspan, president of a firm specializing in
ferreting out corporate fraud and corruption, and the Chamber of Commerce of the United States estimate that kickbacks, bribery, and extortion in the food, retail, and building
industries alone amount to $5 to $8 billion annually. The
building trades have traditionally been a fertile field of corruption.[69] According to Jaspan, it is standard practice in the
building trades to add 8 to 10 percent to a contract bid "as a
cushion to cover the cost of kickbacks" to government officials
and union officers. Jaspan also says that competition for
supermarket shelf-space is so intense that "nationally ad-
vertised drinks, beers and other well-known products are
kept off shelves unless vendors of these products buy display
shelf-space and location by paying off store managers, grocery
managers, or even district managers on some predetermined
basis."

An area of business-government relations that cries out for
investigation by U.S. journalists is whether or not *foreign*
companies domiciled in the United States are required, as a
condition for doing business, to make political payments—

42

and to whom. It may well be that political payments are not made to, or solicited by, government officials, and union leaders do not receive or extort payments from foreign firms. If this is indeed the fact, would it not be useful public information? And if this is the prevailing state of public morality, would not the United States be justified in a little self-congratulation?

Socioeconomic Development and Political Payments

What emerges from our brief survey of examples of irregularities in the business-government relationship around the world is a sense of their pervasiveness. Political payments by business enterprise are made in poor and in rich countries, in less- and more-developed nations, in communist and in capitalist societies.

One conclusion, supported by much evidence, is that perversion of the business-government relationship, at least in obvious forms, declines as a society advances in its awareness and support of nationhood, in wealth and income, in political and legal stability, and in the building of strong social institutions. This is not to say that corruption *ends* at some stage of socioeconomic development. That cannot be expected in a world populated by human beings with all of their moral frailties. Yet socioeconomic development does tend to curb practices that most civilized men and women agree are morally wrong and economically inefficient. It also tends to transform them into more subtle practices, as we shall observe in the following chapter.

Another conclusion that may be drawn from our global panorama is that political payments by business enterprise cannot be eliminated solely by actions of the United States, or even by actions taken in concert with other industrialized nations. Extensive experience with providing economic aid to less-developed countries has shown that socioeconomic development cannot be *imposed* on a country from without. It must emerge from the will of the people of the developing nation. External assistance can only fortify and accelerate an internal process. So it will likely be with political payments by business organizations. They probably can be substantially curtailed by measures that bring about socioeconomic development. Such developments include:

The shifting of loyalties from family, clan, and tribe to nation-states.

The opening of institutionalized channels to enable business enterprise to influence political decision making.

The diffusion of education.

The emergence of an economically strong and politically articulate middle class, which historically has found corruption inefficient and morally repugnant.

The transfer of wealth and power from a small circle of politicians or dictators to other social groups.

Rising living standards.

The growth of local industry, which will reduce the importance of contraband markets.

The paying of adequate salaries to civil servants, thereby reducing their dependence on a private system of political payments.

The development of strong, independent legal traditions in which uniform, impersonal rules and standards prevail instead of the arbitrary discretion of civil servants.

The growth of the professions—accounting, law, engineering, teaching, civil service—which infuse their members and eventually, widening circles of society, with strict canons of professional behavior.

These would seem to be some of the basic remedies for corruption.[70] The historical experience of Europe and the United States is ample evidence that there is no overnight cure.

2

The Emerging Censorship
of Foreign Political Payments

THE emerging censorship of political payments by U.S. business corporations is a potentially important, but little noted, aspect of the recent controversies about these payments. The operating behavior of American business overseas is becoming a new dimension of the public regulation of business. Until recent years, this regulation was concerned with such matters as healthy working conditions for employees, safe and reliable products, and enforcing competition. The disclosure of political payments abroad has led federal agencies to increase still further their role as arbiters of business behavior.

Spokesmen for federal regulatory agencies, of course, claim only that they are the watchmen of the statutory laws. Securities and Exchange Commission officials maintain that they only enforce the securities laws, which call for full disclosure of "material" facts bearing on investment decisions. The Internal Revenue Service contends that its sole concern is with the collection of taxes due from multinational companies. And the Federal Trade Commission intervenes, it says, only to ensure fair business practices and competition. The Senate Subcommittee on Multinational Corporations, which has also taken an interest in foreign political payments, holds that its interests are restricted to the impact of these payments on U.S. foreign relations.

These official declamations by federal regulators and the political rhetoric employed by congressmen are *not* motivated mainly by concern with financial disclosure, tax payments, international relations, or competition. Nor have the many reform proposals emanating from Washington been solely inspired by these matters. *Government officials have been primarily seeking to minimize foreign political payments by American corporations.*

Federal regulation of business—which has greatly expanded in scope and intensity during recent years—is now intruding into another aspect of the operating conduct of American businessmen overseas. A brief review of the involvement of a number of federal agencies with this issue reveals how this federal regulation has developed.

The SEC Investigations

As a result of the Watergate revelations, during 1973 the Securities and Exchange Commission (SEC) began to investigate domestic political payments by the 9,000 publicly owned companies coming under its jurisdiction. Several companies and their officers were charged with using corporate funds to make contributions to the reelection campaign of former President Nixon. The SEC's inquiry revealed that corporate financial records had been falsified to conceal such contributions, and that "slush funds" had been set up outside the corporate systems of financial accountability.

Digging deeper, the staff of the SEC learned that these secret funds were used in a number of instances for transferring payments to foreign government officials or for making foreign political contributions, some of which were legal, others clearly illegal, and some of doubtful legality.[1] The resulting investigations led to the SEC bringing, as of May 10, 1976, injunctive actions against twenty-two companies.[2] All of these elected to make consent settlements, neither denying nor admitting guilt, rather than to engage in time-consuming and expensive court battles with the SEC. Though the agency has been praised by some journalists and members of Congress for its aggressive role in investigating corporations that have made overseas political payments, the fact remains that the SEC had not (at the date of writing) litigated any of these twenty-two cases and, thus, had not won a single conviction. Its dubious theory of the materiality of foreign political payments, discussed below, has thereby escaped judicial determination.

The SEC Disclosure System

The "disclosure system" used by the SEC in these investigations had its birth in the "Truth in Securities" Act of 1933, which was enacted during the New Deal's "First Hundred Days" of unprecedented legislative reform. In asking Congress for this new securities legislation, President Roosevelt declared that

> . . . This proposal adds to the ancient [common law] rule of *caveat emptor*, the further doctrine "let the seller beware." It puts the burden of telling the whole truth on the seller.[3]

Roosevelt, an admirer of Supreme Court Justice Louis D. Brandeis, who believed that "sunlight" was the most effective cleansing agent for "social and industrial diseases," informed newspapermen gathered in his office that the bill before Congress offered "publicity rather than any guarantee to the investing public."[4] The President explained:

47

"What we are trying to do is to get the kind of information as to each issue before the investing public so that, if they then invest, they will know at least that the representations that have been made to them are true."[5]

For some forty years, disclosure has been the prophylaxis used by the SEC to safeguard the investor against misleading or untruthful information.[6] The cardinal canon of the disclosure system is Schedule A of the Securities Act of 1933. It specifies thirty-four items of information that are to be supplied by the issuer of securities to the public in proxy materials and in registration statements filed with the Commission. These items include the capitalization of the issuer, outstanding funded debt, remuneration received by the officers and directors, offering price of the securities to be sold, rights of security holders, and a recent balance sheet and profit-and-loss statement.

In addition, under the Securities Exchange Act of 1934, corporate issuers are required to file two pivotal disclosure statements: Forms 8-K and 10-K. The former is a monthly "current report" in which the registrant is expected to supply information on any new developments, such as changes in the control of the company, acquisition or disposition of assets, significant litigation in which the corporation is a party, and other "material" financial data. The 10-K Form is an "annual report" designed to pick up previously unreported legal, business, and financial activities.

In sum, the corporation contemplating a public sale of its securities or whose securities are already traded on a registered stock exchange is obliged to supply the SEC with a series of X-rays of its economic and financial condition. The objective of this elaborate disclosure system is to enable the "prudent investor"—an idealized character invented by the courts, accepted by the Congress, and catered to by successive generations of commissioners and their staffs—to be protected from his own gullibility and ignorance. The prepara-

48

tion of the various reports and statements to the SEC has reached gargantuan proportions. It continues to expand as lawyers for corporate issuers and investment bankers endeavor to protect their clients against future charges of misrepresentation or incomplete disclosure.

But nowhere is there a specific requirement for disclosure of political payments to foreign officials. No mention of such payments was made in Schedule A for a very simple reason: it was never contemplated that they should be reported. The legislative draftsmen, the key members of the Congress in charge of the bill (particularly Sam Rayburn, a Texas populist for whom Wall Street was an anathema) did not have in mind anything more than placing controls over the truthfulness of information about securities, the stock exchange's bucket-shop behavior, insider trading, and speculation.[7]

There is an additional reason why it was not contemplated that the federal supervisory agency—it was originally the Federal Trade Commission—should extend its jurisdiction to political payments made overseas. In 1933, when the "Truth in Securities" legislation was enacted, overseas investment by U.S. companies, other than in natural resources and plantation industries, was in its infancy.[8] It would be another quarter of a century—the mid-1950s—before the U.S.-based multinational company and its overseas subsidiaries would be exposed in a major way to the varied national environments·in which political corruption flourishes.

How, then, does it happen that foreign payments, which the SEC characterizes as "questionable and illegal," must now be disclosed? The SEC, in effect, has conceded that Schedule A does not contain any specific requirement to disclose foreign payments. The Commission, however, has *assumed* that it is *implicit* in the disclosure requirements that foreign payments be reported to investors because, among other things, a failure to disclose such transactions reflects upon "the quality of a registrant's business" and on "the quality of a registrant's earnings"—in a word, on "the quality of management."[9]

What Is a "Material" Fact?

The SEC grounds its tenuous legal authority to compel disclosure of foreign payments on the assumption that it must ensure that all "material" information is made available to investors. But "materiality" is a slippery, elusive, and elastic term. The SEC defines it as encompassing all "those matters as to which an average prudent investor ought reasonably to be informed before purchasing securities."[10] In including foreign payments, the SEC commissioners have been criticized by a former commissioner, A. A. Sommer, Jr. He observed in December 1975, prior to his resignation, that, as a concept, materiality "will bear virtually any burden and . . . justify almost any disclosure." He warned his fellow commissioners to proceed with caution in expanding its scope. The danger of widening the circle of materiality to encompass overseas political payments, irrespective of the amounts, circumstances, or the cultural environments in which they are made, "may result in significant changes," Sommer pointed out, "in the role of the Commission, the role of other enforcement agencies, and our ability to carry out our statutory duties."[11]

To the Commission's incumbent chairman, Roderick M. Hills, there was, however, a "delicious ambiguity" about exactly what is material for the purposes of disclosure.[12] When it came to payments made overseas, this ambiguity was resolved, for him, in favor of disclosure. "The behavioral pattern of management" in making and/or concealing such payments, Hills believed, is important to investors. "In some ultimate sense," Hills has said, "that may get to be a moral judgment. We make moral judgments," he added.[13]

Investor Reaction to Disclosures

Do investors perceive political payments in the same way that Washington's officialdom does? If disclosure of the making and the concealing of such payments engendered doubts over the integrity of corporate managements, investors would presumably sell their shares in the transgressor companies. And selling pressure would produce a discernible decline in the market price of securities.

To test this hypothesis we selected five U.S. corporations whose overseas payments were substantial and who were subjected to intense media publicity: Exxon, Gulf, Lockheed, Northrop, and United Brands. For each company, the date of the initial disclosure of foreign political payments was identified. Charts 1, 2, 3, 4, and 5 present the weekly ranges of the common stock prices of these companies on the New York Stock Exchange. The average of the daily closing prices of the company's common stock was computed over the five-day and thirty-day periods preceding and succeeding the date of disclosure. These averages were divided by the respective averages of the New York Stock Exchange composite stock price index for the same periods in order to purge movements in each company's stock price of general market influences. Percentage changes in stock prices were then computed. The results appear in Table 1.

TABLE 1   Five-Day and Thirty-Day Relative Changes in Stock Prices Around Dates of Disclosure of Foreign Political Payments for Five U.S. Multinational Corporations, 1975

Company	Date of Initial Disclosure	Percentage Change in Stock Prices	
		Five-Day	*Thirty-Day*
Exxon	5/16/75	−0.6	4.3
Gulf	5/16/75	−0.2	3.2
Lockheed	9/12/75	−3.7	−2.4
Northrop	6/9/75	−12.9	−8.9
United Brands	4/25/75	1.8	−21.4

51

Chart 1
Weekly Ranges of Common Stock Price on the New York Stock
Exchange, 1974–76

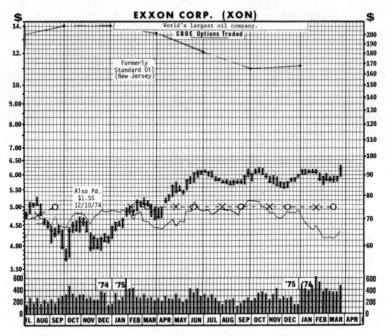

Chart 2
Weekly Ranges of Common Stock Price on the New York Stock
Exchange, 1974–76

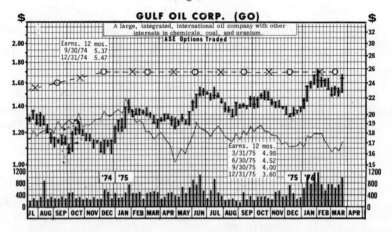

Source: Charts by permission of Securities Research Co.,
208 Newbury St., Boston, Massachusetts 02116

Chart 3
Weekly Ranges of Common Stock Price on the New York Stock
Exchange, 1974–76

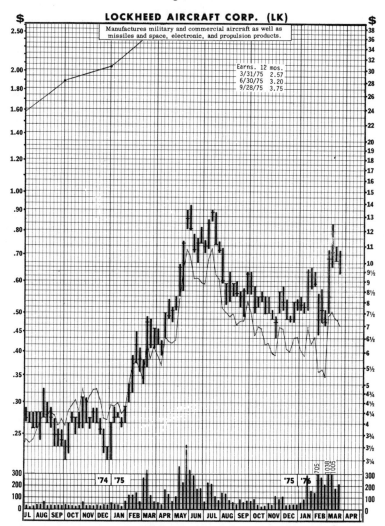

Source: Chart by permission of Securities Research Co.,
208 Newbury St., Boston, Massachusetts 02116

Chart 4
Weekly Ranges of Common Stock Price on the New York Stock
Exchange, 1974–76

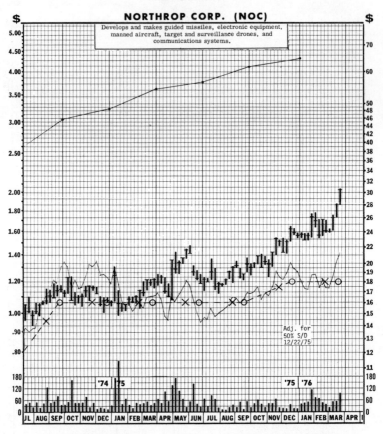

Source: Chart by permission of Securities Research Co.,
208 Newbury St., Boston, Massachusetts 02116

Investor short-term (five-day) reaction was negligible for
Exxon, Gulf, and United Brands, but somewhat more pronounced for the two aerospace companies, Lockheed and
Northrop. The moderate 30-day decline in Northrop's stock
may have been affected more by investor uneasiness over the
defense budget than by any serious dismay over the company's management for having made a large number of over-

Chart 5
Weekly Ranges of Common Stock Price on the New York Stock
Exchange, 1974–76

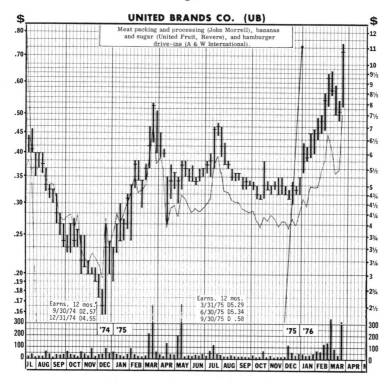

Source: Chart by permission of Securities Research Co.,
208 Newbury St., Boston, Massachusetts 02116

seas payments in connection with the sale of fighter aircraft.

Investor medium (30-day) reaction was only mildly negative for Lockheed's stock, and industry analysts attributed this market activity to the company's shaky financial condition rather than to any loss of confidence arising from media publicity of overseas payoffs. Investors were so little concerned that, at the height of the publicity about Lockheed's massive payoffs during the week of March 1, 1976, the stock rose three points! Medium (30-day) investor reactions were favorable for Exxon's and Gulf's stock. Though United Brands's shares showed the largest decline (21%) over the 30-day period, this may well have been a consequence of investor uneasiness over the company's weakened financial condition and management turmoil following the suicide of its chairman, Eli Black. The price of the stock later rebounded.

We conclude from this analysis that investors did not make any significant disposal of their stocks on learning of the overseas political payments by the managements of the selected five companies. In other words, investors generally do *not* consider these payments as adverse reflections on the integrity or competence of the managements of companies in which they have invested, or on the quality of their earnings. It is possible, although unlikely, that the *long-run* reactions of investors will be different.

Our limited analysis was confirmed by a more extensive study, made at the request of the SEC's Advisory Committee on Corporate Disclosure, by Professor Paul A. Griffin of the Stanford Graduate School of Business. Professor Griffin observed the price movements of the stocks of 74 companies during the eight weeks preceding and succeeding their disclosures to the SEC of political payments. His central conclusions were:

> Firms disclosing sensitive foreign payments appeared to experience a small decline in the value of their common stocks. The effect was temporary and within two weeks after the week of disclosure the firm's security price reverted back to normal levels.

With gentle irony, Professor Griffin added:

> The finding suggests that the degree of concern by those in government . . . does not appear entirely commensurate with the small temporary impact of the disclosure on the value of the corporation.[14]

These analyses raise several questions: Is the SEC talking in a vacuum when it insists that disclosure of foreign payments must be made for the protection of investors? And if investors are not registering their disenchantment with managements who make overseas payoffs—and even find aerospace stocks (Lockheed's in particular) attractive buys—*who* is really agitated about foreign payoffs? The answer appears to be mainly the anti-business segments of the media, the public, and the Congress. That investors do *not* believe that overseas political payments reflect adversely on the integrity and quality of corporate management was confirmed, ironically, by the SEC's own chairman. Speaking at a symposium on May 16, 1976, Chairman Hills stated:

> One large multinational corporation that had disclosed some questionable payments conducted a stockholder vote to determine whether it should disclose all foreign [payments] and political contributions. Ninety-nine percent of the stockholders voted no—they didn't want to see it.[15]

Indeed, recent research casts doubt on the value to investors of the disclosure requirements of the SEC. It contradicts the orthodox view that traders in financial markets react naïvely to information contained in published statements. It supports the idea that traders look behind and beyond published information to obtain and interpret the data that guides their behavior. This theory of "efficient markets" supports the conclusion that the disclosure requirements of the SEC are much less important to investors than they have been made to appear.[16]

The SEC "Voluntary" Disclosure Program

Recognizing that it lacked the manpower to investigate more than 9,000 companies, the SEC adopted a "voluntary" disclosure program, whereby companies that reported their questionable or illegal foreign payments and accounting practices might diminish the possibility of the Commission taking actions against them.[17] Under this program, a company that believes it might have "material" facts to disclose takes a number of steps. It authorizes an in-depth investigation of all relevant facts by persons not involved in the activities in question. Usually, this investigation has been made by a special committee of the company's board of directors, composed solely of outside (i.e., nonmanagement) directors. Such committees normally have the advice and assistance of independent legal counsel and public accountants. The investigation must encompass at least the preceding five years, or longer if necessary to provide a connected account. The report should include detailed information about each payment investigated. The findings of the special committee must be reported to the board of directors of the company. The board is required to issue appropriate corporate policies that terminate illegal or questionable payments and accounting practices, and establish adequate internal controls and safeguards against future improprieties. At the conclusion of the investigation, a final report must be filed with the Commission, generally on Form 8-K.[18]

In general, the SEC's voluntary disclosure program followed the same procedure used by the Commission in its thirteen injunctive cases taken against corporate defendants as of May 10, 1976, in which consent decrees required the companies to adhere substantially to the procedures outlined above. Consequently, voluntary disclosure was seen as less onerous and costly by the more than 360 companies who had chosen to make such reports up to the end of March 1977.

The SEC Guidelines

In its *Report* to the Senate Banking, Housing and Urban Affairs Committee on May 12, 1976, the SEC, for the first time since it began its investigation of overseas political payments by U.S. companies, offered some illustrative circumstances in which these payments need *not* be disclosed. However, the guidelines were ambiguous on key points, and they troubled corporate managements. They were so hedged with qualifications as to make it doubtful that many companies would feel sufficiently confident to risk omitting disclosures without consulting the SEC staff.

Senator Proxmire, Chairman of the Committee, praised the SEC's guidelines. However, he said that they left " 'large gray areas where both corporations and the commission must make subjective judgments about what facts need to be disclosed in specific cases.' "[19] This hiatus, he declared, fortified his argument for an outright prohibition against foreign payments by U.S. corporations—legislation which the SEC opposed.[20]

Although some informal guidance is available to companies participating in the voluntary disclosure program, the statement of principles contained in the SEC *Report* is the culmination of more than a year of internal debate among the commissioners and key members of the staff. Among the commission members who sought to release specific guidelines was Chairman Hills; he was supported in this endeavor by Commissioner Phillip Loomis. Commissioner John Evans, a former Congressional staff member, and Commissioner Irving Pollack, a longtime associate of the Director of the Enforcement Division, Stanley Sporkin, have condemned overseas political payments and were unwilling to grant any official approval to the practice, no matter how small the payments. (At the time of the transmittal of its report to Senator Proxmire, the Commission's fifth seat was vacant owing to the resignation of A. A. Sommer, Jr., earlier in 1976.)

The criteria laid out in the SEC *Report* are in the main a reiteration of rules that have heretofore guided the Comission's enforcement of disclosure. Thus the core of proscribed corporate conduct remains "the deliberate falsification of corporate books and records," which prevents auditors, directors, and shareholders from learning of foreign political payments. Disclosure under the SEC's statement of principles is also mandatory in the following circumstances:

> If "corporate officials have been willing to make repeated illegal payments without board knowledge and without proper accounting," thereby raising questions about "the quality of management."
>
> If the termination of payments or their being made public would jeopardize a "material" amount of the company's business, profits or sales (a figure sometimes interpreted to mean about 5 percent of each category, but which has also been interpreted to mean an amount that might be of interest to a "reasonable" or "prudent" investor).

As the *Report* of the Commission stated, "In attempting to determine whether a specific fact is 'material' there is 'no litmus paper test'." Each case presents unique combinations of facts. Whether particular information should be disclosed depends on the context in which the question arises. Falsification of books and accumulation of funds outside the system of corporate accountability are of paramount concern. Knowledge or participation of top corporate management and the board of directors is important. The size of such payments, and the amount of business affected by them, are pertinent. Defects in the system of corporate accountability must be taken into account. The legality of a payment under U.S. law or under the law of the foreign country in which it is made has a bearing. Whether payments are isolated events or there is a pattern of payments over a long period is an important consideration. The disclosure obligation depends on the presence of any one or more of all these factors.[21]

The guidelines call for the disclosure of payments "where they are significant in amount," but they fail to define "significant." Conversely, however, the *Report* suggests that a payment regarded by management and directors as insignificant need not be disclosed, provided it is accurately reported on

60

the company's books and if the transaction does not have significant "economic implications" to the company or to a significant line of the company's business.[22]

The discussion of fees or commissions paid to foreign agents or consultants also is ambiguous. On the one hand, the *Report* states: "There is nothing inherent in this practice [of utilizing the services of an agent] that gives rise to a disclosure obligation. . . ."[23] On the other hand, the guidelines confuse the issue by suggesting that the necessity for disclosure would depend on such factors as "the relationship of the agent to the government entity or contracting party." For example, would there be a tainted conflict of interest requiring disclosure where the agent has a member of his family in the ministry or department of the government that could award contracts to the company for which he works? The SEC seems to be moving in the direction of requiring a prospective investor or exporter to obtain an "advisory opinion" before undertaking to do business in those world regions where family connections are a sine qua non.[24] Further hedging its approval of the use of foreign agents, the *Report* indicates that whether or not a company should make disclosure of political payments hinges on whether or not steps have been taken by management to assure itself that foreign agents are not "conduits for improper payments."[25] The *Report* further asserts that a company cannot "remain indifferent" to the possibility that its agents are conduits for the transmission of political payments; but it does not set forth what it must do to avoid a charge of "indifference."[26]

In articulating its position on agents' fees, the SEC merely reiterated its long-held position that companies are expected to monitor an agent's use of his commissions. The Commission's attitude presents, however, both legal and practical difficulties. Requiring accountability from an agent on the expenditure of his fees is a departure from the settled rule of the common law that a principal is not responsible for the acts of his agent—a departure that some courts may not be willing to countenance. A more critical problem is that a demand on a well-known agent to make a detailed accounting to a foreign-based company of his disbursement of fees will be rebuffed indignantly as none of the principal's business. To require this information is a sure way to lose the services of experienced and well-established agents—a contingency that is immediately relevant in Middle East markets, probably the fastest growing and most lucrative in the world.

The SEC guidelines say that companies need not always disclose political payments to foreign officials "with the intent to assist the company in obtaining or retaining governmental contracts." The need for disclosure would depend, they assert, on distinguishing between *improper* "payments intended to secure the favorable exercise of judgment or discretion on behalf of the governmental body" and proper payments to an official "under applicable laws, regulations or customs" to act for suppliers in "connection with governmental contracts."[27] Having given its blessing to a venerable practice, however, the Commission quickly removes its benediction by declaring that disclosure may be required by other factors, such as "the recipient's insistence on the maintenance of secrecy or the inaccurate reflection of the payments on corporate books." Presumably the fact that a foreign government employee doesn't want it known in the U.S. press how much he received from a U.S. company for his intervention or assistance will be considered as a suspicious circumstance and will "suggest that the payment is in fact a form of bribery."

Still another type of payment that need not be disclosed is the small "lubrication" payoff used to expedite administrative services to which business enterprises are legitimately entitled but which may be refused or delayed until officials are compensated.[28] Addressing themselves to political contributions, the commissioners state only: "Where these contributions are illegal under local law, they can be assimilated to bribery."[29] This sweeping judgment ignored the prevalence of *extortion* by government officials, which at common law is clearly distinguishable from bribery. Nor did it cover situations in which an American ambassador acts as the instigator of a political payoff, or countenances the practice.[30]

Critics and Criticisms of the SEC

Numerous members of the securities bar—the lawyers who specialize in securities law and practice before the SEC—were disquieted by the Commission's expansion of the scope of "materiality." They believed the Commission was exceeding its statutory authority by the manner in which it applied its own definition of the components of disclosure. They thought the Commission was no longer just enforcing the securities laws but was trying to reform age-old business practices abroad. A former Chairman of the SEC, Ray Garrett, did not believe that the Commission had a mandate "to enforce, even indirectly, through compulsory disclosure, all of the world's laws and all of its perceptions of morality and right conduct."[31]

The sharpest criticism of the SEC's disclosure policy came from the Secretary of Commerce, Elliot Richardson, a former Attorney General, holder of numerous cabinet posts and a recent Ambassador to the Court of St. James. In a letter to Senator Proxmire, dated June 11, 1976, not only did Richardson suggest that the SEC's enforcement policy with respect to foreign political payments "may be based on tenuous legal grounds," but he also asked whether the "expansive definition of materiality has not raised serious questions as to the purpose and scope of the securities laws and the statutory role of the Commission." Richardson wrote: "There may be virtue in a legislative scheme which does not depend for its viability on the continued zeal or militancy of its administrators."[32]

That Secretary Richardson's remark touched a sensitive nerve is evident from the shrill denunciation of his letter by the SEC's incumbent chairman.[33]

Another critic was Milton V. Freeman, a former member of the SEC's staff and a partner in the prominent Washington law firm of Arnold & Porter. Freeman argued that the Commission had become an arbiter of legality and had promulgated a new legal doctrine: if something is done that is illegal, this illegality is material information to be disclosed to investors.[34] Not only was this novel doctrine unsupported by judicial decision, Freeman contended, but it was being applied capriciously. It was being used to expose foreign political payments, not because of their materiality in the traditional sense but only because the Commission now considered illegality to be material.

The problem with this new legal doctrine is that it leaves the Commission, as it is constituted at any particular time, free to determine when and how the doctrine will be applied. Thus, the current Commission has determined that a corporation need *not* make disclosure of its violation of laws against discrimination in hiring: "There is no distinguishable feature," the SEC says, "which would justify the singling out of equal employment from among the myriad of other social matters in which investors may be interested."[35] Compounding its own inconsistency, the SEC has listed a hundred "social matters" in which it suggests investors may be interested. They include activities which are illegal in the U.S. but which, if conducted abroad, are not *per se* material.[36] The Commission's inconsistency has been commented on by former chairman Garrett who observed: ". . . if you require disclosure of all violations of law against bribery or political contributions on the ground that illegal payments are material *per se*, we may be hard pressed to explain that other illegal corporate acts are not equally material for the same reason."[37]

Suppose a construction company has been forced to pay off

union officials and government inspectors to avoid incurring heavy penalties under its completion bond. Should the company be compelled to disclose this payment? And, let us take the situation of an American company with an assembly plant in Israel. As a consequence of this, it was placed on the Arab blacklist and barred from doing business in the Middle East—the most lucrative market in the world. It retains a well-known Middle East go-between to intervene with the Arab League to have its name removed. Again, should the company be required to disclose the payment of corporate *baksheesh* to officials of the Arab League in Damascus, lest the transaction be pronounced "improper" or "questionable"?

In our age of egalitarian democracy, the business corporation and other large institutions are, to be sure, popular targets of criticism. The corporate citizen has few legal rights and is not protected against self-incrimination under the Fifth Amendment. Nevertheless, to require a business corporation to confess to an illegal action even before charges have been brought by the appropriate law enforcement agencies or a trial has been held to determine whether a law has been violated—such a requirement violates elementary justice and due process of law.

That the SEC is substituting itself for local law enforcement authorities is not a fanciful idea. The Commission's investigation of political payments has been expanded to include inter-business payments within the United States. The SEC has charged a Maryland-based restaurant chain and two of its former executives with taking bribes from brewing companies for promoting certain brand-name beers.[38] And the Commission has charged Foremost-McKesson, the nation's largest wholesale wine and liquor distributor, with giving retailers illegal cash payments and free merchandise during the past five years as an inducement to buy the company's products.[39] The movement from statutory watchman of the securities markets to prosecutor of companies for offering liquor dealers trade discounts signals a fundamental change in the Commission's administration of the federal securities laws!

"We Have a Problem"

The day of avoiding litigation by obtaining out-of-court settlements from defendants through an aura of invincibility and fear of reprisals may be ending for the SEC. Increasing numbers of corporations charged with violations of the federal securities laws are taking their cases into the courts and winning many of them. Chairman Hills' declaration during October 1976 that his agency has "an obligation to clarify the law even if we are going to lose" will, it is to be hoped, lead the Commission to eschew the easy route of negotiation and settlement of payment cases and to test its interpretation of materiality in the courts.[40] The growing loss of legal credibility by the SEC among the bar and bench for its poor courtroom performance, and particularly its amicus curiae briefs filed with the U.S. Supreme Court, prompted Chairman Hills to say, "We have a problem, and I am concerned about it."[41]

A considerable part of this "problem" in its broader context is of the SEC's own making. It has shown little understanding of the varied cultures of the world, which sanction and enforce payments by foreign investors and traders. And its parochial view that overseas political payments are *not* a "material factor in the capacity of American business to compete abroad,"[42] along with its contention that making such payments reflects on the quality and integrity of management, have contributed to the disillusionment by the business community with the agency.

Nettled by a crescendo of criticism that the SEC had placed U.S. companies at a competitive disadvantage in foreign markets, Mr. Hills began, during 1976, a retreat from his previous tough position. In an address to the board of editors of the *New York Law Journal* he proposed that American companies, facing "unfair competition" from foreign companies who made payoffs, should be assisted by the full panoply of existing U.S. laws.[43] What Mr. Hills proposed was to aid U.S. firms, required by his agency to disclose their payments, by making life more difficult for foreign firms not under a similar constraint. He would accomplish this through the tariff laws and the U.S. government's power to inspect the books and records of foreign firms supplying goods to the U.S. federal government. The Secretary of the Treasury, he pointed out, has the power to investigate foreign competition that could weaken the domestic economy; and the President, he said, can apply trade sanctions against countries that permit the use of "unfair business tactics."

That Chairman Hills believed it necessary to deploy the government's heaviest artillery against foreign companies who use political payments in their competition with U.S. firms suggests that, contrary to his earlier views, U.S. business was, indeed, significantly handicapped by the policies of the SEC! Moreover, foreign suppliers to the U.S. government are only a minute fraction of the number of foreign companies competing with U.S. firms.

By September 1976, Hills was urging the federal government to do more than " 'rap our own people on the hand.' " He then sought to mobilize the combined resources of the executive branch—the Departments of State, Treasury, Justice, Commerce, and Agriculture—in a crusade to protect American business from the unfair practice of foreign companies using payoffs in their international business transactions. He proposed an escalating arsenal of retaliation against foreign companies: first, private protests to foreign governments; then, public protests, naming the offending company; and, ultimately, a refusal by this country to have any dealings with countries whose companies are permitted to engage in payoffs.[44]

Chairman Hills' belated defense of U.S. business abroad is to be welcomed. However, would it not be simpler to release American companies from the burdens placed on them by his own agency than to adopt the impractical remedial measures he has proposed? It would be virtually impossible to obtain proof *outside* the United States that *foreign companies* were making payments to officials of foreign governments to assist them in obtaining business. American companies may engage in mea culpa breastbeating in this country, but it is not a popular addiction abroad. Moreover, for U.S. officials to attempt to obtain such evidence against non-U.S. firms would be deeply resented by foreign governments as an intrusion into their sovereignty. The United States would appear to have enough troubles without inviting the justifiable wrath of other nations by playing the role of moral busybody.

The IRS Investigation: Policing Corporate Morality

The Internal Revenue Service cooperates closely with the SEC. It has stationed special agents in the office of the SEC to ascertain whether the companies found by the Commission to be derelict in disclosing overseas political payments were also in violation of the tax laws. Prior to the enactment of the Tax Reform Act of 1976, the sole responsibility of the IRS in this area was to enforce Section 162 (c) of the Internal Revenue Code. This section provides, in practical effect, that bribes and kickbacks, including payments to government officials, wherever made, *cannot* be deducted in computing taxable income.

The Tax Reform Act of 1976 introduced a new concept in the taxation of corporate income—so-called "bribe-produced income." U.S. corporations deriving income from the payment of a bribe are denied foreign tax credits, tax deferral, or tax benefits heretofore available to the Domestic International Sales Corporations (DISCs) organized by such companies. Thus, if a foreign-controlled corporation pays a bribe to obtain business, any income resulting therefrom will be taxed *immediately* to the U.S. parent, which is also deprived of the privilege of using any foreign tax imposed on such income as a tax credit against U.S. income tax liability. Similarly, a DISC will be unable to realize tax deferral on income resulting from the payment of a bribe. By failing to distinguish between a bribe initiated by a U.S. company and one paid in response to extortionate demands, the new law is equally punitive in its treatment of companies that are victims of extortion and those that initiate bribes. This is strange justice!

Though Donald C. Alexander, head of the IRS, has declared, "We are not concerned with policing corporate morality," actions of his organization belie his words. In August 1975, the IRS issued guidelines to its field examiners to aid in the identification of "slush funds" and "off book" devices used in making political contributions at home and abroad. And, in April and May of 1976, additional instructions were issued for field examiners to focus their attention on payments to foreign officials for which improper deductions may have been taken.

Three hundred veteran auditors, with a backup force of additional specialists from the Washington IRS headquarters, were placed at the disposal of the field auditors. The auditors' operating manual described techniques for ferreting out the payment of bribes or kickbacks or the making of political contributions. They included: talking with top officers, past and present, especially those who have been fired; interviewing the pilots of company planes; checking with company security personnel; examining executives' itineraries for stopovers in places with strict bank secrecy, i.e., the tax haven countries; sifting company cables to detect transferred funds; paying extra attention to subsidiaries located in tax havens; being suspicious when a company uses foreign products or services rather than those readily available in the United States; and watching for padded prices in foreign transactions.

The Eleven IRS Questions

In April of 1976, the IRS sent out a list of eleven detailed questions to be answered by executives, outside directors, and key employees of more than 1,200 companies, as well as the managing partner of each company's auditing firm. The targeted individuals were requested to respond by an affidavit. Here we summarize the thrust of those tortuously phrased questions (emphasis added); their full text is given in Appendix A to this chapter.

A. Did the company make any payment to *any entity* to obtain favorable treatment in securing business or for special concessions?

B. Did the company make any payment to a *government official or employee*, domestic or foreign, to obtain favorable treatment in securing business or to obtain special concessions?

C. Did the company give or loan any *money* to support or oppose any political party, candidate or committee, domestic or foreign?

D. Did the company give or donate any *property* to support or oppose any political party, candidate or committee, domestic or foreign?

E. Was any corporate employee *compensated for time spent* or *expenses* incurred to support or oppose any political party, candidate or committee, domestic or foreign?

F. Did the company make any *loans or gifts to corporate employees* for the purpose of contributing support, or opposing, any political party, candidate, or committee, domestic or foreign?

G. Did the company make any loans or gifts to any corporate employees to *reimburse them for contributions* they made to support, or oppose, any political party, candidate or committee, domestic or foreign?

H. Did any employee of the domestic corporation have signatory or other authority over disbursements from *foreign bank accounts?*

I. Has the company ever maintained a bank or other account, domestic or foreign, *not reflected on the corporate books?*

J. Did any employee of the corporation maintain a domestic or foreign *numbered account* or an account in a name other than that of the company?

K. What other present or former corporate directors, officers, or employees *may have knowledge* of any of the above subjects?

The sweeping nature of these questions and their ambiguity provoked a loud chorus of indignation from American businessmen, public accountants, and corporate lawyers. Does question A, for example, require a company to report payments to its advertising agency, marketing consultants, or salesmen—all of whom are attempting to "obtain favorable treatment in securing business?" Or consider question K. The respondent may not, in fact, know whether other persons now or formerly associated with the company have any knowledge of some detail embedded in one or more of the eleven questions. However, if subsequent investigation discloses such knowledge by a former colleague or a discharged employee, there is the possibility that he may be charged with perjury.

The respondent is thus confronted with a cruel dilemma: if he refuses to answer the questions, he will be exposed to criminal sanctions and even imprisonment. On the other hand, if his answers should be erroneous—even inadvertently so—he may be exposed to the penalty of perjury. Whether the IRS will garner much additional revenue from its inquisition is questionable, but there is no question about the heavy costs it has imposed on society. Lawyers and accountants are particularly incensed because they are being asked to breach their confidential relationships with clients. Arthur Young & Co., Peat, Marwick, Mitchell & Co., and Touche, Ross & Co.—three of the eight largest U.S. auditing firms— refused to answer the IRS questions. The American Institute of Certified Public Accountants sent a delegation to Washington to protest to Commissioner Alexander. Bowing to these protests, Alexander agreed to permit the auditors to sign a letter stating that, to the best of their knowledge, belief, and recollection, management's answers to the eleven questions are accurate. (Arthur Young & Co. even refused to sign this letter.)

On December 10, 1976, the IRS announced the first results of its year-long investigation. Of 900 companies checked thus far, it had found evidence that "slush funds" were maintained by 300 companies, ostensibly to funnel payments to domestic or foreign government officials. Among these firms, the IRS stated, "There are over 50 companies so far where we have reason to suspect there may have been tax evasion," and it indicated that it would bring tax fraud charges against some of them. IRS Commissioner Alexander stated that political payments were uncovered by detecting significant changes in amounts paid by companies to foreign consultants, discrepancies in the amounts paid to different consultants performing essentially the same services, unusual investments or loans, sudden write-offs of loans, foreign subsidiaries showing minimal revenues or accumulated deficits, and transfers of large amounts of cash to foreign units.[45] Should the IRS bring charges and succeed in convicting one-third of the companies it suspected of willful tax evasion, this would implicate about 2 percent of the 900 firms it audited—a regrettable but still small percentage of the multinational companies investigated.

The gravamen of the complaint against the IRS investigation of improper payments is that the inquiry assumed a criminal intent and was too sweeping and indiscriminate. It is hardly appropriate, the critics say, to the national tax collecting agency of a democratic nation whose beginnings had something to do with arbitrary taxation.

From Trust-Busting to Bribe-Busting

An American corporation that pays a bribe to gain favorable legislative treatment from a foreign government or to facilitate a sale of its product or services at the expense of a *foreign competitor* will not as a general rule be in violation of the U.S. antitrust laws. Within the legal and judicial netherworld of antitrust law, such economic behavior by a U.S. firm overseas has no adverse competitive efforts on U.S. commerce. On the other hand, a payment by a U.S. firm designed to prevent *another U.S. firm* from sharing in a market, or a payment intended to prevent *a U.S. competitor* from being awarded a contract, may well be an unfair method of competition within the purview of Section 5 of the Federal Trade Commission Act. Indeed, the FTC has probed allegations that General Tire & Rubber made payoffs in Morocco to prevent a competitor, Goodyear Tire & Rubber, from obtaining a permit to do business in that country.[46]

"If corporate bribery isn't an unfair method of competition, I don't know what it is," remarked Stephen Nye, an FTC commissioner. He is reported to have said the entire FTC shares the view that overseas bribery that affects U.S. commerce is within FTC jurisdiction. The FTC has announced that it is expanding its investigation of unfair methods of competition to include "illegal political contributions, kickbacks and bribes," which may have been made by aerospace companies, especially Lockheed and Northrop.

A conspiracy among several U.S. companies to bribe a foreign official with the objective of preventing another U.S. company from entering a particular market would probably be held to violate Section 1 of the Sherman Act.[47] That a payment involving one company and one foreign government official also constitutes a conspiracy under this section of the Sherman Act is dubious. However, payments made by one company for the purpose of monopolizing a foreign market might well be in violation of the Act.

The Clayton Act prohibits the payment of commissions or other allowances, except for services actually rendered, in connection with the sale of goods in which either the buyer or seller is engaged in commerce, including commerce with foreign nations. This section encompasses commercial bribery and bribes paid to state government officials to secure business at the expense of U.S. competitors. It is a conceivable, though remote, possibility that this section could be held to be applicable to the payment of a bribe for the purpose of preventing a U.S. competitor from being awarded a contract by a foreign government.

Although the Antitrust Division of the Department of Justice has been quiescent, it has expanded its interest in criminal investigations of companies that have reported making payoffs to foreign officials. Richard L. Thornburgh, Assistant Attorney General for the Justice Department's Criminal Division during the Ford Administration, has indicated that criminal charges—other than for violations of the tax laws—are under consideration in several cases.

Following the reporting of the Lockheed payoffs in Japan and the resultant political crisis among the factions that constitute the ruling and governing Liberal Democratic Party, the Justice Department established a modus operandi for a mutual exchange of information. Its agreement with Japanese officials has served as a prototype for similar arrangements with ten other governments (at this writing) where foreign payments to government officials may be involved. The four-page agreement with Japan provides that information to be exchanged will be limited to evidence that can be used in criminal, civil and administrative" proceedings. This means that Japan (and other governments who have signed the Mutual Cooperation Pact with the Department of Justice) will supply evidence sought by the SEC as well as the

Criminal Division of the Department of Justice. Member countries have agreed that they must notify each other when they plan to use any of the exchanged information in legal proceedings. However, under the pact, countries would not seek information aimed at helping "third parties," such as stockholders or others, who could use this information for private class action or antitrust suits.

The Subcommittee on Multinational Corporations Enters the Scene

A fourth federal investigation into foreign political payments was conducted by the Subcommittee on Multinational Corporations of the U.S. Senate Foreign Relations Committee, whose chairman was Senator Frank Church of Idaho.[48] Elsewhere, we have noted the origin of this Subcommittee during 1973, as an aftermath of the offer of funds by International Telephone and Telegraph to the CIA to help prevent a socialist takeover of the Chilean government. Following the disclosures to the Watergate investigating committee during 1974, this Subcommittee seized on political contributions to foreign governments by U.S.-based corporations as a topic for investigation. Such an opportunity for national publicity was not to be missed by Senator Church, then a man with presidential ambitions.

The Subcommittee on Multinational Corporations held a series of hearings during 1975. At these hearings, which were widely publicized, testimony was taken on the foreign political contributions of Gulf, Northrop, Exxon, Mobil, and Lockheed. Masses of company documents were released to the press. We shall not here recount the findings of the Subcommittee; they are treated elsewhere in this book. What concerns us here is the theory underlying the investigation. How did a Subcommittee of the Senate Committee on Foreign

Relations justify its concern with foreign political payments by multinational companies?

In opening the hearings, Senator Church supplied the Subcommittee's answer. He said: ". . . what we are concerned with is not a question of private or public morality. What concerns us here is a major issue of foreign policy. . . ." He quoted from Gunnar Myrdal's *Asian Drama*, which advanced the thesis, Senator Church said, that ". . . the habitual practice of bribery and dishonesty tends to pave the way for an authoritarian regime," and that "the Communists maintain that corruption is bred by capitalism, and with considerable justification they pride themselves on its eradication under a Communist regime." "Thus," Gunnar Myrdal concluded, "it is obvious that the extent of corruption has a direct bearing on the stability of governments."[49]

Senator Church's effort to connect corruption in the business-government relationship with governmental instability and the spread of communism is more disingenuous than it is convincing. Bribery and extortion have persisted in one form or another from time immemorial in *both* communist and noncommunist societies. Who will contend that they have been absent from the United States—the world's oldest and most stable capitalistic democracy? Or that corruption is absent from the Soviet Union, whose sixty years make it the oldest and stablest of the world's communist societies? To describe U.S. corporate involvement in these ancient practices as "a major issue of foreign policy" surely is to transcend the boundaries of permissible political rhetoric!

A second justification offered by Senator Church for his Subcommittee's investigation was that "illicit corporate contributions, bribes and payoffs create unfair conditions for scrupulous competitors."[50] This argument, too, fails to convince. Fairness in competition is the province of the Federal Trade Commission and the Antitrust Division of the Department of Justice—not of the Senate Committee on Foreign

Relations. An even more basic criticism, however, is that Senator Church's remarks implied that American multinational companies were bribers—instigators of the foreign political payments that created unfair competition for other American companies. However, the majority of such payments are, in fact, extortions by foreign government employees, as will be seen. What usually creates a problem for the U.S. company is not an "unscrupulous" competing U.S. company but an "unscrupulous" foreign government employee.

The printed transcript of the Hearings shows that, contrary to the Chairman's disavowal of interest in moral questions, he employed strong rhetoric condemning the alleged behavior of the American companies under investigation on moral grounds. Moreover, the Hearings fail to disclose that primary interest, which he professed, in the effect of foreign political payments on U.S. foreign relations and the stability of foreign governments. Indeed, one may ask, what *were* the probable effects of the Church Subcommittee's inquiries on the stability of foreign governments? Considering the serious impacts of its disclosures upon the governments of Japan and The Netherlands—discussed elsewhere in this book—it can plausibly be argued that the Subcommittee's work was itself a much stronger destabilizing influence than were the payments themselves!

The Media and the New Morality

In any account of the new moral censorship of American business, attention must be paid to the role of the news media. Although this role has been that of a resonator and amplifier rather than an originator, the particular events that the media choose to publicize and their interpretations of those events are matters of importance to the nation. They help to mold public opinion, regulatory actions, judicial decision, and the law.

During the decade of the 1970s, the print and electronic media emerged as an institution comparable in power and influence to the three coordinate branches of government. Shielded by the First Amendment to the U.S. Constitution, the press has become almost invulnerable to the criticism and legislative curbs that limit the power of such other social institutions as business or government. Congressmen, who depend upon the radio and television networks for national visibility, are loath to level criticisms at the media.

In its two most dramatic conflicts with the Nixon Administration—publication of the purloined Pentagon Papers and of the Watergate scandal—the Washington-based press corps and the New York-Washington press axis not only challenged but defeated a President of the United States. Indeed, Professor Huntington has asserted that the media were able to accomplish what no other group of politicians or disgruntled citizens had previously done in American history—bring about a journalistic coup d'etat that forced the resignation of a President.[51]

Emerging from their triumph with a strong sense of hubris, media moralists proceeded to castigate multinational corporations for making political payments overseas. The record shows that they exploited and sensationalized the revelations of the SEC and of the Church Subcommittee. *Time* and *Newsweek* printed special cover stories on the payoff "scandal." *Time* spread across the cover of its February 23, 1976, issue: "The Big Payoff, Lockheed Scandal, Graft Around the Globe." The *Los Angeles Times* editorialized on foreign payments as "the spreading poison." The *Washington Post* sonorously warned that American confidence in business institutions and leadership was in a "process of disintegration" and involved a "national crisis." And *Time* intoned that foreign payments by American companies "strike at the very heart of democratic government." These declamations were repeated by the television networks and the wire services. Naturally, this overblown editorializing has influenced the thought of tens of millions of Americans.[52]

Although the media editorials have roundly condemned corporations for making political contributions at home and abroad—payments which were legal in many jurisdictions—they have yet to express equal indignation about the congressmen and public officials of this and other nations who received these payments and who, in many instances, solicited them. Media voices have also been muted about violations of the Corrupt Practices Act by the big labor unions. As John J. McCloy—the distinguished American who recently served as chairman of a special committee of the board of directors of Gulf Oil to investigate its questionable payments—observed in an address to the Bar Association of the City of New York on March 15, 1976, failure to enforce the law against political contributions by labor unions may have been a significant cause of its violation by some business corporations.

Exaggerated accounts in the media of corporate misbehavior have helped to create a hostile environment for American business. Out of this environment have come ill-considered and ineffective proposals for new business regulations. Another regrettable consequence has been a further deterioration in public confidence in the business institution and a further weakening of the bonds that hold together our democratic society.

Results of the New Censorship

What have been the consequences of the new governmental censorship of foreign political payments by American companies? Has it reduced their number? If so, has it caused American companies to lose business to foreign-based competitors, with adverse results for U.S. employment and the balance of international payments?

So far, the evidence is inconclusive. During February 1977 the *Wall Street Journal* surveyed twenty-five large corporations that had disclosed questionable payments abroad and had later forbidden their employees from making any more of them. None reported that it had lost a significant amount of business.[53] Without doubt, the strong stand taken by U.S. government agencies against the making of such payments did sharply curb the practice. However, the reports of no loss of business should be viewed in the light of a general cyclical upswing in world business and of the difficulties of disentangling its effects from those associated with the cessation of political payments. At a conference of senior business executives held at UCLA during the same month, the concensus was that the governmental crackdown on political payments had, indeed, caused foreign governments to divert many orders away from U.S. companies. As one executive expressed it, "foreign governments prefer to deal with companies whose governments do *not* require them to 'kiss and tell'—and that means nearly every other government than ours." But the long-run effects of unilateral efforts by the U.S. government to stop foreign political payments cannot yet be assessed with confidence.

Guidelines for Censors

We have seen that federal government inquiries into corporate political payments abroad constitute a tale of impetuous action, accompanied by high rhetoric and moral indignation, followed by a good deal of backtracking and withdrawals, all leaving in their wake much confusion.

The U.S. government should *not* be criticized for a concern with moral issues, including those that arise in business-government relationships at home and abroad. We strongly believe that our government should address problems of ethical behavior in business—and in government and the media as well. When federal agencies do deal with these issues, however, they should do so openly and candidly, and without hypocritical denials of such interests. They should display objectivity and a becoming humility in the face of complexity. Their inquiries should show sensitivity and sophistication regarding the social, cultural, and ethical values of other societies, rather than the parochialism and ethnocentricity too often displayed. Finally, those who undertake to assess the morality of others would do well to recall the words of Matthew: "Judge not, that ye be not judged."

Appendix A: Text of the Eleven IRS Questions

A. Did the corporation, any corporate officer or employee or any third party acting on behalf of the corporation, make, directly or indirectly, any bribes, kickbacks or other payments, regardless of form, whether in money, property, or services, to any employee, person, company or organization, or any representative of any person, company or organization, to obtain favorable treatment in securing business or to otherwise obtain special concessions, or to pay for favorable treatment for business secured or for special concessions already obtained?

B. Did the corporation, any corporate officer or employee or any third party acting on behalf of the corporation, make any bribes, kickbacks, or other payments regardless of form whether in money, property or services, directly or indirectly, to or for the benefit of any government official or employee, domestic or foreign, whether on the national level or a lower level such as state, county or local (in the case of a foreign government also including any level inferior to the national level) and including regulatory agencies or governmentally-controlled businesses, corporations, companies or societies, for the purpose of affecting his/her action or the action of the government he/she represents to obtain favorable treatment in securing business or to obtain special concessions, or to pay for business secured or special concessions, or to pay for business secured or special concessions obtained in the past?

C. Were corporate funds donated, loaned or made available, directly or indirectly, to or for the use or benefit of, or for the purpose of opposing, any government or subdivision thereof, political party, candidate or committee, either domestic or foreign?

D. Was corporate property of any kind donated, loaned, or made available, directly or indirectly, to or for the use or benefit of, or for the purpose of opposing, any government or subdivision thereof, political party, candidate or committee, either domestic or foreign?

E. Was any corporate officer or employee compensated, directly or indirectly, by the corporation, for time spent or expenses incurred in performing services for the benefit of, or for the purpose of opposing, any government or subdivision thereof, political party, candidate or committee, either domestic or foreign?

F. Did the corporation make any loans, donations or other disbursements, directly or indirectly, to corporate officers or employees or others for the purpose of making contributions, directly or indirectly, for the use or benefit of, or for, the purpose of opposing, any government or subdivision thereof, political party, candidate or committee, either domestic or foreign?

G. Did the corporation make any loans, donations or other disbursements, directly or indirectly, to corporate officers or employees or others for the purpose of reimbursing such corporate officers, employees or others for contributions made, directly or indirectly, for the use or benefit of, or for the purpose of opposing, any government or subdivision thereof, political party, candidate or committee, either domestic or foreign?

H. Does now or did any corporate officer or employee or any third party acting on behalf of the domestic corporation have signatory or other authority or control over disbursements from foreign bank accounts?

I. Does now or did the corporation maintain a bank account or any other account of any kind, either domestic or foreign, which account was not reflected on the corporate books, records, balance sheets, or financial statements?

J. Does now or did the corporation or any other person or entity acting on behalf of the corporation maintain a domestic or foreign numbered account or an account in a name other than the name of the corporation?

K. Which other present or former corporate officers, directors, employees, or other persons acting on behalf of the corporation may have knowledge concerning any of the above areas?

Appendix B: Other Governmental Controls of Fees and Commissions Paid on Foreign Sales

Though other departments and agencies of the U.S. government do not maintain a disclosure system as elaborate or far-reaching as that of the SEC, several agencies have available to them a broad federal statute imposing criminal or civil liability for making false statements. Section 1001 of the Fraud and False Statements Act provides:

> Whoever, in any matter within the jurisdiction of any department or agency of the United States knowingly and willfully falsifies, conceals or covers up by any trick, scheme, or device a material fact, or makes any false, fictitious or fraudulent statements or representations, or makes or uses any false writing or document knowing the same to contain any false,

fictitious or fraudulent statement or entry, shall be fined not more than $10,000 or imprisoned not more than five years, or both.

In addition to this blanket coverage, the Export-Import Bank, the Agency for International Development, and the Department of State have specialized statutes governing false statements made by persons conducting business with these agencies under the special programs that they administer.

U.S. firms whose goods are purchased through Export-Import Bank loans are required to furnish a certificate to the Bank that declares any commissions, fees, or other costs of goods sold over and above the actual price. The Agency for International Development (AID), under a special statute authorizing loans of hard currency to foreign countries for purchase of U.S. commodities, requires an American exporter to file a supplier's certificate, also certified to by AID, that no kickbacks or commissions were paid.

The International Security Assistance and Arms Export Control Act of 1976 requires reports to be filed with the Secretary of State, pursuant to regulations issued by him, of political contributions, gifts, commissions, and fees paid to agents and others in order to secure sales of military equipment in government-to-government sales. The statute also provides that such payments are not to be reimbursed unless found to be reasonable, allocable to the contract, and not made to an intermediary for the purpose of using improper influence. Similar reporting requirements are imposed for commercial sales of hardware and equipment handled directly by military contractors. All such information is to be transmitted to the Congress, through quarterly reports released by the President, and is to be deemed to be "confidential." (This is no guarantee that the information will not be leaked to the media.)

It should be noted that, even without this statute, the Department of Defense requires disclosure of all fees and commissions paid in the sale of military equipment under the Military Sales Act of 1968. Moreover, the general statute on false or fraudulent statements applies.

The use of agents and payment of agents' fees is not eliminated under the disclosure requirements of the new Act. Payment of "reasonable" agents' fees as part of "cost of sales" on Foreign Military Sales (FMS) is still operative, and guidelines of the Armed Services Procurement Regulation (ASPR) continue to be the source of authority for the practice.

There is an exception in the case of Iran. The Iranian government has stated categorically that it will not permit a fee for an agent in the pricing of any U.S. equipment purchased under Foreign Military Sales. (U.S. arms sales to Iran average between $2 and $3 billion annually and are expected to continue at this rate over the next four years.) This declaration of policy has led to the issuance of Defense Procurement Circular #117, November 23, 1973, which, in turn, requires inclusion in all Letters of Offer to Iran of the following language:

> Notwithstanding any other provision of this contract, any direct or indirect costs of agents' fees/commissions for contractor sales or agents involved in FMS to the Government of Iran shall be considered as an unallowable item of cost under this contract.

3

Classes and Cases
of Foreign Political Payments

Hᴀᴠɪɴɢ surveyed the role of political payments in societies around the world and reviewed the U.S. government investigations into the involvement of American multinational corporations with these payments, we come now to classify these payments and to illustrate each class with examples drawn from world business.

By a "political payment" we will mean *any transfer of money or any thing of value made with the aim of influencing the behavior of politicians, political candidates, political parties, or government officials and employees in their legislative, administrative, and judicial actions.* Our central concern is, of course, with *foreign* political payments. Such payments include those made to induce favorable action by foreign officials or to deter harmful action (or inaction), and contributions to candidates for foreign political offices or to foreign political organizations or to news media affiliated with them. Also included here are payments made to private businessmen of foreign countries who act as local agents or representatives of American-based companies, but who may serve as conduits for political payments to those mentioned above.

The Classes of Foreign Political Payments

The whole category of foreign political payments has been variously labeled by U.S. government regulatory agencies and by the news media as "sensitive," "questionable," "improper," "unethical," "immoral," or "illegal." The general impression made on the American people by the publicity given these payments is that U.S.-based multinational companies practice massive bribery and corrupt foreign government officials for profit. As a result, many believe that Congress should pass a law imposing severe penalties on corporate officials for engaging in these practices.

This is, as we shall see, a simplistic diagnosis of the problem, followed by a naïve prescription for its remedy. It reflects ignorance of what, in fact, is a very complex phenomenon. And it falsely depicts the American multinational company as a moral pariah, corrupting the honest and efficient officials of foreign governments. We shall show that foreign political payments are, in fact, small in relation to the total volume of international business and relatively infrequent; that they are made to a wide variety of persons for a multiplicity of reasons; that they take on a bewildering variety of forms; that many are lawful and those that are not involve varying degrees of extortion as well as bribery; and that they present real ethical dilemmas to the managers of multinational corporations.

Table 2 presents a classification of foreign political payments by U.S. multinational corporations in which such payments are classified by legal type, by type of foreign recipient,

TABLE 2   Classification of Foreign Political Payments by U.S. Multi-national Corporations

1. *By Legal Type*
   A. Lawful payments
   B. Bribery
   C. Extortion
   D. Hybrids of bribery and extortion

2. *By Type of Foreign Recipient*
   A. Major government officials—legislative, executive, or judicial
   B. Minor government employees
   C. Employees of government-owned corporations
   D. Political organizations
   E. Candidates for government offices
   F. Politically affiliated news media
   G. Agents, finders, consultants, or representatives

3. *By Mode of Payment*
   A. Cash
   B. Deposits in numbered foreign bank accounts
   C. Overbilling of sales with kickback to the buyer
   D. Gifts of property (watches, jewelry, paintings, "free" samples)
   E. Gifts of services (use of automobiles, aircraft, hunting lodges, payments of rent on homes, country club dues, etc.)
   F. Payment of travel and entertainment expenses
   G. Making unsecured loans—never collected
   H. Putting relatives on the payroll as "consultants"
   I. Providing scholarships and educational expenses for children
   J. Making contributions to charities of the payee's choice
   K. Purchasing property from the payee at an inflated price
   L. Selling property to payee at a deflated price

4. *By Purpose of Payer*
   A. Obtain or retain business
   B. Reduce political risks
   C. Avoid harassment
   D. Reduce taxes
   E. Induce official action

by mode of payment, and by purpose of the payer. Evidently, we are dealing with a fabric of rich texture and intricate design. A discussion of the purposes of the many kinds of payment, illustrated by examples, will reveal the full panoply of such transactions. It will lay a foundation for analyzing these payments in economic and political terms, and for constructing positive proposals for reforms that can elevate the ethical plane of multinational business in the future.

Foreign Political Payments by Legal Type

The most basic legal distinction with respect to corporate political payments is between those that are lawful and those that are not. Payments made as a result of bribery or extortion are, of course, generally outlawed. But the American states and foreign nations differ in their treatment of corporate contributions to political parties or candidates of political parties. For example, such payments can lawfully be made in Canada; but in the United States they are illegal when made to candidates or parties in federal elections, and also in the state and municipal elections of many states.

John J. McCloy summarized well the state of the law in his address to a Conference Board meeting on Preventing Illegal Corporate Payments, held in New York City, during June 1976.

> With regard to political corporate contribution payments made domestically, they are generally illegal under the Corrupt Practices Acts, which have been in the Federal and a number of state statutes for many years. There are some states—nine, I believe—in which political contributions are not illegal. Moreover, generally speaking, political contributions are not considered illegal in most foreign jurisdictions—although frequently restrictions are imposed on the size of the contributions and the manner of payments.[1]

The point is that some types of corporate political payments—notably contributions to political parties or candidates for election to public office—are lawful in most foreign countries and in some American states. Even in jurisdictions where these contributions are unlawful, they are not "bribes." Although they may be made for the purpose of acquiring influence and the sympathetic exercise of political power, they are not conditioned on the abuse of governmental authority, which is the essence of bribery or extortion. Likewise, payments by a company to its foreign agents are political payments within our definition, but they are generally lawful.

Fundamental to a discussion of *unlawful* political payments is the legal distinction between bribery and extortion. The journalistic habit of describing all such payments by American companies as "bribery" is a serious error.

Black's Law Dictionary defines a "bribe" as "Any valuable thing given or promised, or any preferment, advantage, privilege or emolument, given or promised corruptly and against law as an inducement to any person acting in an official or public capacity to violate or forbear from his duty, or to improperly influence his behavior in the performance of his duty."[2] It states that "to extort" means "to compel payments by means of threats of injury to person, property or reputation" or "the corrupt demanding or receiving by a person in office of a fee for services which should be performed gratuitously; or, where compensation is permissible, of a larger fee than the law justified, or of a fee not due."[3] In short a bribe is a payment made to *induce* the payee to do something for the payer that is improper; an extortion is a payment made to *deter* the payee from harming the payer in some way. In a bribe, the initiator is the payer, the object is an improper favor, and the motivating influence is an offer of something of value. In an extortion, the initiator is the recipient, the object is a thing of value, and the motivating force is a threat of harm to the payer.

Obviously, the burden of guilt in bribery is borne by the payer (here, the multinational company), whereas in extortion it is borne by the recipient (here, the foreign political or governmental figure). This often-overlooked distinction is vital in any effort to assign blame for improper political payments for American companies abroad. As we shall see, the evidence shows that most of these payments have more of the characteristics of extortion than of bribery.

Pure bribery and extortion have the characteristics we have noted; but many foreign political payments are *hybrids* of the two types. Consider the case of a small payment by an American business executive to the customs officer of a foreign government to expedite the clearance of imports into the country. This type of payment has been called euphemistically a "facilitating payment" and is colloquially known as "grease." If, in fact, the businessman offered payment in return for *specially rapid* service by the customs officer, it would be a bribe. If, on the other hand, the customs officer indicated that he would *delay* a *normal* clearance unless he were paid off, it would be an extortion. But it is often difficult to classify particular transactions because they involve aspects of both types of payments. Most, however, are made to induce foreign officials to perform their regular duties, and not to procure special favors for the multinational company.

It is illuminating to compare tipping with bribery and extortion, because all three are alternative types of payments for services. The dictionary defines a "tip" as "a gift or gratuity of money" or "a small present of money," such as is given to a waiter or servant. But this fails to define accurately the nature of a tipping transaction. *Pure tipping,* in the ideal sense, is the giving of a small gratuity in appreciation of good service, voluntarily and without expectation of *any* quid pro quo. Here, neither its being given nor withheld influences the quality of services rendered. In purpose and effect, *pure* tipping is quite distince from either bribery or extortion, being given neither to induce the servant to perform services *beyond* his normal duties nor to deter him from withholding *normal* services.

But anyone whose travels have brought him into extensive contact with service employees around the world will testify that pure tipping is rare. "Impure" or conventional tipping encompasses varying combinations of bribery and extortion. In the real world, many tips take on the color of bribes, as when the patron slips the restaurant captain $5 to be seated favorably, and another $5 to the waiter to ensure specially prompt and attentive service. And even more frequently, tipping becomes basically extortion, as the traveler who has waited long for delivery of his luggage because he failed to tip the bell captain will sadly testify. Indeed, there *is* a quid pro quo for most tips. If it takes the form of especially attentive service, the tip becomes a bribe; if of the avoidance of subnormal service, it becomes an extortion.

This same analysis can be applied to the "grease" paid by multinational companies to lubricate the wheels of commerce. "Greasing," like tipping, is an ingrained custom in most countries of the world, and the foreigner ignores it at heavy cost to himself. For the multinational corporation to eliminate "greasing" from its foreign business would have consequences as serious as those that would befall the traveler abroad were he to stop tipping!

The Recipients of Foreign Political Payments

The foreign political payments made by American multinational companies may also be classified by the type of recipient. Among foreign recipients, it is convenient to distinguish major political and governmental figures, government employees, employees of government-owned corporations, political party organizations, candidates for public office, news media affiliated with political organizations, and business agents, finders, and consultants, who may serve as conduits for payments to government officials.

Major political leaders of foreign nations come first to mind as recipients of corporate payoffs. For example: newspaper headlines have trumpeted the charges that Prince Bernhard of The Netherlands or former Prime Minister Kakuei Tanaka of Japan requested payments from Lockheed for promoting the purchase by their governments of that company's military or civilian aircraft.[4] As a result, the public has come to suspect that bribery of high foreign political figures by American companies is rampant. Yet the number of *proven* cases of bribery involving misconduct by high officials of foreign governments is very small. And many instances of misconduct are more extortion than bribery. The truth, however, is always hard to discover because of the clandestine nature of the transactions.

Rank-and-file employees of foreign governments are undoubtedly the most frequent recipients of these payments, albeit small ones. Most of this "grease" goes to customs officers, port employees, railroad employees, and other functionaries whose actions or failures to act put them in a position to grant favors or to threaten harm to multinational companies that must deal with them. Generally, such payments are relatively small in amount, but some assume large dimensions.

One actual case involved payments by the foreign affiliate of an American chemical company to the local employees of a railroad owned by a Latin American government. The plant of the company depended entirely upon rail freight cars to bring in its raw materials and to haul out its finished product. The local railroad employees assessed heavy "switching" charges against the company for switching loaded cars into and out of its terminal, and "moving" charges for keeping loaded cars moving toward their destination. Switching and moving freight cars were, of course, part of their assigned duties. They offered to cancel these charges in return for under-the-table payments. The local plant manager made these payments because the only alternative was to shut down his plant. He did not appeal to higher authorities in the railroad because he suspected that they too were "on the take"; and, if they were not, this action would make his relations with the local railroad employees even more costly! Although these payments were clearly prohibited by the laws of the country and cannot be condoned, the unhappy dilemma of this plant manager evokes sympathy.

Similar tales can be told about payoffs to obtain the clearance of imports or urgently needed machinery, to move equipment off the docks of a port, to obtain visas for foreign workers, or to expedite the issuance of building permits. And "grease" is by no means confined to foreign business operations. As any American construction contractor will testify, it is also rife at home.

Another class of recipient is that of employees of corporations owned by foreign governments. Although their legal status may be different than that of regular civil servants, they too possess discretionary authority, which can be used to favor or to penalize multinational firms. Government-owned corporations play an important role in many nations. This is especially true where governments attempt to control key sectors of their economies through ownership of petroleum, mining, steel, fertilizer, aluminum, and other basic industries. The larger this public sector, the greater is the potential for extorting improper payments from multinational firms. Payments made to influence the actions of *full-time* employees of government-owned corporations are normally illegal under the laws of the foreign countries concerned. But the status of payments to *part-time* employees, to consultants, or to relatives of full-time employees is frequently unclear.

In one case, an American coal company retained an agent to represent it in sales of its metallurgical coal to a steel company owned by a South American government. It paid the agent a commission that was normal in the trade and reasonable in the light of the services rendered. Later, the company learned that its agent was a part-time consultant of the steel company. Because this involved an apparent conflict of interests, it thereupon terminated the relationship.

The same American coal company appointed as its agent

to sell coal to the national steel company of an Asian country an Asian businessman who turned out to be a relative of the prime minister of that country. The commission paid him was also normal in the trade and reasonable in relation to the services he performed. Believing that the arrangement might be subject to criticism, however, the company in time terminated the agency. Its sales of coal to the Asian steel company thereupon declined. Later, it considered the matter still again. Reasoning that the agent was not a government employee, that no American or foreign law prohibited the relative of a government official from engaging in a lawful business activity, and that there was nothing in the relationship to arouse suspicion, it reinstated the agent. Coal sales soon resumed their former level. Here, again, were close decisions, and opinions will differ about the propriety of each.

Contributions to candidates for foreign public office, to foreign political organizations, or to their affiliated news media constitute still another class of recipient of political payments by American corporations. Unlike "grease," which most observers have accepted as an inevitable but minor social peccadillo, these payments are meant to protect the company against the passage of adverse laws and regulations by foreign governments. They have provoked a loud chorus of criticism. Critics condemn interference by an American-based company in the internal political affairs of foreign countries. The well-publicized cases of International Telephone and Telegraph in Chile, of Exxon (then Standard Oil of New Jersey) in Italy, and of Gulf in South Korea—which we shall examine in detail —have become focal points of controversy. To some degree the opposition to such payments is based on an erroneous belief that they are prohibited abroad as they are in the United States. However, certain kinds of political payments are lawful in many foreign nations, as we have seen. Criticism has also been directed to the cover-up of such payments, by American companies, with improper accounting. But, the *basic* issue these payments raise is the mode and the degree of political involvement that is appropriate for the business corporation in a foreign country. We will return to this issue later on.

The final class of recipient to be discussed is the business agent, finder, representative, or consultant of the U.S.-based company in foreign countries. He is a businessman rather than a governmental employee, but he may serve as a conduit for the transmission of funds to governmental employees. There is, of course, nothing improper about the mere employment by an American company of agents or representatives to advance its business interests. In most countries this is desirable and, in some, essential. When an American company proposes to enter a foreign nation, it ordinarily needs the assistance of persons who are familiar with the language, laws, and commercial customs of that country, and who have personal acquaintance with its businessmen and government officials. Such representatives can perform services of great value. They can expedite business operations and shorten the time span between initial investment and returns from it. They can arrange introductions and meetings, supply information, make local market studies, and conduct involved negotiations leading to business agreements.

Representatives are paid a commission for their services, usually a percentage of the value of sales they have negotiated. When transactions range into hundreds of millions of dollars, the commissions can range into millions of dollars. These large payments give rise to the suspicion that, if earned from sales to the government, the agent has bribed officials to get the order. Unfortunately, these suspicions are sometimes well founded, as the case of Lookheed illustrates. Nevertheless, it would be unjust and inaccurate to characterize all fees and commissions paid to foreign agents as "bribes" or "payoffs." Most are legitimate business outlays for necessary services of value to the company.

The American multinational company faces a dilemma in

dealing with its foreign agents and consultants. No company can *guarantee* that none of its payments to an agent is passed on by him to government officials. Neither an American company nor the U.S. government has the legal right to compel a foreign agent to submit to an investigation of the uses he makes of his fees or commissions. If such rights exist, they are possessed by the foreign government involved. For these and other reasons, hasty proposals for the public disclosure or U.S. governmental review of all foreign agency agreements or payments should be rejected.

Yet, these payments raise difficult issues. To what extent, in fact, are they passed on to government employees? What are the legal and moral responsibilities of an American company for assuring that they are not improperly transmitted? Examples of the problems raised by payments to agents are described later on, as are proposals for action by multinational companies for dealing with them.

The Modes of Payment

The methods of making foreign political payments are legion. Because many are known by the parties to be illegal or unethical, a multitude of stratagems has been devised to disguise their true nature. Most payments are made in currency rather than by check, in envelopes personally delivered by a trusted emissary to the recipient or his representative at an agreed rendezvous. (Claude C. Wild, Gulf's Washington lobbyist, reported that some payments had been made behind rural barns!) Payments are made into numbered Swiss bank accounts at the order of the payee. Double assurance of the payee's anonymity is gained if he puts title to the Swiss bank account in a Liechtenstein trust. Offshore corporations are used to make and to receive payoffs.

Payments can also be made in the form of expensive gifts

of property, such as watches, jewelry, oil paintings, negotiable securities, country homes, objets d'art, automobiles, or aircraft. Because payments in property are visible and are even more open to discovery and criticism than payments in currency, gifts of *services* are a popular mode of payoff. These can be as varied as are the wants and the ingenuity of man.

Some examples of gifts of services include: a rent-free villa on the French Riviera; the occupancy of a fashionable London flat complete with servants and a chauffeured Rolls-Royce; picking up the tab for an Arab or African minister and his entourage at the George Cinq Hotel in Paris or the Dorchester in London. It is not unusual for a European arms supplier to provide a Middle East defense minister or an influential Asian politician with a small fortune in gambling chips to be used in an evening's divertissement at a Monte Carlo casino, or to place a yacht and a bevy of international *poules de luxe* at the disposal of high-ranking Third World politicians vacationing in Nice. Russian trade officials who visit the United States are not infrequently taken to Las Vegas on expense-free weekends by their U.S. business hosts. Slot machine and other gambling winnings—no out-of-pocket losses are permitted by the hosts—are used by the Russian guests to purchase much-prized American luxury goods, electronic equipment, and clothing. "Entertainment" can be a method of obtaining influence without incurring the disadvantages of covert political payments. Moreover, entertainment is sanctioned under the laws and mores of the West.

Entertainment of communist officials is not invariably initiated by Western firms; trade officials from the Soviet Union and Eastern European bloc countries have been known to *coerce* their business hosts into providing lavish expense-free vacations and furnishing expensive luxury-type gifts. A French manufacturer, for example, who met an Eastern European trade delegation at the Paris airport, in accordance with prior arrangements for the trade officials to inspect the company's plant in Marseilles, was informed that the delegation wished to be taken to Cannes on the French Riviera for the weekend. And West European and Japanese firms doing business with officials of the communist state enterprises are expected to pay for hotels, meals, and transportation, when these officials arrive with insufficient funds in Stockholm, Paris, Bonn, or Tokyo. "Entertainment expenses" have been stretched to include blatant requests for television sets, home appliances, or other luxury items not readily available in Moscow, Belgrade, Bucharest, or Warsaw.

Companies can finance other valuable services for government officials and politicians. Their children are given scholarships and educational expenses at American universities. Ailing members of their families receive paid-up medical care at the best American hospitals. Their indigent relatives are put on the corporate payroll as "consultants" with a handsome annual fee for performing ephemeral services. Contributions are made to the payee's favorite charitable organization. (This is rare because the payee's favorite "charity" usually is himself!) Still another ploy is the making of a corporate loan to the foreign official, evidenced by an interest-bearing note, which the company never intends to collect!

An ingenious way in which a company can bribe a public official, or in which the official can extort a payment, is through the sale of property owned by the official to the company at an inflated price. In a recent case, an American company was seeking a site in England on which to build a factory. The local Town Council withheld its approval on trumped-up environmental grounds. When the company purchased an (unneeded) parcel of property from the key member of the Town Council at four times its market value, the site was quickly approved. This strategy of concealment can be quite successful, because all of the accounting is above board and real estate values range widely, even in the judgments of experts.

Of course, a bribe or an extortion may also be transmitted to the payee in a reverse of the above transaction. The payer can *sell* the recipient property at a *deflated* price under the market value. Gulf Oil Company was suspected of having disguised a payoff to officials of the South Korean government by this stratagem. In 1972, it sold a very large crude oil tanker, the Chun Woo, to a Korean business group, and then leased the vessel back for twenty years on terms that practically guaranteed the owners a fat profit. Gulf said its motive was to help the South Korean government realize its desire to develop a Korean flag tanker fleet. The Gulf Oil Report found that "there is no evidence that the profits were actually used for political contributions." However, it conceded that the transaction "had obvious political overtones."[5]

An ingenious mode of transmitting a bribe or an extortion is by *overbilling and kickback*. This is frequently done where a company sells goods or services to a foreign corporation. Let us assume that a company sells a foreign government corporation goods with a value of $100. By prearrangement between the employees of the seller and the buyer, the company establishes an account receivable on its books for $110 and bills the government corporation for $110. Later, the foreign corporation pays the company $110. The company then credits its accounts receivable with $110, but credits its sales account with $100, and "kicks back" $10 into an account designated by the buyer. This $10 "kickback" may be a bribe to, or an extortion by, the employees of the foreign corporation; or it may simply be a method by which the foreign company seeks to avoid its own country's exchange regulations, or to accumulate foreign funds to defray the costs of foreign business travel. Even if the purpose of overbilling and kickback is legitimate, the practice does involve misleading and incomplete bookkeeping. It is thus subversive of accounting controls, on the integrity of which efficient business management depends.[6]

Because the parties to a bribe or an extortionate payment generally violate the law, they often go to great lengths to conceal the true nature of the transaction. Great ingenuity is displayed in devising methods of payment that might permit of a plausible excuse in the event of discovery. The commercial counselor of a European government told the following story after long—but unsuccessful—efforts to sell his country's road machinery to the Minister of Public Works of a certain Caribbean nation. Finally, his ambassador suggested a payoff to the Minister. The counselor pondered the method of payment. Obviously, an outright proffer of money would be gauche—even dangerous.

After much thought, he hit on the answer. Knowing the Minister was a bibliophile, he acquired a first edition of a classic book and inserted $20,000 between its pages. He then called on the Minister and presented the book "with the compliments and best wishes" of his country. The Minister thanked him, thumbed through the pages of the book, noted the contents, and calmly laid down the book with the remark, "Mr. Counselor, I understand that this book has been published in a two-volume edition." The counselor had not expected such avariciousness, and he knew that he could not double the bribe. Being quick-witted, however, he replied: "Mr. Minister, my government is unable to give you the two-volume edition, but we will supply an appendix." An order for the machinery was soon executed!

The Purposes of Foreign Political Payments

Foreign political payments made by American multinational companies may also be classified according to the purposes for which they are made. The common belief that all are made simply to gain business is quite wrong. One can distinguish at least five broad objectives: to reduce political risks, to avoid threats and harassment, to reduce inflated taxes, to induce foreign government employees to perform their duties, and to obtain or retain business. Of these motives, only one—gaining and retaining business—has a positive thrust; the other four are essentially defensive in character. That this is the case will become clear as we examine these purposes in detail along with some well-known cases of each.

Payments to Reduce Political Risks

All business activities involve risks and uncertainties. Markets may shrink. New products may fail. Costs may accelerate unexpectedly. Trusted customers may default on their debts. Essential supplies may become unavailable because of man-made or natural disasters. Employees may strike. This list can be extended indefinitely. These are the normal "business risks" that the management of an enterprise lives with day by day.

When a company goes abroad, however, a whole congeries of *political* risks is added to these normal business hazards. They arise out of the larger uncertainties in the foreign political environment of business. The foreign government may impose punitive taxes or regulations. It may limit the amount of dividends or capital that a company can repatriate, i.e., bring home. It may unilaterally change the terms of investment agreements in onerous ways. It may expropriate or nationalize the company's properties without paying prompt and just compensation. In a world in which nations cannot be sued without their consent, and in which many nations assert the right to "perpetual sovereignty"—which means essentially the right of a country to change investment agreements unilaterally at any time—it is not surprising that multinational companies seek to reduce the risks of adverse actions by foreign governments.

To illustrate these points, let us briefly examine four well-known instances of foreign political payments by large American corporations for the purpose of reducing or averting risks of political action that would be adverse to their interests.

The Case of International Telephone and Telegraph in Chile. In 1970, fearing a socialist takeover of Chile, International Telephone and Telegraph offered the U.S. Central Intelligence Agency $1 million to help prevent the election of the Marxist leader, Dr. Salvador Allende Gossens, as President of Chile. The case was unusual in that the offer was not made to a Chilean opposition candidate or party but to the CIA— which refused it. Later, after Allende was elected President, he expropriated ITT's Chilean telephone company without subsequently paying prompt and just compensation, as required by international law.

The revelation of ITT's offer by a Washington newspaper columnist during 1972 led to a meeting of the Senate Committee on Foreign Relations. It quickly formed a Subcommittee on Multinational Corporations under the Chairmanship of Senator Frank Church, whose first task was to investigate ITT's behavior in Chile. As the investigation proceeded, ITT was pilloried by the American news media and by domestic and foreign politicians in the United Nations for "intolerable interference" in the domestic affairs of a foreign nation.[7] The Report of the Subcommittee was critical of ITT, but it was cautious in its conclusions. In brief, it found that the company's behavior was improper but not unlawful:

> . . . the company's concern was perfectly understandable. So, too, was its desire to communicate that concern to appropriate officials of the U.S. Government . . . . But what is not to be condoned is that the highest officials of the ITT sought to engage the CIA in a plan covertly to manipulate the outcome of the Chilean presidential election. In so doing the company overstepped the line of acceptable corporate behavior.[8]

There is a sequel to the story. ITT had insured its investment in Chile against expropriation with the semipublic Overseas Private Investment Corporation (OPIC). After its properties were expropriated, it claimed $92 million in reimbursement. OPIC resisted the claim on the grounds that the expropriation had resulted from the "provocation" of the Chilean government by ITT. The case was arbitrated by a distinguished panel appointed by the American Arbitration Association. In upholding the company, the arbitrators stated:

> The contracts did not require ITT to remain supine and impassive in the face of threatened and almost certain expropriation if the Marxists won . . . ITT could act, and on the record did act, to enlist the assistance of the U.S. government without committing a breach of any obligation . . . . It has long been regarded as a legitimate function of the United States, as a government, to assist its nationals in the protection of their persons and property abroad. The Supreme Court has expressly recognized this function of the State Department.[9]

The arbitrators drew attention to the default by the U.S. government of its historical role to assist in the protection of U.S. property abroad. In recent years, the U.S. Department of State has gone to extreme lengths in maintaining a hands-off attitude toward the foreign investments of American corporations. It has not even uttered a mild reproof to foreign governments that have committed arrant acts of depredation against U.S. investors.

This official indifference to lawlessness has led American multinationals to intervene in foreign political affairs to protect their property. It has compelled them to buy the protection their own government has failed to supply. It has expanded the pressure for the involvement of the CIA in *covert* actions to accomplish what the State Department should be doing *overtly*. The U.S. government should call on the governments of other countries to honor their treaties and investment agreements. This will help the world to develop a stable international economic order. These aspects of the case of ITT in Chile have been generally overlooked by the critics of American business.

The Case of United Brands in Honduras. A spectacular—and tragic—case of a U.S. multinational corporate political payment abroad to reduce political risks was that made in Honduras by United Brands, a food conglomerate put together by the late Eli Black. United's principal asset was the United Fruit Company, a leading dealer in Central American bananas, which became part of United Brands in 1969. As *Fortune* relates the story:

> Black's testing time came in 1974 when Honduras, Costa Rica, Panama, Guatemala and Colombia, emboldened by the success of the OPEC countries, formed the Union de Países Exportadores de Banano, or UPEB. Three of them, Honduras, Costa Rica, and Panama, which together accounted for more than half of United Brands' banana supplies, declared a $1 tax on every forty-pound box. The taxes would have cost the Company some $20 million, a sum almost equal to its net income the previous year. [And United Brands was then heavily in debt.] As is by now well known, Black authorized a $1,250,-000 bribe to a Honduran official in a calculated attempt to split the UPEB's ranks. The Honduran government in return cut the tax to 25 cents a box. And when the story was about to break early in 1975, Black jumped forty-four floors from the Pan Am building to his death.[10]

A more complete account of the Honduran payoff by United Brands was disclosed on December 13, 1976, when a special committee of the company's board of directors filed its report with the SEC. The report stated that, in May 1974, Mr. Black offered General Oswaldo Lopez Arellano, the Honduran President, several hundred thousand dollars if the Honduran banana tax was reduced. General Lopez reportedly dismissed the idea and "changed the subject." Harvey Johnson, vice-president of United Brands, told the committee that subsequently he was approached by Abraham Bennaton

Ramos, the Honduran Economics Minister, to discuss the banana tax. Bennaton conceded that the tax was too high and said it could be reduced if United Brands paid him $5 million. The Company rejected that amount. Later, Johnson met with Bennaton and they agreed on a $2.5 million payment. Black approved the deal, and, in September 1974, United Brands transferred half of this amount, $1,250,000, to a numbered Swiss bank account opened by Bennaton. Black never reported the payment to his board of directors. The second payment of $1,250,000 was never made.[11]

Whether this transaction was in fact a case of bribery or of extortion could be a subject for fine-honed legal debate. Manifestly, there was culpability on both sides. The facts suggest one of those curious mixtures of bribery and extortion that are not uncommon in world business. As the oldest and largest multinational company operating in Central America, United Fruit had for many years been a whipping boy of Central American politicians and communist propagandists. All of the facts about governmental pressures on United Brands probably will never be known. For several years before 1975, Black had been under intense pressure from the Panamanian and Honduran governments to relinquish United Fruit properties in those countries. He had, in fact, before his death agreed to sell United Fruit properties to the Panamanian government at their artificially low book values. Later, according to *Fortune*, his successor did sell them for $151,000 and lease them back at $2 million a year!

His successor also transferred to the Honduran government the company's 190-mile railroad, in return for its agreement to limit the increase in the banana export tax to 5 cents a box per year, up to a ceiling of 50 cents per box. Evidently, "gifts" of property were made by United Fruit to the government of Honduras to keep down the banana export tax. Black's action, it appears in retrospect, was to apply a solution illegal in Honduras to a very difficult problem of corporate security, which his successor resolved in a lawful, but essentially similar, way. What course events would have taken *if* the U.S. government had *not* been officially indifferent to foreign governmental pressures on United Brands is an interesting subject for speculation.

The Case of Gulf Oil in South Korea. Gulf Oil has become known as a notorious practitioner of corporate corruption since the public disclosures during 1973 that it made large political payments both at home and abroad. The contributions made by Gulf that are of interest here are $1 million paid during 1966 and $3 million paid during 1970 to the Democratic Republican Party (DRP) of South Korea.

The first payment was solicited by a high official of President Park's secretariat as a contribution to help the party finance a forthcoming election campaign. Bob R. Dorsey, Chairman of Gulf Oil, testified about it to the U.S. Senate Subcommittee on Multinational Corporations:

> Our investigation indicates that the demand was made by high party officials and was accompanied by pressure which left little to the imagination as to what would occur if the company would choose to turn its back on the request. At that time the company had already made a huge investment in Korea. [Over $200 million.] We were expanding and were faced with a myriad of problems which often confront American corporations in foreign countries. I carefully weighed the demand for a contribution in that light, and my decision to make the contribution of $1 million was based upon what I sincerely considered to be in the best interests of the company and its shareholders.[12]

In 1970, there came another demand by the DRP for a contribution of $10 million—this time attended by a much more blunt approach. Chairman Dorsey testified that S. K. Kim, now deceased, the head of the DLP party, told him that

> ". . . we were doing exceedingly well out there and that basically, our continued prosperity depended on our coming

up with a ten million [dollar] political contribution to the party." [Later, as a result of acrimonious discussion, the figure was negotiated down to $3 million.] [Dorsey testified that] "I just thought that the opportunity to continue a profitable business, without unwarranted and inhibiting government interference, required it."[13]

These payments appear to have been lawful under both American and Korean law. The Special Committee of Gulf's Board of Directors, whose chairman, John J. McCloy, was not affiliated with Gulf, concluded that

> . . . it is quite clear that Gulf was in no sense a volunteer seek-ing to suborn favors by means of largesse. Neither the first nor second payment was in any sense initiated by Gulf or treated by Gulf as anything other than a distasteful effort on the part of the government or the party to obtain a contribu-tion which Gulf had no desire to make.[14]

In other words, it considered the payments to have been ex-torted by the ruling party of South Korea rather than to have been bribes for special favors to Gulf.

The Gulf case raises again the fundamental issue: what action should an American multinational company take when its property or rights to do business are threatened by the government or ruling party of a foreign country—unless it pays off? In the days of President Theodore Roosevelt, a com-pany would probably report attempted extortion to the U.S. ambassador, and the U.S. government would quickly lodge an official protest with the offending government. Unless redress were made, sanctions would follow. But this old-fashioned response has been replaced by one of official passivity. The U.S. company is now left to fend for itself. We leave to the reader the decision he would make if confronted by the ethi-cal dilemma faced by Chairman Dorsey.

The Case of Exxon in Italy. During 1975, Exxon's top man-agement publicly disclosed that it had *authorized* Esso Italiana, its Italian affiliate, to make $27 million in secret political payments between 1964 and 1971, and that during the same period an additional $29 million to $31 million of *unauthorized* payments had been made. A special committee of three Exxon board members investigated these and related payments. In its report the committee wrote that these payments were made largely from forty secret bank accounts known only to Dr. Vincenzo Cazzaniga, former managing director of Esso Italiana. These off-the-books funds had been built up by secret rebates and bank overdrafts.[15]

Exxon asserted that these payments were political contributions, which are legal in Italy.[16] It appears likely that most of them were made to political parties or their official news organs in an effort to influence political trends and the outcomes of elections in Italy. These were matters about which Exxon had good reason to be concerned. The Communist Party had a strong and growing following in Italy. The risk of a communist takeover of the Italian government, to be followed by a large-scale nationalization of industries, was substantial. All through the 1950s and the 1960s, the U.S. government heavily supported anti-communist parties. Could it fairly criticize Italian affiliates of U.S. corporations for doing likewise? Nor was Exxon the only multinational company to try to prevent a communist takeover. The Royal Dutch–Shell Group and British Petroleum also disclosed that they had persistently made payments to Italian political parties.[17] Exxon's political contributions in Italy were, however, ended in 1971.

What made Esso's authorized political payments in Italy censurable was not their purpose—to reduce political risk—but two other facts. They were *secret* payments, covered up by deceptive accounting and off-the-books funding, which impaired the integrity of Esso's financial reports. Secondly, as the *Wall Street Journal* reported:

... the secrecy surrounding these payments ... freed Mr. Cazzaniga to wheel and deal in ways that Exxon said it did not authorize. Company documents indicated that, through hidden kickbacks, 40 secret bank accounts and other devices, Exxon's normal accounting controls were subverted, and Mr. Cazzaniga allegedly siphoned another $29 million to $31 million from the coffers of Esso Italiana S.p.a., ...[18]

Although at least some of Exxon's top managers had known and approved of the $27 million of political payments, they were apparently unaware of the *additional* $29 million or more of company funds diverted to other channels. How could Exxon's internal controls have been so loose as to enable Cazzaniga to divert millions of the company's money to unknown recipients for so many years without detection? The answer is that, having approved of secret and deceptive accounting for political contributions, Exxon's top management in New York lost effective control of its Italian executives. The moral of the tale is clear: *If an American company finds it necessary to make political contributions in a foreign country where such contributions are lawful, it should make them openly and account for them in the regular channels.* This policy will bring dual benefits. It will avoid deceptive bookkeeping, which subverts efficient business management; and it will help to prevent fraudulent diversions of company funds by managers of foreign affiliates.

Payments to Avoid Threats and Harassment

Payments by American multinational companies to local police and security forces for protection against harassment of their employees or business operations are another form of political payment. Confronted with civil security risks in many countries, the foreign concern must turn to government security forces for protection. Because regular protection is often inadequate, or lacking, companies have no

110

recourse but to employ the local police and security personnel.

Acts or threats of harassment take many forms. Kidnapping of American executives of foreign affiliates for ransom is a recent spectacular example. Several American companies have had to pay kidnappers in Argentina and some other countries millions of dollars for the safe return of their executives. Harassment usually takes less violent forms, however, such as threats to sabotage production plans, block needed transportation, or frustrate the operations of the company in other ways.

The Case of Castle and Cooke. Castle and Cooke, a multinational grower and processor of food products, revealed during 1976 that the largest single classification of its payments to foreign government employees—$300,000 over the five-year period from 1971 to 1975—were those made to military guards and to local police for security purposes. We let the report speak for itself:

> This type of payment dates back more than 20 years and clearly arose from the Company's concern about the risk of physical harm to its personnel and risk of loss or destruction of Company property. It must be remembered that many of the Company operations in foreign areas are necessarily conducted in rural areas where little or no governmental services exist, and incidents of murder, robbery and vandalism (particularly in the earlier days) are not uncommon. In one country where the law requires payment of all wages in cash, the Company is required to handle payrolls in the hundreds of thousands of dollars on a regular basis and therefore needs armed guards to safely fulfill its payroll responsibilities. In at least one country, the Company is prohibited from maintaining a private security force and therefore has no alternative but to look to the military to provide soldiers to serve as security guards for the Company. In countries where civilian police forces existed, the Company sometimes felt it necessary to make private payments to police officials to be assured of timely and adequate police protection in emergency situations

such as occurred during an unruly labor strike. Although the laws of the various countries varied somewhat, legal opinions from independent attorneys in the principal countries involved have advised the Company that virtually all such payments were lawful and customary in the countries involved.[19]

Payments to Reduce Inflated Taxes

Multinational companies also make under-the-table payments to foreign government officials to settle their tax liabilities. Such payments violate the laws of most nations; but they are condoned and commercially practiced in many. While usually described as bribes, more often they are really shakedowns of business firms by local tax officials. Consider the typical circumstances.

The tax laws and regulations of a certain foreign country are very general and uncertain in their application. They leave wide latitude for interpretation. Local tax officials are thereby able to make plausible—and extravagant—tax assessments against business firms. Lack of effective judicial processes means that there is no effective appeal from their decisions to higher authorities. The incentive to the local manager of an American multinational company is very strong to try to make a quick settlement. The competitive position of his firm in its market, even its very survival, may be at stake. The "negotiation" of tax liabilities between local officials and taxpayers is an accepted practice in this country. Not infrequently, the local tax official will suggest that a favorable settlement can be reached, if the local manager will pay him a specified sum under the table, or perhaps into a numbered Swiss bank account. Often, such hints are taken by the hapless taxpayer.

Whether we apply the term "bribery" or "extortion" to this transaction is unimportant. What is important is that managers of the foreign affiliates of U.S.-based corporations are confronted with serious ethical dilemmas. Should they pay oversized tax bills, which may threaten the viability of their businesses and their jobs? Should they risk imprisonment on a spurious charge of tax evasion? Should they withdraw from business in the country? Or should they do what they see many local businessmen doing: paying the tax assessor to reduce their tax bill?

The ultimate resolution of this dilemma lies as much with the government of the host country as with the multinational company. Only if its tax laws are clear and certain, if it provides established procedures for prompt review of the decisions of local tax officials, if tax appeals are equitably decided, and if penalties are imposed on tax officials for soliciting or taking bribes, only then will the temptation to make improper payments be removed. *Neither an American company nor the U.S. government can unilaterally resolve the dilemma.*

Payments to Induce Foreign Government Employees to Perform Their Duties

Foreign political payments are made more frequently to induce foreign government employees to perform their official duties than for any other purpose. Most are small, but in the course of a year they can cumulate to substantial "taxes" on the American multinational company. The SEC has described them as "facilitating" payments, but they are more graphically known as "grease" because they "lubricate" the machinery of business. Examples are payments to clerks and customs inspectors to procure timely inspection of travel documents, to clear baggage or household goods through customs, or to approve import documents covering essential machinery and equipment. These facilitating payments are more akin to extortion than to bribery because they are paid to deter the recipient from damaging the payer by his inaction rather than to induce him to do a special favor for the payer. The underpaid lower officials of many foreign governments must routinely collect such private "taxes" in order to support their families.

Payments to Obtain or Retain Business

A major purpose of foreign political payments by American companies—and the only one stressed in the news media—is to establish businesses, to develop resources, or to sell products to foreign governments. Business-getting payoffs have evoked the most indignation and condemnation among federal officials. The SEC's *Report on Questionable and Illegal Corporate Payments and Practices* to the Senate Committee on Banking, Housing and Urban Affairs on May 12, 1976, tabulated the "questionable" payments abroad voluntarily disclosed by 89 U.S.-based multinational corporations.[20] Most of this group of reporting companies were on the "*Fortune* 500" list of leading industrial corporations. The reports showed that most of the *disclosed* payments were for business-getting purposes. Of course, an even larger number of "facilitating" payments probably were *not disclosed* because they were individually under $1,000.

An analysis of these reports by industry is revealing. Although American technological leadership is unquestioned in the fields of jet aircraft and electronic data processing, political payments to get business appear frequently in the reports of firms in those industries. The reason is that *comparatively large parts of the sales of these industries are made to governments.*

Other industries in which business-getting foreign political payments are frequent are petroleum and drugs. Firms in both industries are subjected to very extensive governmental regulation, and they also purvey comparatively large amounts of their products to governments. The U.S. oil company that goes abroad in a search for petroleum confronts the need to obtain drilling concessions or service contracts from foreign governments; and this makes necessary frequent contacts with many governmental officials over extended periods of time. Pharmaceutical companies are likewise prolific dispensers of political payments abroad, because foreign governments and their agencies are large buyers of pharmaceutical products, and the sale of drugs is everywhere subject to close governmental control. However, where companies deal directly with consumers in markets, rather than with governments, political payments appear to be rare.

Business-getting foreign political payments raise special problems of law and ethics, because they usually involve foreign agents or consultants who are not government officials but whose commissions may be funneled in part to governmental officials. The case of Lockheed Aircraft sharply raised these issues.

The Case of Lockheed Aircraft. In May 1975, it was disclosed that Lockheed Aircraft had paid $22 million over a five-and-a-half-year period to foreign government officials and political parties to win sales contracts for its aerospace products.[21] Among those named were former Prime Minister Tanaka of Japan and Prince Bernhard of The Netherlands.[22] The Securities and Exchange Commission charged Lockheed with violation of the Securities Exchange Act of 1934. It alleged that the company had disguised and concealed foreign political payments by false accounting entries, channeling funds through "consultants," and making payments through corporate entities created solely to disguise the true recipients of the payments. It charged that the two chief executives had created a secret Swiss bank account from which foreign payoffs were made. These disclosures, along with Lockheed's financial troubles, led to the resignations of Daniel J. Houghton, the company's chairman, and A. Carl Kotchian, its president, in February 1976. In April 1976, the SEC suit was settled by an injunction against Lockheed, in which the company neither admitted nor denied that it had acted illegally in the past.

In evaluating Lockheed's behavior it should be remembered that the payment of commissions to agents for negotiating sales of aircraft to foreign governments or to government-owned or private airlines is an established commercial practice throughout the world. Ordinarily such commissions range from 4 to 6 percent of the sales price, but they can be 10 percent or more.[23] Because individual sales transactions often run to hundreds of millions of dollars, commission payments are large. Since 1970, Lockheed reportedly paid more than $200 million in commissions to consultants, commission agents, and others.

Most of Lockheed's payments to foreign government officials appear to have involved the purchase of military aircraft by such countries as Indonesia, Saudi Arabia, and the Philippines. These payments were investigated by the Senate Subcommittee on Multinational Corporations. Its published documents relating to them suggest, as the *Wall Street Journal* reported, that Lockheed did *not initiate* the bribes and kickbacks. For the most part it followed the advice of its consultants in various countries to make payments rather than to risk loss of business.[24]

What made Lockheed's foreign political payments so controversial was their large amount, the secret and deceptive accounting for them, and the apparent violation of the laws of some foreign countries. However, it should be noted that the company was hard-pressed to finance its wide-bodied commercial jet program and was deeply in debt to its bankers. Financial pressures no doubt led its management to adopt these aggressive marketing practices.

The Case of Boeing. Close issues of corporate propriety were raised by the case of Boeing.[25] The company disclosed, in March 1976, that it had paid nearly $70 million in commissions to foreign representatives since 1970 to help sell its aircraft, and that "in four or five instances" those commissions went to foreign government employees. However, Boeing defended the payments as proper because none of the foreign government employees was in a position to approve of aircraft purchases. For example, on December 9, 1976, Boeing disclosed that it had retained José A. Pigna, a vice-president of Viasa Airlines, majority-owned by the Venezuelan government, as a sales consultant. Pigna, a Venezuelan national residing in the United States, represented Boeing in an effort to sell its helicopters to the Venezuelan government.[26]

The SEC commenced an investigation of Boeing and demanded that the company produce full details of its foreign payments, including the names of its agents, some of whom it suspected had channeled funds to foreign government officials. Boeing refused to supply their names, arguing that such disclosure would cause foreign governments or foreign government-owned airlines to delay or cancel their orders for Boeing equipment, would unfairly damage the reputations of the agents, and would impair Boeing's competitive position in the aircraft industry. Although a federal court issued a temporary order keeping the names of the agents under seal for the time being, the issue of how much Boeing will have to tell the public about its overseas payments remained unsettled at time of writing.[27]

The Frequency and Importance of Foreign Political Payments

Are political payments by U.S. business corporations widespread and significant? Do they constitute the major national scandal that some journalists have alleged?

The most thorough collection of information to date about foreign political payments by American companies was presented to the Senate Committee on Banking, Housing and Urban Affairs on May 12, 1976, by the Securities and Exchange Commission.[28] It reported the disclosures made up to that time by 95 corporations, of which 89 were made voluntarily and six were required by the courts as a result of SEC action. These were the primary findings:

1. *Domestic political contributions.* Twenty-six companies, or 27 percent of the total number, reported having made domestic political contributions. The responses did not reveal which of them were legal and which were illegal.

2. *Foreign political payments.* Fifty-four companies, or 56 percent of the total number, reported having made payments to officials or employees of foreign governments. Some were legal and some not. In addition, 27 companies, 28 percent of the total number, stated that they had made foreign payments of "questionable" legal status. Thus 84 percent of the reporting firms disclosed foreign payments or practices that were either illegal or questionable in character.

3. *Inadequate or deceptive accounting.* Of the 89 companies that voluntarily reported to the SEC, 64 disclosed how foreign political payments were treated on their books. Forty-four of these companies, more than 67 percent of those disclosing their bookkeeping practices, admitted that some payments were inadequately or deceptively recorded through the devices of overbilling, off-the-books slush funds, or misleading entries. Only 20 companies, one-third of those reporting, stated that all payments were regularly accounted for. The high incidence of secrecy and falsification of records in accounting for foreign political payments is, indeed, their most disturbing aspect. It was properly criticized by the SEC as an "apparent frustration of our system of corporate accountability. . . ."[29]

4. *Relative importance of political payments.* Although questionable political payments, foregin and domestic, may have been a material factor in a few companies such as Exxon, Gulf, and Lockheed, they have certainly been *de minimis* among U.S. multinational companies as a group. The authors tabulated the total questionable payments by those 34 of the 89 companies reporting to the SEC that had gross sales revenues of $1 billion or more during 1974. (See Table 3. Lockheed was not included in the group by the SEC.) The total of such payments over the reporting periods of the companies (which varied from three to five years) was *$93.7 million.* During the same periods, the total sales revenues of the 34 companies were *$679 billion.* Thus questionable payments—foreign plus domestic—formed only 0.014 percent of aggregate revenues, or only about one dollar for each $7,250 of sales revenue. Even when they are related to the *foreign* sales of the companies—estimated to be approximately 33 percent of total sales—the ratio is 0.04 percent or one dollar for each $2,400 of sales. Manifestly, this cannot be considered "material" for the companies as a group.

Did the 89 companies reporting to the SEC constitute a representative sample of the approximately 9,000 American corporations that regularly file reports with the SEC? Or even of the 3,000 U.S.-based multinational corporations?[30] We believe that the *reporting* companies were *more* likely to have made political payments abroad, and to have made them in relatively larger amounts than were *non-reporting* companies. The SEC was conducting a program of investigating questionable payments by American companies. When it publicly proposed that companies might avoid future problems by "voluntarily" disclosing their questionable payments, those firms with something questionable to report would be most likely to file a report. Hence, the sample of reporting companies is undoubtedly biased toward the inclusion of those

TABLE 3 Questionable Political Payments Reported to the Securities and Exchange Commission by Companies Having 1974 Gross Revenues of $1 Billion or More

Name of Company	Total Revenues for 1974 (in thousands)	Reporting Period (calendar years)	Gross Revenues During Reporting Period (in thousands)	Total Illegal or Questionable Payments (in thousands)	Total Questionable Payments as a Percentage of Gross Revenues During Reporting Period
American Airlines	1,641,307[1]	1971–1973	4,081,126[3]	55	.00134
American Cyanamid	1,779,872	1971–1975[4]	7,822,880[3]	1,180	.01508
American Home Products	2,182,991[5, 15]	11-1-70–12-31-75[4]	3,935,992[3, 5, 6]	6,462	.16418
American Standard	1,676,973	1972–1975[3]	6,283,737[3]	266	.00423
AMF	1,026,871[15]	1971–1975[4]	4,709,030[3]	1,500	.03185
Burroughs	1,532,627[15]	12-1-70–12-31-75[7]	6,589,489[3, 6]	1,500	.02276
Carnation	1,886,828[15]	1968–1975[4]	10,901,429[3]	1,261	.01156
Cities Service	2,846,672[15]	1971–1975[4]	11,847,888[3]	645	.00544
Coastal States Gas	1,315,265	1971–1975[4]	4,865,062[3, 6]	8,000[8]	.16443
Colgate-Palmolive	2,615,448	1971–1975[4]	11,265,229[3]	865	.00768
Dresser Industries	1,397,970	1971–1975[4, 9]	6,146,900[10, 11]	24	.00039
Exxon	45,729,858	1963–1975[12]	216,897,000[3, 10]	29,948	.01380
General Telephone & Electronics	5,661,510[15]	1971–1975[4]	24,945,448[3]	13,075	.05241
General Tire & Rubber	1,726,199[13, 14, 15]	1969–1975[9]	9,014,739[3, 11, 13, 14]	1,265[15]	.01403
B. F. Goodrich	1,966,239[13, 15]	1971–1975[9]	8,159,151[3, 13]	124	.00151
Goodyear Tire & Rubber	5,256,247	1964–1975 (Domestic)[4, 16] 1970–1975 (Foreign)	11,853,000[3]	1,105	.00264
Honeywell	2,626,000[15]	1971–1975[4]	50,000,000[16]	1,840	.01555
ITT	11,154,401[1]	1971–1975[16]	8,353,395[3]	3,864	.00773
Johnson & Johnson	1,967,885	1971–1975[4]	41,742,958[3, 13, 17, 18]	1,002	.01200
Kraftco	4,471,427[13, 15]	1970–1975[4, 9]	21,837,894[3, 11, 13]	546	.00250
Merck	1,329,550	1968–1975[4]	7,786,384[3, 10, 13]	3,761	.04830
Occidental Petroleum	5,537,505[13]	1969–1975	23,000,000[3, 13]	570	.00248
Ogden	1,858,119[1]	1970–1975[4]	7,877,256[4, 19]	2,471	.03137

Pfizer	1,571,887	1971–1975[3]	6,694,503[3,20]	262	.00391
Pullman	1,425,587	1971–1975[3]	5,917,430[3]	2,275	.03845
Rockwell International	4,408,500	10-1-71–9-30-75[4]	17,699,400[3,11,13]	668	.00377
Rohm & Haas	1,021,736	1971–1975[3]	3,982,247[3]	749	.01881
Singer	2,103,000[15,24]	1971–1975[9]	9,700,200[10,24]	15	.00015
Standard Oil of Indiana	10,156,428[15]	1970–1975[4]	42,833,580[3]	1,668	.00389
Tenneco	5,001,470[21]	1970–1975[4]	23,211,688[3,21]	1,052	.00453
United Brands	2,020,526[13,15]	1971–1975[9]	9,008,563[3,13]	2,000	.02220
Warner Lambert	1,946,063	1971–1975[4]	8,737,223[3]	2,255	.02581
Westinghouse Electric	5,838,118[22]	1971–1975[4]	25,728,612[3,22]	243	.00094
White Consolidated Industries	1,016,621[13]	1971–1975[9,23]	4,494,537[13,23]	1,180	.02625
Totals—34 companies			$679,000,000	$93,700	.01380

1. SOURCE: SEC Report.
2. SOURCE: SEC Report. Excludes amounts or payments reported by the company and disclosed in the SEC Report as legal or apparently legal. Includes all other amounts disclosed in the SEC Report.
3. SOURCE: One or more Forms 10K of the company containing financial statements for the Reporting Period.
4. SOURCE: One or more Forms 8K and/or Forms 8 of the company containing information regarding the Reporting Period.
5. This amount represents "gross sales" reported by the company.
6. This amount was calculated with respect to all portions of the Reporting Period, other than regular fiscal years, by computing the average monthly revenues for such periods.
7. SOURCE: Form S–7 filed January 12, 1976, and Form 8K of the company.
8. The company states that, based on an unconfirmed report, only part of this amount is involved .
9. SOURCE: One or more annual reports to shareholders of the company containing financial statements for the Reporting Period.
10. This amount is based upon results reported for fiscal years ended during each calendar year of the Reporting Period and does not necessarily correspond to results for such calendar years.
11. SOURCE: Form S–7 of the company.
12. SOURCE: Form S–7 of the company.
13. This amount represents "net sales" reported by the company.
14. This amount excludes the revenue of RKO General, Inc.
15. Source examined differs from the SEC Report. Amount contained in sources used in this table.
16. SOURCE: proxy statement.
17. SOURCE: Form S–8 filed by the company.
18. This amount represents "net sales" reported by the company for fiscal years 1964–1975.
19. This amount represents "aggregate sales" reported by the company for the Reporting period.
20. This amount represents "net sales and other income" reported by the company for the Reporting Period.
21. This amount represents "total net sales" and "operating revenues" reported by the company for the Reporting Period.
22. This amount represents "total income" reported by the company for the Reporting Period.
23. SOURCE: Form S–14 filed by the company on March 23, 1976.
24. This amount represents "total sales" reported by the company.

that had made substantial political payments abroad.

Considering the bias in the sample of companies that "voluntarily" filed reports with the SEC and the comparatively small amounts of reported payments by those companies in comparison with the totality of their business, the SEC was amply justified in stating in the conclusion of its *Report* that ". . . the present evidence of corporate abuse, while indeed serious, does not support any general condemnation of American business."[31]

PART II

Analysis of the Problem

4

The Economics
of Political Payments

Since political payments involve the transference of money
or other things of value, one cannot understand them fully
without examining them from an economic perspective. So
far, however, the economics of political payments has not at-
tracted much attention from economists. Hence, we are required to take some first steps to bring the phenomenon of
political payments within the scope of economic thinking. In
making such an economic analysis, we will employ the basic
economic concepts of a "commodity," which is traded in a
"market" and for which there exists both a "supply schedule"
and a "demand schedule" that intersect to produce an
"equilibrating price." By applying these basic analytical concepts of economics to the actual circumstances within which
these payments are made in a country, we believe that we can
derive insights into the forces that determine the frequency
and amount of political payments in that country. These
insights can be useful in formulating corporate and public
policies that can reduce the volume of private and official
corruption, and can help to elevate both the efficiency of inter-

national trade and investment and the level of behavior of businesses and governments around the world.

Political Authority and Influence as a Commodity in Trade

From an economic point of view, bribery, extortion, or other payments for political influence and for the sympathetic exercise of political authority may be treated as a single "commodity." "Political authority" may be defined in the most general sense as the legal power to act for the sovereign state, and "political influence" may be defined as the ability to shape the thinking and action of those who possess political authority. Foreign political payments by U.S.-based multinational companies are, in essence, either payments for the exercise of political authority and influence in ways *favorable* to their business activities, or payments to deter the exercise of political authority and influence in ways *harmful* to their commercial interests. This general proposition holds whether we are considering a picayune payment by an American executive of a multinational corporation to a foreign customs official to induce him to act promptly to admit baggage to the country, or a payment of millions of dollars by the foreign affiliate of a U.S.-based multinational corporation to a foreign political party to enhance its chances of success in an election and thereby to defeat punitive taxation, public regulation, or nationalization of its properties.

In both of these cases, the American multinational company is buying political authority and influence—the power to determine the nature, scope, and timing of official actions by a government, its officers, and employees. To be sure, there is never a written contract or agreement covering such transactions, and, in the nature of the case, there can not be. Furthermore, the expectations of the purchaser may often be disappointed or frustrated. Nevertheless, the essence of all such payments is the belief of the purchaser (the multinational company) that the actions of the seller (the foreign official, government employee, candidate, or party) will be so influenced by the payment as to produce beneficial results worth more than their cost or to deter harmful results that would cost more than the payment. What is always involved, in one way or another, is the "sale" of political authority or influence.

The Boundary Between the Marketable and the Nonmarketable

Our analysis begins, then, with the assumption that there is a "market" in which there is trading in segments of the political authority and influence of a nation. We recognize that this assumption is foreign to the ideals of American political thought. The idea that official power vested by the state in a governmental official can be bought and sold is repugnant to the American mind. Americans draw a line between ordinary goods and services that can be traded in markets, and human rights and duties and the exercise of political authority and influence, which should not be the subject of trade.

There have been many examples of this attitude in our public life. Since President Lincoln signed the Emancipation Proclamation in 1862, human beings cannot be bought or sold in markets as chattels. Even contracts for long periods of employment cannot be enforced against persons. Votes in an election cannot lawfully be bought or sold. The sale of public offices is prohibited. "Public office is a public trust" asserts the aphorism. Exemptions from military conscription are not to be traded. "Influence peddling" by government officials is unlawful. A wide range of political powers, as well as the rights and duties of individuals, have deliberately been withdrawn from the arena of market competition. Americans reject the idea that these things can be bought and sold like gasoline or breakfast food. They consider such trade demeaning to the dignity of human beings and subversive of our belief in a pluralistic society in which there is a clear separation between business and government, between the commercial and the political.[1]

Granting the desirability of this separation of domains in American society, we do well to remember two important facts. First, our own society draws the boundary line between the domains of marketable goods and services, on the one hand, and nonmarketable political rights, duties, and authorities, on the other hand, *differently today than in the past.* Second, other societies in the world, whose historical evolution has been along different paths, draw *different boundary lines than we do,* and some appear not to draw any boundary line at all.

Let us not forget that little more than a century ago in the United States human beings were traded in slave markets as chattels. In the Jacksonian period, many federal political offices were openly auctioned off to the highest bidder. During the early nineteenth century, municipal authorities frequently farmed out the right to collect real property taxes to the highest bidder, who then possessed full governmental authority to collect them. And in the present century, "vote buying" by political bosses was openly practiced in the ethnic conclaves of our great cities.

Today, most of these practices are outlawed by statute or condemned by public opinion, and violators suffer punishment. Yet it would be naïve to suppose that in contemporary American society the purchase and sale of political authority and influence have been totally suppressed. Subtle, refined, and devious ways of effecting such transactions have taken the place of the crude and open methods of yore. Although the sale of public office is illegal, it is a matter of record that many U.S. ambassadors to foreign nations previously made very large contributions to the political campaigns of the presidents who appointed them. Similarly, inheritance tax appraisers in some states are legally entitled to keep enormous statutory fees, and they naturally make commensurately large "campaign contributions" to those who appoint them. Although a federal official would commit a criminal offense by accepting money to recommend the governmental purchase of a military weapon, many have accepted lavish entertainment and vacations at the expense of supplier corporations.

The Washington Legal–Political Corps as Influence Vendors

And what should be said of the role of the enormously influential Washington legal-political corps, whose stock in trade is "influence"? Corporations are confronted with an endless procession of problems involving the federal government—a securities controversy with the Securities and Exchange Commission, a merger or acquisition question with the Department of Justice or the Federal Trade Commission, difficulties with the Federal Communications Commission in renewing a radio or television broadcasting license, or the need for authority from the Federal Power Commission to build a nuclear power plant.

These and a host of similar business-government problems can usually be resolved with the help of an experienced, influential—and expensive—Washington law firm, one or more of whose partners usually has been a member of the regulatory agency involved. Plainly, when a former Secretary of Defense, Secretary of State, Attorney General, Justice of the Supreme Court, Chairman of the SEC, or legal counsel to a former President telephones a former colleague in government regarding a problem of his corporate client, nothing as crude as bribery is involved. What transpires is more subtle. A favorable decision or a satisfactory compromise is reached owing in large measure to friendship, to ideological affinity, to affiliation with the majority political party, or to an unspoken, unarticulated understanding of reciprocity for favors rendered. It is the latter, when translated into reality, that can become a subtle, but insidious, form of bribery.

More than a few members of regulatory agencies—especially ambitious young lawyers—expect to retire from their federal agency into the practice of law before that agency. They expect to capitalize on their former relationships and acquired expertise. They will realize these opportunities by becoming a partner in one of the established, prestigious law firms, or by setting up their own law practices. Each generation of federal officials perpetuates the same set of subtle relationships. And the Washington law firms continue their existence while Presidents come and go and administrations change.

The ethics of some practices of the Washington political-legal corps have recently been questioned. Monroe H. Friedman, Dean of the Hofstra Law School and Chairman of the Ethics Committee of the District of Columbia Bar Association, called for the adoption of a rule by the Bar Association to discourage influence peddling. It would require a Washington law firm to withdraw from any case before a federal regulatory agency whenever it hired a lawyer from the regulatory agency who had had a major role in the proceeding. Although this rule appears reasonable and modest in effect, the proposal was reported to have been "stirring an uproar" in the Washington legal-political establishment. Evidently, it touched that most sensitive of nerves—the pocketbook![2]

In sum, the Washington legal-political corps includes among its functions sophisticated "influence peddling." Like their counterparts in Latin America, Africa, and Asia, they are the mediators between those seeking favors and the federal officials with the power to confer them. In practice— as distinguished from the mythology surrounding the practice—the Washington legal-political establishment is not essentially different from similar sources of influence in the older traditional societies. Although it does not itself generate either a supply of, or a demand for, political authority and influence, it performs an important *mediating* function in the market under consideration.

Comparison of the Washington legal-political corps with the influence establishment in other countries is illuminating. In many foreign nations, especially those in the Third World, political and social evolution has been such as to produce a monolithic state that lacks any clear division between a public and a private sector. Indeed, throughout much of the world today, official political ideology is hostile to the concepts of the private-enterprise market economy. To the extent that there is a private sector, it is generally quite undeveloped, and it must compete with the more favored and highly subsidized public sector. Social evolution has proceeded from the extended family, to the tribal organization, to the establishment of a national government. Meager fiscal resources result in an inadequate and poorly paid civil service. Statutory law is rudimentary and unclear, leaving wide discretionary authority in the hands of government officials and civil servants. An effective judiciary is lacking, as are judicial interpretations of the law. Appointment to government office is perceived, in these circumstances, as a legitimate opportunity to wield political authority for personal gain.

The government official is seen as a kind of *private* tax collector, entitled to levy imposts on business firms, particularly foreign corporations, much as the nineteenth-century tax farmer was viewed in our own country. In effect, public authority is treated as a private property right, freely disposable by the public official. In many of these nations there are no laws prohibiting payments by U.S. corporations to public officials; and in many of the nations that have such laws, the enforcement is weak or nonexistent. It is in these countries that the "market" for segments of political authority and influence is the largest and most flourishing.

The theory that foreign political payments by American multinational companies are, from an economic point of view, purchases of political authority and influence is analogous to the theory, advanced some years ago by Anthony Downs, that a politician in a democracy is essentially an entrepreneur selling policies for votes instead of products for money.[3] Down's theory has been criticized as a cynical interpretation of democratic political action; but it is a plausible extension of economic theory to explain political transactions, which, in our culture, normally lack stated monetary values, but which, nonetheless, can be—and often are—evaluated in economic terms.

The Market for Political Authority and Influence

In its essence, a "market" is a system of communication between buyers and sellers of a distinct commodity or service, within which information about prices and terms of sale is transmitted, and within which purchases and sales of the commodity or service take place. A market may be located at a particular place (hence, the familiar term, "marketplace"); but it need not have a unique location and does not in many instances, as witness the markets for money and credit or the over-the-counter market for stocks and bonds.

It requires some stretching of our ordinary categories of thought to think of a "market" for political authority and influence, in which selling public officials and buying business firms communicate with each other and conclude transactions. And, indeed, very little is known about this market primarily because it is a "black market," either prohibited by

132

law or frowned on by public opinion even when tolerated. Neither the buyers nor the sellers of political authority and influence publicly announce their bids and offers; nor, unless required to do so by some public agency such as the Securities and Exchange Commission, do buying companies reveal the "prices" they paid for segments of political authority and influence in foreign countries. And we do not know how extensively foreign public officials communicate to prospective buyers the terms on which they will sell their influence, or how extensively foreign multinational companies make known to public officials their offers to purchase it.

No doubt, this market is a very rudimentary and imperfect one, shot through with monopolistic and monopsonistic elements because of the wide gaps in the traders' knowledge of competing bids and offers. Nonetheless, those informal sub rosa channels of communication known as "the grapevine" often function quite effectively; and one may conclude that a market for political authority and influence in a country can possess a rudimentary system of communication, which permits of some degree of competition in the formation of prices.

What determines the supply of, and the demand for, segments of political authority and influence in a country, the size of the market, and the price paid for this "commodity"? Let us first look at the demand side of the market. What factors determine the *amount* of political influence and sympathetic exercise of political authority effectively *desired* by multinational companies in a foreign country?

Determinants of Demand

We can readily identify three important determinants of demand in this market: the extent of *perceived business opportunities in a country*, the extent of *governmental regula-*

tion of the private sector of the economy, and the degree of *uncertainty in the administration of governmental regulations. Company characteristics,* including the industry type, policies, internal controls, and competitive relationships, will also influence the demand for political authority and influence. However, company characteristics do not appear to be *systematically* related to the characteristics of host countries, and thus are not *general* factors in demand.

It is our hypothesis that, other factors remaining the same, foreign multinational companies will demand *more* political influence and exercise of political authority on their behalf in a country the *more* extensive the perceived business opportunities it contains, the *greater* the governmental control over the private sector of the economy, and the *less* certain the administration of such governmental controls. Other factors may be involved, such as the quality of law enforcement, but the three we have cited appear to have the major weight.

Let us consider these factors in order. Manifestly, a small country with meager natural and human resources and low per capita income offers foreign multinational corporations relatively limited business opportunities. The natural resource base of such a country will not support much investment in the development of an export trade; and its small poverty-stricken population will limit the size of its domestic markets. Constricted business opportunities mean, *ceteris paribus,* a weak demand for political authority and influence by foreign firms. The converse will be true if a country's perceived business opportunities are extensive. For example, the relatively large business opportunities in Indonesia and Nigeria can be contrasted with the more limited scope for business enterprise in Tunisia or Liberia. Therefore, one would expect larger "markets" for political authority and influence in the former than in the latter countries, assuming other factors were the same.

The extent of governmental regulation of the private sector of an economy is also a factor in determining the demand for political authority and influence by foreign companies. The more extensive such regulation of industries and business functions, and the more detailed it is, the greater will be the demand by foreign companies for the political authority and influence needed to cope with it, other factors being equal. Thus, a relatively unregulated market economy such as Taiwan's will generate less demand by foreign companies for political authority and influence than will a highly regulated economy like India's. The rapid growth of governmental regulation of business during recent years, in the United States and in many other nations, has undoubtedly tended to increase this demand and the amount of corruption in the business-government relationship. Indeed, it has enlarged both the demand for, and the supply of, political authority and influence for sale. As the political scientist Edward C. Banfield has written: "Whatever their causes, every extension of governmental authority has created new opportunities and incentives for corruption."[4]

Finally, the degree of certainty in the administration of government regulation is an important determinant of multinational corporate demand for political authority and influence. Certainty of governmental regulation normally rises with the political and economic development of countries, as their legal and administrative systems grow in competence, and as commercial customs and traditions become established. It also rises as the quality of law enforcement improves. The more certain the legal and socioeconomic environment, the less the foreign company will seek to purchase governmental authority and influence. Canada and Angola may be contrasted as extreme cases with respect to this factor.

Although it does not appear possible to assert the existence of any *general* relationships between the characteristics of the companies doing business in a foreign country and the demand for political authority and influence, there appear to be some characteristics that contribute to such a demand. For example, intense competition between American companies in supplying goods and services to a foreign government has led to large political payments; consider the case of Lockheed. Conversely, outstanding technological and financial leadership seems to reduce the vulnerability of a company to foreign payments; consider the case of IBM.[5]

Determinants of Supply

Turning to the supply side of the market for political authority, we inquire what are the major factors in determining the supply of this "commodity." Again we can identify three important determinants; namely, the *political stability of government*, the *competence and remuneration of governmental officials and employees*, and the *amount of discretionary administrative authority governmental officials possess*. Other factors may be involved, such as historical traditions, but they appear to be of less importance.

The relative stability of government clearly influences the attitudes of public officials toward the taking of bribes or the exaction of extortions. If the history of a country is one of rapid turnover of governments, often accompanied by violence and the assassination of political leaders, the short and uncertain tenure of public officials will lead them to expand the supply of political authority and influence that they are willing to offer for sale in the market. They will reason that they have only a limited time to capitalize on their official positions and see to the financial security of their families. The contrary will be true in countries with a history and an expectation of relatively stable governments.

Similarly, the competence and remuneration of a country's civil servants is an important determinant of the supply of political authority and influence offered for sale. For the most part, the older industrialized nations pay their civil servants adequate—sometimes excellent—compensation and attract competent people into government service; because of this civil servants are not under financial pressure to augment their incomes by accepting or soliciting bribes. But new nations usually lack competent civil servants, and they egregiously underpay them. In such countries governmental employees feel privileged—indeed, economic necessity compels them—to accept bribes offered for special favors or to extort payments from foreign firms. Thus, the supply of political authority and influence available for sale in the market is expanded.

The third important determinant of the supply of political authority and influence is the extent to which a government delegates discretionary decision-making powers to its officials, rather than narrows the range of their discretion by the enactment of clear and specific statutes and regulations. The wider and the more numerous such delegations of discretionary authority, the greater will be the supply of political authority and influence that public officials are able to offer for sale.

A large fraction of the political payments made by American multinational companies to foreign government officials appears to arise from the exercise of bureaucratic fiat by those officials. For example, many governments use procurement and concession policies that leave decisions in the hands of single administrators rather than subject them to competitive processes, such as the submission to procurement boards of sealed bids that are opened publicly. Some foreign governments appear to maintain these practices deliberately, in order to generate opportunities for "extracurricular" income for their public officials. When a single official holds plenary power to admit or deny entry of goods or persons into a country, to approve or disapprove of a factory site, to raise or lower a tax assessment, or to grant or withhold a concession, the temptation to misuse such power becomes almost irresistable.

Another prolific source of bribery and extortion arising from the discretionary authority of governmental employees has been the administration of tax laws in countries that lack clear and certain laws, that have no tradition of strict enforcement, and that delegate power to local officials to negotiate tax settlements. Mexico and Italy are prime examples. Their tax officials are in a position to make extravagant assessments, which are reduced when the taxpayer makes an appropriate payoff.

Another delegatory situation that is tailor-made for bribery or extortion is the lodgement in a public official of full authority to grant or withold mineral exploration rights. Here, again, the large potential supply of political authority that is opened up by this practice can be radically reduced if the foreign government withdraws discretionary power from officials and requires a competitive bidding procedure that leaves little or no room for personal favoritism. Professor Murray L. Weidenbaum has written, concerning the eradication of political payments *in the United States*, that it will require far more than new laws or tighter auditing standards. "Rather, we need to reduce the arbitrary decision-making authority that many Federal agencies now possess in their dealings with business firms."[6]

The Price of Political Authority and Influence and the Quantity Traded

Having identified the principal determinants of the demand for, and supply of, political authority and influence, we are now in a position to make some generalizations about the relative frequency, size, and total amount of political payments that will be made in a country by foreign multinational companies. A familiar economic law tells us that a strong and inelastic demand for a commodity combined with a small and inelastic supply will lead to a relatively high price. Conversely, a weak and elastic demand combined with a cheap and elastic supply produces a relatively low price. Let us apply this principle to the market for political authority and influence in a country. Conceive of a country possessing extensive business opportunities and very extensive and uncertain governmental regulation of the private sector, but also a stable government and a competent and well-paid civil service having little discretionary authority—in economic terms, a situation with strong and inelastic demand and costly and inelastic supply. One would expect to find that in this country political payments by foreign companies were relatively few in number but individually large in amount, i.e., the commodity has a high price. Conversely, a country with meager business opportunities and a laissez faire policy, but with an unstable government and an underpaid civil service possessing wide discretionary administrative authority (i.e., a situation with weak and elastic demand and a cheap and elastic supply), may be expected to have a high incidence of political payments, but the individual amounts of such payments would be relatively small, i.e., the commodity has a relatively low price.

It would, of course, be desirable to test this theory of the market for political authority and influence by quantifying the various supply-and-demand determining factors for each nation, and then ascertaining whether the volume and average amount of political payments predicted by the theory is borne out by the facts. Unfortunately, organized knowledge of the actual markets is insufficient to enable us to test the validity of the theory in this rigorous manner. The theory does, however, conform to a priori logic; and it is borne out by the incomplete information we do possess.

The *Report* of the Securities and Exchange Commission to the Senate Committee on Banking, Housing and Urban Affairs on May 12, 1976, recorded "questionable" payments by some 95 U.S. multinational companies to foreign governmental officials.[7] This tabulation revealed that foreign political payments by aerospace and pharmaceutical companies were relatively frequent and substantial in amount; and, in contrast, payments by automobile and food product companies were relatively infrequent and unsubstantial. Because the aerospace and pharmaceutical industries are highly regulated both by the U.S. and foreign governments, whereas the automobile and food industries are lightly regulated by comparison, a correlation between the extensiveness of governmental regulation and the frequency of foreign payoffs is indicated. This result is predicted by the theory we have advanced.

The preceding result is also confirmed by an analysis of more comprehensive information covering the 300 companies that had, up to the end of 1976, filed reports with the SEC indicating that they had made questionable payments. Of these companies, about 200 appeared on Standard and Poor's list of companies. Of this group, the number of the companies reporting to the SEC in each industry was then compared with the total number of companies in that industry listed by Standard and Poor. (The results appear in Table 4.) The industries with the highest proportions of companies reporting questionable payments were the health care, drug, and cosmetics, tobacco, oil and gas drilling, petroleum, rubber, and chemical industries. At the other extreme, the industries with the lowest proportions were the insurance, banking, food retailing, apparel, and automobile and automobile parts industries.

TABLE 4   Relative Frequency with Which U.S. Companies Reported
Questionable Foreign Payments, by Industry

Industry[1]	(A) Number of Companies Reporting Questionable Payments[2]	(B) Total Number of Companies in Industry[2]	Percentage of Total Companies (B) Reporting Payments (A)
Aerospace	9	29	31.0
Air Transport	6	27	22.5
Apparel	2	34	5.9
Automobile and Automobile Parts	4	64	6.25
Banking	1	65	1.5
Beverage	7	38	18.4
Building	7	74	9.5
Chemical	18	63	28.6
Communication	3	56	5.4
Container	2	35	5.7
Electronics and Electrical	10	65	15.4
Food Processing	12	73	16.4
Health Care, Drugs, and Cosmetics	29	63	46.0
Insurance	0	40	-0-
Leisure Time	9	40	22.5
Machinery	15	85	17.6
Metals, Nonferrous	8	60	13.3
Office Equipment	9	50	18.0
Oil	19	62	30.6
Oil and Gas Drilling and Services	10	32	31.25
Paper	1	30	3.3
Railroad	2	16	12.5
Retailing, Food	1	48	2.1
Rubber Fabricating	5	17	29.4
Steel and Coal	4	29	13.8
Telephone	2	19	10.5
Textile	2	19	10.5
Tobacco	3	9	33.3

[1] Standard and Poor's *Classification of Industries.*

[2] Excludes companies not included in Standard and Poor's *Classification.* Includes all other companies that reported to the SEC up to December 31, 1976, that they had made questionable payments, according to tabulation of Charles E. Simon and Company, Washington, D.C., *Sensitive Payments by Corporations.*

Some Practical Implications

Putting morality to one side, bribery by, and the extortion of, business corporations in their relations with public officials are clearly uneconomic in character. By benefiting individuals rather than the people of a country as a whole, they are burdens imposed on international trade and investment for private instead of public benefit. Moreover, the *uncertainty* regarding their amount and effect on underlying transactions, and the time and expense incurred in negotiating improper political payments, are additional costs of doing business with other nations, which do not produce countervailing advantages. In contrast with open and aboveboard trading, free of corruption, they involve unproductive uses of resources. They constitute wasteful barriers to international economic intercourse, which diminish the welfare of people in both the host country and the home country of the multinational company. For example, bribes are not infrequently made to bring about the purchase of inferior goods or services. For economic reasons alone, it is in the interest of all countries to reduce the size and frequency of improper political payments.[8]

Looking at business bribery and extortion as a market in which governmental authority and influence are traded enables us to identify the factors that lead to corruption of the business-government relationship. It points to the basic actions needed, by governments and by multinational corporations, to reduce the volume of such corruption in the future. It also helps to evaluate many reforms that have been suggested. *Only reform proposals that fundamentally reduce the supply of, and demand for, political influence and authority will be effective in changing the behavior of world business.* To this subject we shall return in Part III of this book.

142

Appendix A: An Elementary Model of a National Market for Political Authority and Influence

For those readers who find line diagrams of economic concepts helpful in clarifying economic ideas, a diagrammatic explanation is provided here. Those who are put off by such constructions can skip this appendix and still understand the thrust of argument.

Figure 1 illustrates the status of a national market for political authority and influence, both *prior* to reforms and as such a market would operate *after* reforms have been made in the behavior of corporations and governments.

Solid lines and letters without suffixes denote the hypothetical state of the market *prior* to reforms of policy. The demand curve for political authority and influence in the country, DD, slopes downward to reflect the probable decline in demand as the number of purchases of political authority and influence per year rises. The supply curve, SS, is drawn to rise in reflection of the probability that more political authority and influence will be offered in the market the higher the price. Market equilibrium is established at the intersection of DD and SS, with an average (bribe or extortion) price of MP and OM transactions per year. The total size of the market, in annual monetary volume, is OMPR.

We now assume that reforms are made in the national policies and in the behavior of governments and corporations. Dotted lines and letters with suffixes denote the post-reform market situation. The reforms have the effect of reducing demand (shifting the DD curve to the left) to D_1D_1, and of reducing supply (shifting the SS curve to the left) to S_1S_1. As a consequence, there is a new market equilibrium at the intersection of D_1D_1 and S_1S_1, with an average price of M_1P_1, significantly lower than before; and an annual rate of transactions of OM_1, also significantly lower than before. As the

Figure 1
An Elementary Model of a National Market for Political
Authority and Influence

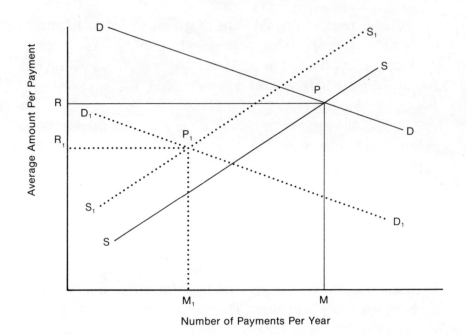

Number of Payments Per Year

Pre-Reform Market: DD: Demand Curve
SS: Supply Curve
AM: Number of Payments
MP: Average Amount of Payments
OMPR: Dollar Amount of Trade

Post-Reform Market: D_1D_1: Demand Curve
S_1S_1: Supply Curve
OM_1: Number of Payments
M_1P_1: Average Amount of Payments
$OM_1P_1R_1$: Dollar Amount of Trade

demand and supply curves have been drawn here, the size
of the market has been reduced to little more than one-third
of the former market, to $OM_1P_1R_1$.

5

The Politics of Corruption in Business-Government Relations

In the preceding chapter we examined political payments from an economic perspective. Since there is no developed economic theory of such payments, we attempted to make sense of them by the use of such familiar economic concepts as market, supply, and demand. In brief, there they were seen to constitute a "black market" in segments of political authority and influence. Like economics, political theory also does not provide a well-developed general framework for the analysis of political payments by business enterprises. But political scientists have concerned themselves with the general phenomenon of corruption in political activity, including that found in the interface between business and government. Accordingly, we shall in this chapter analyze the politics of bribery and extortion in business-government relations, making use of such tools of political science and anthropology as seem relevant.[1] From the perspective we will take, corruption may be described as an "informal political system," existing alongside the formal political system with its familiar apparatus of legislative, executive, judicial, and

145

bureaucratic institutions.[2] Corruption will thus be seen as a pathological state or deformation of the basic economic and political institutions of human society.

Corruption in Government and Business Organizations

The distinguished political scientist Edward C. Banfield contrasts business and governmental organizations, and draws implications about the relative frequency of corruption among employees of the two types of institutions.[3] The business corporation's objective, Banfield observes, is sharply focused on the optimization of returns on investment. It offers personal, material incentives to its employees. It has a well-defined hierarchical system of control, under which higher-echelon executives define goals for lower-echelon executives, limit their discretionary powers, give or withhold rewards or penalties, and monitor their performance. Normally, its management continues in office so long as returns on investment are satisfactory. Except as the business organization must make disclosures to comply with governmental regulations, its affairs are secret.

The business corporation, he suggests, will incur costs to prevent corruption only insofar as it expects them to yield returns equal to those that could be obtained from other investments. That is, its objective will be to reduce corruption to the point that it is consistent with profit optimization, rather than to eliminate it. It will normally tolerate petty pilfering or other minor forms of graft. In dealing with personal corruption among its higher officials, it will shun publicity, for fear that a bad reputation might scare away investors or invite a takeover bid.

Banfield points out that the governmental organization, in contrast, has numerous objectives that are unordered, vague, and mutually antagonistic, if not contradictory. Power and glory are strong incentives for its top officials, and job security for its lower-level functionaries. Its "top management" usually consists of an unstable coalition of individuals, among whom authority is fragmented. Because of civil service constraints, it lacks power to reward or penalize lower-level employees effectively. Terms of office of top governmental officials are limited. The organization operates in an environment of publicity and public participation, and has few secrets.

As an ideal, the governmental organization, especially in the United States, will aim to eliminate corruption—no matter what the cost. In practice, however, as we show later in this chapter, many governments throughout the world condone corruption. Nevertheless, in Banfield's model, where the duties of government employees are often mutually incompatible and superior officials do not resolve their dilemma, these employees often must act corruptly. A loose system of internal monitoring (i.e., control) permits of more corruption than in the business corporation. Most monitoring of government agencies is done by the news media and other external agencies. Inflexibility in the pay scales of civil servants makes them more amenable to the acceptance, or solicitation, of graft. Paradoxically, the political "machine" tends to *reduce* corruption in government. It replaces fragmented top management with the informal central authority of the "boss." He has a well-defined objective—to enhance his organization —and his tenure is reasonably secure. He defines the authority of subordinates, maintains an incentive system, and monitors members of his organization to check unauthorized graft.

The structural and behavioral differences between business and governmental organizations, noted by Banfield, tend to make corruption relatively more frequent among governmental employees than among business employees. This conclusion conforms to our previous findings, and suggests that more political payments are initiated by governmental than by business employees and are, from a legal point of view, more extortions than bribes.

Corruption as an Aspect of Politics

Like the use of force and violence, corruption is a pervasive part of most political systems in the world, whether capitalist or communist, authoritarian or democratic. It is a persistent and well-nigh universal characteristic of political activity, growing out of the values and mores of societies.[4] Thus it is not merely the deviant activity of a few unscrupulous businessmen, as some journalists and politicians would have it.

In these times, when criticism by the media and public officials focuses on the transgressions of American multinational corporations, it is well to recall that political corruption was endemic in the past among European nations and in the United States. And the West's moral repugnance to corruption is a relatively recent social development. As the Swedish sociologist, Gunnar Myrdal, has observed: "Great Britain, Holland, and the Scandinavian countries were all rife with corruption two hundred years ago."[5] In Great Britain, between 1751 and 1760, bribery was the foundation on which Walpole and Pelham operated the parliamentary system of government. Political payments were used by the Whigs to create an ". . . elaborate system of governmental favors, ranging from direct payments to voters and members of Parliament, to patronage and the various favors available in foreign trade and the privileged trading companies."[6] Indeed, political corruption on both sides of the Atlantic helped bring on the American Revolution.[7] Professor Carl J. Friedrich has suggested that the colonists might better ". . . have attacked this corruption rather than King George in their Declaration of Independence."[8] Corruption of state legislators, representatives, and senators was pervasive in the last century. And current newspaper stories are a reminder that there are still aberrations by public officials from the legal and moral standards of acceptable conduct.[9]

Gift-Giving and Kinship Ties in Traditional Societies

From Western moral perspectives, the exchange of gifts in traditional societies is often seen as an act of corruption. In these societies, however, elites are often obliged to make gifts to their poorer clienteles or to the community. The less affluent are expected to make token offerings to their patrons or leaders as a sign of their allegiance.[10] This ancient practice of gift-giving still prevails in the traditional Middle East desert societies. It is employed to seal the loyalty of the gift-giver to the throne or to the seat of a ruling emir. Where traditional gift-giving as a symbol of fealty leaves off and becomes bribery in the modern Western sense is not readily apparent.

The practice of political payments is regarded by many traditional populations as no different from the "gifts" or "tribute" to officials sanctioned by age-old customs. Indeed, the payoff is seen as a latter-day equivalent of obeisance to higher authority. "Tea money," *cumshaw* (literally "thank you"), or an actual gift of a chicken, for example, laid at the doorstep of a village headman by a peasant farmer in need of a favorable decision in a land dispute, or a jade bowl presented by a Japanese businessman to a cabinet minister from whom he seeks a favor—these offerings are not so much bribes in the Western legal and moral sense as expressions of the difference in status between the one who does the asking and the one who confers the favor.

In Japan, for example, a money payment can serve as a means for regaining the goodwill of an individual whose feelings have been injured and who has thereby lost face. This is not unlike the analogous situation in the United States where an aggrieved party sues in the courts and is awarded money damages in satisfaction of his alleged emotional and mental distress. Thus, when Coca-Cola appointed a Japanese national as the president of its Japanese company, one of his first steps in ending a major source of the U.S. company's distribution troubles was the payment of $550,000 to protesting local bottlers as a "conciliation gift." This was a traditional gesture for satisfying the loss of face that the local bottlers had incurred because Coca-Cola had bypassed their distribution facilities.[11]

Traditional kinship ties also create demands and relationships that appear corrupt to modern Western eyes. Thus, in many new African and Asian states, as well as in Latin American countries, where loyalty to the state is secondary (if it exists at all), and the family, village, tribe, and clan command the primary loyalty of the individual, public office is exploited for the benefit of the nuclear or extended family.[12] In these countries, the demands of the "family social security system" compel an educated member of the family, holding a government job, to be "corrupt" in the modern Western sense. On his meager pay, he has no means of fulfilling the financial importunities of his family or clan. Familial bonds prevent him from refusing a plea for a job, or a license, or some other governmental favor. In consequence, he is forced to engage in nepotism, to accept bribes, and to extort money from individuals and business enterprises—indigenous and foreign —who appear before him. Indeed, in China the Confucian tradition countenanced the use by the mandarins—the world's first elite civil servants—of public office for personal aggrandizement. Their acceptance of gratuities (graft) to supplement their low government salaries was officially sanctioned.

Dominant Governments and Corruption
in the Third World

Throughout much of the Third World, corruption is expanded by the dominant role that governments play as dispensers of business privileges and as major sources of nonagricultural employment. In Africa, Asia, and Latin America, government employment confers exceptional status and prestige. A governmental job is, therefore, a prize eagerly sought, not infrequently paid for, and, once obtained, carefully safeguarded. Public office is not only a key to supplemental income; it unlocks the national treasury as well.

The pressure for public employment in many Third World governments is not unlike the situation prevailing in seventeenth-century England when government officials, drawing inadequate salaries and often burdened with debts incurred in buying their jobs, used their official posts to extort fees, solicit bribes, and pocket state revenues. Samuel Pepys, Secretary to the Admiralty in 1673, succinctly stated the advantages of an officeholder when he observed: "It was not the salary of any place that did make a man rich, but the opportunity of getting money while he is in the place."[13]

In many less-developed nations, governments are not only major employers, but they are also responsible for economic planning, social welfare, and, through their public sectors, for the actual production of goods. The role of governments as distributors of privileges, such as import and export permits, franchises, authorizations to establish a business, and obtain foreign exchange, has vastly increased the corruption in business-government relations. Accounts of corruption in many new states are replete with examples in such branches of the public service as customs offices, public works departments, excise and tax offices, loan agencies, and foreign exchange control boards.[14] These are all agencies that dis-

151

pense valuable privileges to enterprises, or handle sizeable amounts of revenue, or whose administrative personnel are vested with wide discretionary power.

The governmental bureaucracies of the underdeveloped countries are rarely subjected to the countervailing restraints that exist in the industrialized nations, such as political parties, functioning legislatures, strong judiciaries, trade unions, business lobbies, and other groups that can make their political influence felt. In consequence, the civil services of many Third World nations operate as feudal baronies, exploiting those with whom they deal. In the absence of institutions or organized groups capable of restraining official venality, the employees and officials of these bureaucracies possess virtually untrammeled power for obtaining personal wealth.

In the industrialized countries, the status and education of civil servants is not significantly different from that of many private citizens, businessmen, or professional practitioners such as lawyers and accountants. In the preindustrial societies, on the other hand, the civil servant is a high school or university graduate, while the bulk of the citizenry is illiterate. The rural peasant or the city dweller, who is usually a transplanted countryman, approaches the civil servant not as a citizen seeking a service to which he is entitled but as a supplicant seeking a favor. The wide educational and social gap that separates civil servants and the citizenry in the underdeveloped countries tends to engender corruption. Because his position puts him beyond effective criticism or restraint, the administrator is free to make arbitrary decisions in favor of a supplicant from whom he can extort payments. A low-status, impotent private citizen appearing as an applicant or supplicant is apt to offer a bribe with the hope and expectation of obtaining a favorable decision.

In the regimes in which legal systems offer tenuous security for business enterprise, the existence of a corrupt bureaucracy, amenable to pecuniary blandishments, may be, paradoxically, the only means for obtaining relative stability in business-government relations. Payments made to, or extorted by, a corrupt bureaucracy can enable a socially chaotic system to function.

Open versus Covert Business Influence on Government

Political influence is exerted differently in the industrialized countries than in the agrarian, preindustrial societies. In the former, demands by individuals and special interest groups normally reach the political system *before* the enactment of legislation. Indeed, legislation is usually a consequence of such demands. *Bribery of officials by businessmen is considerably lessened by the existence of open channels for the exercise of political influence.* Examples of such channels are campaign contributions to candidates for election or to political parties, public relations campaigns to arouse public support for or against pending legislation, and direct lobbying in legislatures. The decline of corruption during modern times in many liberal-democratic countries can thus be traced, in part, to the institutionalization and legitimization of political influence by business enterprise.

In Third World countries with socialist-statist regimes, private enterprises, and particularly foreign-based corporations, are afforded little or no opportunity to exercise an influence on the formulation of legislation, even where popularly elected legislatures exist. Hence, such political influence as they are able to exercise must be exerted at the stage when laws are *enforced*. It is at this juncture that corruption occurs. Laws or decrees are not applied impersonally, but at the discretion of government officials whose favors are available for purchase. Because the political systems of many underdeveloped countries do not provide for the "institutionalized influence" of business, enterprises are obliged to deal with political power—often concentrated in hands ideologically hostile to business—by means of the payoff. To put this differently, corruption in many parts of the world is simply the "uninstitutionalized" political influence of the private sector.

The Misty Line Between Bribery and Extortion

In overseas business-government relations, the distinction between bribery and extortion is frequently blurred, as we have noted. In the marketplace, the actor who initiates the political payment is not always apparent. Consider this situation. A minister responsible for the defense of a desert emirate on the Arabian Peninsula has had before him a proposal to buy from company Y, an American aircraft manufacturer, a squadron of sophisticated jet fighter aircraft. A decision has been withheld for months. There have been rumors of a pending visit by a high-ranking Soviet military delegation who, it is understood, will offer the Ruler a squadron of MIG fighter aircraft, defense missiles, and a training program on far more favorable terms than those proposed by company Y. In response to increasingly anxious inquiries on the status of its proposal, Y's local agent informs the company's home office that a decision by the minister can be expedited by the judicious application of the Middle East's magic elixir—*baksheesh*—in the form of a million dollar check deposited in a numbered Swiss bank account. (In accordance with the prevailing custom in the former Trucial States, this money payment will be shared with the Ruler.)

It is not clear from the agent's communication whether this method of expediting the ministerial decision is his own idea or reflects an intimation conveyed to him by the minister's aide. Subsequently the *Wall Street Journal* carries a short paragraph reporting that the Y company has been awarded a hundred million dollar contract by the Emirate of Khalish.

The whole transaction raises many questions. Did the transaction involve bribery or was it extortion? Was the payment made to induce the minister to accelerate the performance of his duty? Was it made to ensure a decision favoring a U.S. supplier? Did the Department of State and the American embassy play a part in turning the decision to the Y company? Or was the payment made in response to pressure exerted by the minister on the Y company through its agent?

In the black market for political influence, *who* did *what* to *whom* makes much practical difference. But as the scales of justice are seen by the media world, guilt is not evenly assigned. It is useful to note that, in their coverage of political payments by American companies abroad, *who* initiates a political payment has not seemed to make much difference to the U.S. media—and, until recently, to the Securities and Exchange Commission. Payments have often been described indiscriminately as "bribes," and the implication has been drawn that the guilty party to the transaction was the corporate payer. Somehow, the payee (who may have instigated the demand for the payment) is rarely mentioned; or he is treated as having been corrupted by American businessmen and their agents.

With the worldwide growth of terrorism, the American company abroad has in recent years become the victim of an *unofficial* form of extortion—ransom demands for the release of executives or members of their families after kidnapping. In one case involving the kidnapping of an Exxon executive in Argentina, a ransom of $14 million was demanded and paid to guerrilla abductors for his release. And in a recent bizarre case in Venezuela, the Owens-Illinois Glass Company had its property expropriated by the Venezuelan government because—contrary to the wishes of the government—the company negotiated with the kidnappers to save the life of its plant manager and paid the ransom! The local terrorists also demanded that the company take out ads in the *New York Times*, the *London Times*, and *Le Monde* of Paris denouncing itself and the Venezuelan government!

Foreign corporations, particularly those whose parents are located in the United States, are perceived throughout most of the Third World as cornucopias of wealth, some of which legitimately may be siphoned into the pockets of deserving but impecunious civil servants and their political masters. The rationalization for using the international corporation as a milch cow is the Robin Hood syndrome of taking from the rich for the benefit of the poor.

The Political Cycle of Corruption and Cleanup

In coup-prone societies in which political instability is chronic, regimes come and go with bewildering rapidity. But the foreign corporation remains as a target of opportunity, close at hand, and helpless to resist a pecuniary extraction. Ironically, such extractions are usually accomplished by a regime that has seized power pledged to eradicate the corruption of its predecessor.

Thailand is a case in point. The Thai kingdom historically has been one of the most corrupt in Southeast Asia. Early in October 1976, the Thai military executed a coup d'etat and seized power from a civilian government that only recently had superseded a military regime. The new ruling military group named Thanint Kraivichan, a conservative professor of law and supreme court judge, as prime minister. In his acceptance speech, he listed reform of corruption as one of the new "reform" regime's priorities.[15]

Nigeria offers another example of military reformers who placed the elimination of corruption high on the list of their priorities. When the military, led by Major General Yakubu Gowan, ousted the civilian regime of Sir Abubabar Tafawa

Balewa, in January 1966, many Nigerians believed the army would fulfill its pledge to clean up corruption. The ostensible reason for the removal of General Gowan (who ruled from July 29, 1966, to July 29, 1975) by another army faction was that too many high officials continued to engage in corrupt practices. General Gowan, now a student at an English university, is reputed to have deposited several hundred million dollars in foreign bank accounts.[16] The new military regime mounted a broad attack on corruption—as had its predecessor. It established a Permanent Corrupt Practices Investigation Bureau and a Special Tribunal to handle all cases of corruption in all sectors of the nation's economy. In an unprecedented step for an African country, hundreds of civil servants were dismissed, and all high-ranking military officers were required to disclose their finances. Yet, after ten years in power by successive reform-minded military regimes, as Professor Levi A. Nwachuku observes, corruption remains as the perennial Nigerian social malaise.[17]

Brazil provides still another illustration of a military regime that seized power with the intention of cleansing the body politic of corrupt practices by politicians and businessmen. To an editor of the *Wall Street Journal* it is "somewhat surprising that twelve years later corruption is again widespread throughout Brazilian life." On a visit to Brazil, Edwin Mc-Dowell found that even supporters of the military government (whose officer corps is generally considered a model of rectitude) "admit that bribes, kickbacks, and influence peddling are pervasive."[18]

The Rewards of Politics

Politics—at home or abroad—can be a richly rewarding career. It provides the trappings and panoply of power, popular adulation, and—not the least—opportunities to acquire a personal fortune. During the heyday of his power, the late Kwame Nkrumah, the American-educated dictator of Ghana, with exquisite but unintentional irony, caused to be inscribed at the base of his own statue outside the Law Courts in Accra, words that all too often characterize the lives of many who seek political careers:

> Seek ye first the Kingdom of Politics
> and all else shall be added unto you.

Adhemar de Barros, in his time a well-known Brazilian politician, once expressed the same idea more simply and with brutal candor, when he exclaimed to the voters of São Paulo: "I steal, but I achieve!"

In his notable study, *Arms and Politics in Latin America*, Professor Edwin Lieuwin estimated that over a period of five years (1954–59) six Latin American dictators had made off with over $1 billion in personal graft.[19] And some "sons of the Mexican Revolution" are known to have retired from the presidency as millionaires. Argentina under the recent rule of the Peronistas offers another dramatic illustration of corruption on a massive scale by public office holders. Two former presidents—Maria Estella Perón and Paul A. Lastri— were placed in custody and charged with embezzlement and fraud. Along with a string of former provincial officials closely associated with the Peronist movement, seven one-time cabinet ministers, three former state secretaries, a former federal judge, and a prosecutor have been charged with corruption.[20]

That politics can be financially rewarding is especially true in Southeast Asia. In looking at political payments there, it is useful to see those practices through Asian eyes rather than through the lenses of the Western observer whose vision is affected by different standards of probity. What the West calls "graft" is for most Asians merely a natural form of income by which the fortunately placed individual helps his family and the members of his clan, village, class, or trade. These are limited loyalties, to be sure, but they engender unlimited corruption.

For example, the late Thai strongman, Marshall Sarit Thanarat, and his family held the state monopoly on lottery tickets. Together with the members of his family, he had acquired controlling interests in more than a dozen businesses, including a construction firm that became a principal beneficiary of government contracts. By Western standards, Sarit was crooked on a massive scale. When he died, his estate was estimated at between $100 and $140 million. He was posthumously found guilty of having embezzled state funds of about $50 million, which were then siphoned into his private account. Most of this money was spent on a harem of "minor wives." Yet his splendid funeral was attended by the king and queen, and an opposition motion in the Parliament to deprive him of his military rank was defeated.[21]

Contributions to Foreign Political Parties

Payments coerced from overseas affiliates of U.S. firms for political contributions have been substantial. In one country alone, South Korea, over a period of five months, from the end of December of 1973 to May of 1974, about $40 million was extracted from the Seoul business community in which the largest companies have home bases in the United States. Some indication of the toll levied against U.S. corporations may be seen from a compilation prepared by the Securities and Exchange Commission of eighty-nine companies reporting political payments.[22] Of the eleven companies that reported having made contributions to political parties over varying periods, the amount aggregated $47 million.[23]

The foreign political party frequently serves as an instrument of monetary extraction not only from the multinational corporation, but also from the governments of the great powers. Thus the Soviet Union is called on to subsidize overseas communist parties. The U.S. government has financed democratic, anti-communist parties, such as the Christian Democratic parties in Italy and Chile. France provides "aid" for the one-party regimes of her former African colonies. The People's Republic of China makes funds available to friendly political parties and regimes in sub-Saharan Africa, and to dissident groups trying to subvert unfriendly regimes in the Arabian Peninsula.

As has been noted, some members of the international business community also give financial support to foreign political parties. In many countries—Italy, Canada, and Japan are examples—local laws expressly permit business corporations to contribute to political parties. Laws in other countries are murky, and in making a political contribution, the foreign corporation frequently lacks clear legal authorization. Nevertheless, throughout much of the world, corporate political contributions by local and foreign companies are common and—as in Latin America—almost obligatory. The propriety of making such contributions is much more a preoccupation of Americans than it is of people in most foreign countries, who take a more relaxed view of corporate financial support of political campaigns and parties.

To be sure, some corporate managements that have authorized or have had knowledge of political contributions by their overseas subsidiaries have not always exercised good judgment. Others were forced to make contributions under the threat of economic reprisals. In responding to solicitations—however made—for political contributions, management motives can be complex and obscure. Is a particular payment "insurance" against political damage to an existing investment by a ruling party or by an opposition party that is expected to take power? Is it made to retain the goodwill of the party in power and to provide access to the leading figures of the party when, as, and if needed? Is it a response to a political "shakedown"? Is it made to secure future business, or to create a favorable business environment? Is it made— as is so frequently the case in the United States—with the expectation of obtaining changes in government policies, especially in the area of taxes? In Third World countries, where market economies are closely circumscribed, management motives in responding to political solicitations can fill a small catalog. Previously, we examined political payments by Gulf in South Korea, Exxon in Italy, and Lockheed in Japan as *types* of foreign payments. Here, we look more closely at the *political processes* involved in those payments.

A critical point with respect to corporate contributions to political parties is the determination in each case of whether or not they involve bribery or extortion. The point is illustrated by the testimony of Gulf Oil Corporation's former chairman, Bob R. Dorsey, before the Senate Subcommittee on Multinational Corporations. After describing the display of raw Oriental power involved in his shakedown by the late S. K. Kim, financial chairman of South Korea's Democratic Republican Party—"as tough a man as I've ever met," Dorsey said—Senator Dick Clark, nevertheless, persisted in asking: "Do you interpret that payment to have been a contribution or a bribe?"[24]

Senator Clark, Chairman Church, and the Subcommittee's counsel also disregarded the distinction between bribery and extortion when they interrogated Mobil executive vice president Everett S. Checket. Although the Subcommittee categorized inaccurately the payments by the Italian affiliate of Mobil to the Italian political parties as "bribes," it ignored the clear example of extortion by a prominent Italian politician of a U.S. overseas facility. At a truly impartial hearing the information would have been elicited that the former president of Italy's Campania Region, Galileo Barbirotti, was *convicted* of extorting the equivalent of $160,000 from Mobil's

Italian affiliate. He had threatened, for trumped-up ecological reasons, to order Mobil to move its large refinery from a suburb of Naples. Signore Barbirotti is the highest-ranking Italian official thus far to have been fined and jailed for extorting money from major oil companies. The Italian prosecutor, in an interview with the *Wall Street Journal*, pointed out that, under Italian civil law, Mobil was considered the party *against* whom the offense had been committed and was entitled to a restitution of the money extorted.[25]

Lockheed's Political Payments in Japan

It is instructive to examine Lockheed's experience in Japan to see how political contributions were extorted by politicians from an American company as the price of obtaining a contract for the sale of twenty-one TriStar wide-bodied jet aircraft to All Nippon Airways. In an interview in August 1976 with the leading Japanese newspaper, *Asahi Shimbun*, the former president and vice chairman, A. Carl Kotchian, who directed Lockheed's marketing strategy in Tokyo at the time of the political payments, declared: "We can honestly say there was not a single occasion on which we proposed payoffs. All the problems of money were raised as requests from our agent, Marubeni Trading Company, and our confidential consultant, Mr. Kodamo."

In his personal memoir, *Lockheed Sales Mission: Seventy Days in Tokyo,* published in Japanese, Kotchian recounted his Herculean labors to win the All Nippon Airways order in intense competition with McDonnell Douglas. The final chapter contains his poignant observations about the $12 million, paid on his authorization to the company's agents and consultants, which amounted to 2.8 percent of the $430 million order:

162

Was it really possible, from the standpoint of reality, to say "I refuse to pay"? I thought of all the effort expended by the thousands of men and women since the conception and designing of the L-1011 TriStar; our superhuman efforts to avoid bankruptcy because of our own financial difficulties as well as similar difficulties of the engine maker (Rolls-Royce); the successive defeats in both the KSSU and Atlas competitions in the European theater. I thought of the painful final efforts of the last seventy days. And I thought of being told: "If you make this payment, you can surely get the order of as many as 21 airplanes." I must admit that my moral and ethical considerations gave way to the commercial gains we had been seeking for so many hard days and weeks to make.[26]

The former managing director of Marubeni, according to Kotchian, informed him that $1,831,000 would have to be paid to the then Prime Minister, Kakuei Tanaka. This payment was described as a "gift" to induce him to bestow a "special favor" on a foreign company seeking a major contract from a company controlled by the Japanese government. Kotchian was also advised that $100,000 (in yen) would have to be paid to six other politicians of the Liberal Democratic Party as well as a kickback of $300,000 to executives of All Nippon Airways.

The six politicians to whom payments were to be made were not obscure members of the ruling party but ministers and prominent members of the Diet. They were: Susumu Nikaido, Chief Cabinet Secretary; Tomisaburo Hashimoto, Secretary General of the Liberal Democratic Party and a member of the Diet; Hideyo Susaki, Transport Minister; Takayuki Sato, Former Parliamentary Vice Transport Minister and a member of the Diet; Mutsuki Kato, Vice Transport Minister; and Kazuomi Fukunago, Chairman of the Liberal Democratic Special Committee on Civil Aviation.

Japan's federal prosecutors indicted Tanaka, Hashimoto, and Sato for the crime of "solicited bribery." Despite the indictment of three of the Japanese politicians for having *solicited* bribes from an American aircraft manufacturer, Senator Church said in a speech at a Harvard University conference that Lockheed had worked against U.S. foreign policy interests because its payments to Japanese politicians had "contributed to the corruption and subversion of the ruling party, on which the United States relied heavily."[27] But Japanese politicians have a long history of corruption. Political corruption was a major factor in the breakdown of parliamentary government before World War II. It led to the first postwar scandal, the Showa Denho case, in 1948, which caused the downfall of the Ashida cabinet. Lockheed's payoffs were only the latest chapter and, undoubtedly, not the last.[28]

In the national election held in December 1976, only one of the three indicted Liberal Democrats, Takayuki Sato, was defeated, and his failure to win reelection was less a consequence of a linkage to the "Lockheed scandal" than his membership in a weak "machine" or "supporter's association," as political organizations are known in Japan. Indeed, former Prime Minister Tanaka won by a landslide, receiving only 12,000 fewer votes than when he was the incumbent prime minister. Three other Liberal Democrats, who were identified by name as recipients of Lockheed payments but who escaped prosecution on technicalities, also were reelected. Ironically, the official in charge of the Lockheed prosecutions, Justice Minister Osamu Inaba, barely won reelection.[29]

In this election, for the first time since its founding in 1955, the Liberal Democratic Party lost its majority in the lower house of parliament. But it remained by far the largest party in the Diet and was able to continue in control by obtaining the support of independent members. As the *Wall Street Journal* observed in an editorial:

> . . . even without [the Lockheed] scandal, the LDP has been losing ground steadily—from a high of 339 seats to its present 249 seats in the 511-seat lower house. The major reason for

the steady erosion is that the party's strength lay in rural areas and with small businessmen, whose influence has been dwindling.[30]

Contrary to Senator Church's assertions, some observers felt the election would not lead to a major shift in Japan's pro-U.S. stance.[31] The incumbent prime minister, Takeo Miki, however, resigned as president of the Liberal Democratic Party and prime minister owing to the opposition that he incurred for having pressed the Lockheed investigation too hard, for having permitted the arrest of a former prime minister, and ignoring other matters.[32] He was succeeded by his long-time rival, the seventy-one-year-old career bureaucrat Takeo Fukuda, whose selection assured the continuation of Japan's basic domestic and foreign policies.[33]

Exxon's Support of Italian Political Parties

The complications that can result from *concealing* the making of political contributions—in a country in which such contributions are entirely legal—are dramatically depicted in the experience of Exxon's Italian affiliate, Esso Italiana. In Italy, the business community is expected to finance the political parties. The larger political parties—communist and non-communist alike—run schools and youth centers, publish newspapers and journals, and maintain their own publishing houses for the printing of party books, pamphlets, and tracts. Most, if not all, of these activities operate at a loss. The scale of election spending in Italy is massive. At the end of electoral campaigns, there are huge unpaid bills. Even party memberships, subscriptions to newspapers and publications, and the mandatory kickbacks of a part of the members' parliamentary salaries are insufficient to pay the bills.

Instead, the Fiats, Olivettis, Pirellis, Montedisons, the ENI (the huge state oil company), the IRI (a giant state industrial

holding company), the Confidustria (the General Confedera-
tion of Italian Industry), and the Italian affiliates of the
major international corporations from Western Europe,
Japan, and the United States make up the losses. In particular, the affiliates of the international oil companies are an
important source of political funds because oil is big business
in Italy. From 1963 until 1972 (when these payments were
discontinued), Esso Italiana contributed $29 million to the
major parties—the sums ranging from $3 to $5 million each
year.

Oil industry contributions were made in part through the
industry's trade association, Unione Petrolifera. Party leaders
informed the association how much the industry was expected to contribute, and the amount was raised by assessments levied on the members.[34] Contributions were chan-
nelled through the parties' own newspapers—Esso Italiana
even contributed $89,000 to the Italian Communist Party in
this manner. Several leading Italian newspapers are owned
by the big private and state corporations—*La Stampa* (by
Fiat), *Il Giorno* (by the ENI), *La Notta* and *Il Giornale* (by
Pesanti and Italcementi).

In 1974 a law was enacted by the Italian parliament granting public subsidies of about $75 million annually for all
political parties. The new law continued to legalize political
contributions made by corporations, but for the first time
required *disclosure* of the names of the recipients. In prior
years, by mutual understanding of donors and donees, it
was the practice to conceal the names of the recipients.
This led to disguising payments on the corporate books so
that the recipients could not be identified by the prying
eyes of the tax inspectors. As the payments were usually
listed as business expenses, with receipts to show them as
such, tax deductions from Italian income taxes were taken.
In a candid letter to his fellow Exxon employees, dated July
14, 1975, the now-retired chairman, J. K. Jamieson, acknowl-

edged that adherence to this practice by Exxon's affiliate was a "mistake."

Political contributions in Italy—as in many other countries —are conducive to the award of lucrative government contracts, public utility franchises, protection against import competition, and other favors a friendly government can confer. Archie Monroe, Exxon's controller, testified that Esso Italiana's contributions were allocated to "categories relating to business objectives," such as efforts to reduce or defer taxes, to obtain refinery licenses, to import natural gas, or to secure favorable locations for service stations—privileges within the discretionary power of the ruling party of the Italian government to bestow or withhold.[35] The Italian business community supports the political parties for the same pragmatic reasons that prompt the support of political parties by business organizations in other democracies—to influence party attitudes and to exert leverage over party votes.

Some observers of the Italian scene believe that Italian big business also finances the Italian Communist Party, the second largest party in Italy, as insurance against the day when it may take over the government. The Communist Party in 1976 was grappling with the Christian Democrats—no longer the majority party in the Chamber of Deputies—for eventual control of the government. The Italian Communists have been indirectly financed by Italian firms through brokerage fees earned in arranging deals with communist bloc countries and the Soviet Union.[36] The socialists are said to have earned similar commissions for arranging ventures with Yugoslavia and the People's Republic of China. The Italian Communist Party operates a network of highly profitable export-import companies that trade with the communist bloc countries of Eastern Europe and the Soviet Union.[37]

Communist spokesmen contend that these international business activities, along with their profitable domestic businesses, have enabled them to discard Moscow's cash subsidies.

Others in a position to know believe that the Soviets continue to use their diplomatic pouch as a means of transmitting cash to the party. Although the Italian government may have entertained the thought of cracking down on this method of transmitting funds, it was never in a position to take effective action because the other parties were also involved in a similar traffic. In fact, the ruling and governing party—the Christian Democrats—for some two decades has been the beneficiary of financial support by the United States. In essence, the parties tolerate each other's clandestine offshore funding.

As a long-time member of the Senate Foreign Relations Committee, Senator Church was well aware—or should have been from Committee discussions—of the U.S. policy of providing financial aid to the Christian Democratic Party. Yet the same Senator Church, presiding over the Senate Subcommittee on Multinational Corporations, when informed by Mobil Oil's executive vice president, Everett S. Checket, that Mobil Oil Italiana's political contributions were made "to support the democratic process of government," ridiculed the statement, chided the witness, and charged that the payment was a "bribe" to obtain special favors.[38]

Why, it may be asked, is it morally justifiable for the U.S. government to subsidize Italian political parties to prevent the communists from taking power, but morally reprehensible for a private company with a large investment to do the same thing? Despite a holier-than-thou attitude of profound shock over learning of payoffs by U.S. corporations abroad, the U.S. State Department and American ambassadors to foreign countries have long known of the practice and have winked at it.[39] The American Embassy in Rome, when informed of the payments made by the Italian affiliates of the U.S. oil companies, evinced neither shock, surprise, nor disapproval. Indeed, according to the counsel to the Senate Subcommittee on Multinational Corporations, who interviewed members of the Embassy, their attitude was that Esso Italiana was getting a "nice slice of the pie," and, therefore, was "not as bad off as they represented to the Embassy."[40]

Are Italian politics, after all, greatly different from American politics? Business supports political parties in order to minimize the economic damage that might otherwise be inflicted on it—its contributions are a kind of political ransom. Special interest groups in Italy have slipped cash to politicians in the same way that milk producers in the United States have financed Democrats and Republicans alike to hold up milk prices; or the unions have financed Democrats to see things Labor's way.

Perhaps the real difference between Italian and American politics is that the Italian politician is less prone to hypocrisy. In an ancient land that holds few illusions for its people, every Italian *knows* that politicians are corrupt. And the practitioners of the world's "second oldest profession" see no reason to disabuse their constituents of this firmly held conviction.

Should American Companies Make Foreign Political Contributions?

The traumatic experiences of several prominent American business leaders who were coerced into contributing to the reelection campaign of former President Nixon, the SEC's requirement for the disclosure of foreign political payments, and the widespread treatment by the media of many such contributions as "bribes," have led some companies to adopt a policy of abstaining from the making of *any* political contributions abroad.

Such a policy in our judgment is not prudent, and the

ability to sustain it is doubtful. In many countries it is legal and customary for business enterprises to contribute to political parties and to candidates for election. There is little likelihood that foreign politicians will relinquish their solicitations of, or pressures on, U.S. managers to donate funds to their electoral campaigns. Those who believe otherwise are deluding themselves. A refusal to make a political contribution can endanger an overseas investment and provoke retaliatory action. Not only will the declination be construed as a lack of sympathy for the host country's own political development, but it will invite resentment that can be expressed in economic reprisals or "creeping expropriation." Whatever the mode that official displeasure takes, the overseas U.S. facility is likely to suffer. Although the Department of State officially disapproves of political contributions abroad by U.S. companies, it has yet to demonstrate its willingness to shield an American overseas facility from the demands of foreign politicians and officials.

A realistic policy for the U.S. corporation, where it is permissible to do so, and it is believed necessary to protect its business interests, is to participate voluntarily in the electoral processes of the countries in which it is an investor by contributing modest sums to the local parties and their candidates. After all, a concern with the furtherance of democratic elections is a vital attribute of corporate citizenship, at home or abroad. U.S. subsidiaries abroad are organized under the laws of host countries; they are subject to the laws of the countries in which they are domiciled; and for all practical purposes they are *foreign* corporations. As such, they are governed by host country laws and customs respecting political contributions.

If the foreign affiliates of American-owned companies expect to be accorded the same treatment as local companies, they should assume the same obligations with respect to

170

political contributions. Where there is doubt as to the legality of using corporate funds for a political purpose, the local manager should obtain an opinion from local counsel and be guided accordingly.

6

Ethical Perspectives on Foreign Political Payments

THE revelations that several hundred major American business corporations made payments for political influence and special favors to foreign political figures and government employees were hardly news to knowledgeable people in business, in politics, in the news media, and, one must assume, in the Securities and Exchange Commission itself. Indeed, here in the United States, corruption in business-government relations has been fairly common for a long time. And one might well have assumed that, given the size of American investment abroad and the traditions of extortion and bribery prevalent in many countries of the world, considerable sums were being paid out by U.S. companies to pave the way for their entry into, and continuance in, European and Third World economies.

The unattractive fact is that, in most of the countries of the world, companies that have sought to carry on business were traditionally asked for, or sometimes offered, various inducements to the appropriate persons for governmental favors and influence. These long-standing foreign practices of trading in governmental favors and influences have confronted the directors and officers of U.S. multinational corporations with difficult ethical dilemmas. On the one hand, there have been, since the end of World War II, profitable opportunities to expand direct investment abroad. The initiation of such investment has often required large payoffs to politicians. Having once invested, firms have then faced the ongoing need to protect their investments. In many instances, the success of an investment, even the avoidance of expropriation, as well as the more mundane day-to-day relations with governmental agencies abroad, required the constant purchase of favors and influence. On the other hand, the U.S. businessmen who made these payments came from a society that holds that the merit of a product or service should be the determining factor in its choice and that disapproves of the purchase of political and governmental favors and influence. Thus, as a consequence of carrying on business in other countries, American businessmen have frequently violated deeply held personal and social norms.[1]

The SEC investigations also turned up the fact that, in many cases where questionable payments had been made, the responsible corporate officers attempted to conceal them by arranging for the normal accounting procedures to be skirted. The payments were frequently made from so-called off-the-books funds. Many have concluded that no better proof can be offered that those making these payments believed they were wrong than the fact that they arranged for their cover-up.

As a result of these revelations, some members of the news media, the public, and the Congress have become exercised by what are perceived to be the corrupt practices of U.S. multinational companies, and to a much lesser extent, of foreign politicians and governmental employees. Many Americans are confused by the conflicts between the demands of "business ethics" and the desire to respect the values and tradi-

173

tions of other countries, as well as to reap the advantages of international investment. It is the meaning and origins of these conflicts that we examine in this chapter. Before, however, we can be clear about these ethical conflicts we need first to examine more thoroughly just what is meant by "political payments," "bribery," and "extortion."

The Meaning of "Political Payments"

As the subject of U.S. companies making payments to foreign politicians and government employees moved onto the front pages of the country's newspapers in the months and years after the Watergate affair, a number of euphemisms were invented to characterize them. They were "questionable payments," or "improper payments," or "sensitive payments." The SEC entitled its report to the Senate Committee on Banking, Housing and Urban Affairs, *Report on Questionable and Illegal Corporate Payments and Practices.* In the media, allegations were published in which these payments were characterized as bribes; rarely were they characterized as responses to extortionate demands or to the solicitation of bribes, although many were clearly such.

In this study, we have used the phrase "political payments" to cover the whole range of payments for influence and the sympathetic exercise of authority. By characterizing them as "political," we have intended to call attention to a central aspect of all these payments—all have in mind the purpose of influencing the political structure or processes of a country, etiher by reaching the political figures who run the country or by buying the cooperation of those who work in the political structure, i.e., the government, of the country, whatever their level. And in using the term "payment" we mean, of course, to indicate the transfer of anything of value—it need not be cash.

174

As has been noted earlier, some "political payments" are legal and some are illegal. Generally speaking, the payment of agents for proper business services rendered is, per se, legal, although the use by an agent of some of his fee or commission to bribe a government official or employee is generally illegal. In some countries, such as Canada, corporate contributions to political parties are completely legal, but, here in the United States, as was noted in chapter 3, business contributions to political parties on the federal level have been illegal; and most U.S. states have prohibited such contributions, but in nine they have been permissible.

It should be noted that *illegal* corporate contributions to political parties are not thereby to be characterized as bribes; they are simply an illegal form of payment in their own right. There is no question usually that such contributions are made to acquire political influence, but their illegality is not the illegality of bribery.

The point to be made is that "political payments," as we use the phrase, are not, in and of themselves, illegal—some are and some are not. Where they are illegal, as in the case of bribery and extortion, the precise scope of what constitutes ilegal behavior, of course, varies from country to country around the world. Hence, we are not dealing with a phenomenon that has a unique and specific legal meaning in all the jurisdictions of the world, much less a unique and specific ethical meaning.

The Legal Meaning of "Bribery" and "Extortion"

In addition to those political payments that are (legal or illegal) contributions to political parties, or payments to agents, there are, of course, those corporate political payments that are bribes or responses to extortionate demands. While the legal definitions vary to a degree from country to country, bribery and extortion are crimes in most of the countries of the world. As John J. McCloy remarked before a Conference Board meeting on Preventing Illegal Corporate Payments in June 1976:

> I would . . . distinguish . . . those expenditures which constitute outright bribes. Such payments usually constitute crimes, so far as my investigation disclosed, in whatever country they take place. I know of no country where such a bribe would be considered legal. . . .[2]

In chapter 3, the general legal definitions of "bribery" and "extortion" were reviewed.[3] We should note that, from a legal perspective, in both bribery and extortion both parties, the payer and the recipient, are considered to be guilty. Bribery and extortion do differ in that extortion involves threats of harm or duress that bribery does not. In extortion, one person is compelling the other, whereas in bribery we actually have two persons cooperating.

There is an intermediate form of paying for influence and favors, between bribery and extortion, which is characterized legally as the "solicitation of a bribe." Here, without the threat of harm to the payer, which would be extortion, a potential payee solicits a bribe from a potential payer. And, indeed, many political payments involve, strictly speaking, the solicitation and payment of a bribe. The politician or government employee indicates to the corporate executive that, in return for a specified payment to him, he will, for example, obtain a government order for goods or services from the company. There is no threat to carry out a deliberate act of harm—it is rather that a special service will cost so much.[4]

While these legal definitions are clear enough, we should note that there are not infrequently situations in which, due to long-established corrupt relationships, it is difficult to determine whether a particular political payment was an instance of either bribery, the solicitation of a bribe, or extortion. In these cases, the potential briber well knows that he will be asked for a payment in return for a certain service or for a promise not to do harm, or the potential recipient well knows that he will be offered a payment. In such cases, the payment is illegal, but one would be hard-pressed to make a precise and unique determination of the crime that had been committed.

The Psychology of Bribery and Extortion

Before we examine political payments from an ethical perspective, it is useful to recognize how deeply the impulses toward bribery and extortion are rooted in human behavior. This is not the place, of course, to analyze in detail the psychological or emotional roots of these impulses. Suffice it to say that the bribery and extortion that goes on in the business-government relationship is relatively formal and explicit by comparison with the many, complex layers of bribery-like and extortion-like behavior that infuse a significant portion of human interactions. And the bribery and extortion in the business-government relationship that we are discussing here are not so different from similar activities that go on *within* businesses and governments. Thus, negotiations on employment, salary, and perquisites very frequently involve both subtle extortionate demands and the payment of bribe-like settlements. Similarly, negotiations between politicians for committee chairmanships or other purely political plums can often be analyzed in terms of extortion and bribery. The point is that the bribery and extortion that take place during a deal concerning military aircraft in the Middle East are part of a wide spectrum of human transactions that run from the mother "bribing" her child to eat his spinach with the promise of a movie, to the wife "extorting" a mink coat from her husband, to the sports manager who pays off the local hoodlums so that they will refrain from disrupting his operations.

In calling attention to the widespread occurrence of bribery-like and extortion-like behavior among human beings, we hope to make it clear that, whatever the ethical considerations that make bribery and extortion unacceptable, we are dealing with a deeply embedded human tendency. While we would prefer to have a world without the distortions of bribery and extortion, we must gear our expectations of improvement in the human condition to an objective view of what the human condition really is. The steps we propose, we hope, take that understanding fully into consideration.

An Ethical Analysis of Political Payments

Although the phenomenon of foreign political payments is widely called a problem of "business ethics," it is remarkable how little discussion there has been, in the last few years, of the *ethics* of corporate political payments abroad. Rather, most of what has been published on the subject has been divided between accounts of the details of the payments, statements that emphasize how prevalent such corruption is around the world, and, of course, the rhetorical condemnations of politicians. Some have claimed to detect a strain of "moralism" in the U.S. federal investigators. On the other hand, those same investigators all staunchly deny being "moralists" and claim only to be enforcing the law. What is more likely is that the investigators are *neither* particularly moralistic *nor* zealous about enforcing the law—how is it that they did not investigate these payments years ago?—but rather politicians simply taking advantage of the latest hue and cry. In any case, there has been little effort to make an ethical analysis of the phenomenon.

And it is important to carry out such an analysis so that thinkers and policy makers can finally begin to make up their minds about this issue. Due to a failure thus far to deal with the whole subject on a fundamental level, it floats uncomfortably over U.S. and world politics and economics. Perhaps it will turn out that the major issue is how to harmonize, in some rough and ready way, American moral ideals, or pretensions, with the easy ways of the rest of the world. If it seems that we should move toward such a compromise, perhaps Americans should then be called on to recognize that they themselves are not so pure—corruption thrives here at home—and on the other hand, perhaps foreign politicians and government employees should be urged to reevaluate their own age-old customs with an eye to improving their efficiency in a modern world economy.

In any case, the fog that surrounds this matter can hardly be dissipated unless the whole subject of political payments is evaluated in the wider context of the values associated with economic activity and development in general. With this in mind we proceed here to examine the arguments that can be devised *against* making foreign political payments, as well as those that can be developed *for* making them. And we will try to understand how some of them might be countenanced, even if, in some ultimate sense, they are regarded as wrong.

The Arguments Against Political Payments

What, then, is it that is wrong with businesses making payments to political leaders and government employees for the purpose of securing favors, influence, and the sympathetic exercise of political authority? And what is it that is wrong with those same political figures and government employees making extortionate demands for payments on businesses?

Concerning many such payments one is right off tempted to say they are wrong because they violate the law. And at a certain level this is true. But at a deeper level, it is because we believe certain activities to be wrong that we pass the laws we do. Here we want to deal with the subject at this deeper level. What is it about these activities that convinces us that they are wrong? It is thinking at this level that has led us to criminalize certain behavior as bribery or extortion.

To begin such a discussion it is useful to identify what happens in government corruption in the general terms that have been proposed by the political scientist Edward C. Banfield. He notes that it is the role of an "agent" to "serve the *interest* of a *principal*. . . . The agent is a person who has accepted an obligation (as in an employment contract) to act on behalf of his principal in some range of matters and, in doing so, to serve the principal's interest as if it were his own." Here, obviously, the agent is the political leader or governmental employee who is acting on behalf of his principal, his country or its government. The agent has a certain "*discretion*," the range within which he can make decisions, which can be to the advantage or disadvantage of "*third parties*," here, business corporations. Such decisions must be made in the face of "*rules* (both laws and generally accepted standards of right conduct) violation of which entails some probability of a penalty (cost) being imposed on the violator." Banfield suggests that an "agent is *personally corrupt* if he knowingly sacrifices his principal's interest to his own, that is, if he betrays his trust. He is *officially corrupt* if, in serving his principal's interest, he knowingly violates a rule, that is, acts illegally or unethically albeit in his principal's interest."[5]

In these terms, we see then that we are asking why is it wrong for an "agent" (political leader or governmental employee) acting within his official "discretion" (defined by his cabinet post or civil service job) to violate the "rules" (that set his standards of conduct) by sacrificing the "interest" of his "principal" to his own interests or by acting illegally or unethically in his principal's interest.

The making of political payments in general, especially the bribery of politicians and government employees, and the making of extortionate demands by them on business enterprises, all are for the purpose of subverting the intention of government to render justice and provide for the common good. Such payments, whether strictly criminal or just improper, strengthen the apparently ineradicable and inevitable tendency of politicians and government employees to feather their own nests rather than serve their constituencies. By benefiting individuals and making the interests of the citizens of a country secondary, the advantages that could come to a country through the honest exercise of the cooperative processes of government are lost, putting such a country at a disadvantage relative to those countries where such processes work more effectively. In short, tolerance of political and governmental involvement in bribery, extortion, and political payments in general has opportunity costs for those countries that permit it.

More specifically these activities are called wrong because they violate a basic widespread assumption about the nature, function, and purpose of those governments that are, in fact, established to achieve justice and promote the welfare of the people. That assumption might be stated as the principle that governments, through the officials that guide them and the government employees that operate them, should distribute discretionary benefits, whether to individuals or to corporations, solely on the basis of the merits of the particular case, as defined by the relevant laws and regulations, and not as favors accompanied by secret diversions of corporate funds.

We have referred to "those governments that are, in fact, established to achieve justice and promote the welfare of the people." The qualification is important in the current discussion, because there are clearly governments in the world today that are not established for these purposes. They are, despite verbal claims to the contrary, simply devices by which a small social, economic, or military elite exercise control over a country and assure that the major benefits available to the country flow to them personally. Since the actions of the rulers of such a country make it clear that they are not interested in a fair distribution of discretionary benefits, their receipt of political payments is not a violation of a commitment to be just or concerned with the public welfare; it is simply getting the best deal they can. We will not attempt to deal here with the important questions of whether or not foreign companies ought, in the first place, to cooperate economically with such a regime, and whether or not other nations should apply economic sanctions against a political regime viewed as unrepresentative of its people.

When we examine the general assumption that those who rule a country should act fairly in doing so, we find that the more socially and politically developed societies make this assumption because experience has taught them that the government of a country needs to be relatively impersonal and objective to moderate and adjudicate the differences between the various conflicting groups and interests in the society. It is precisely to avoid or control strife between the segments of the society and to attain the higher efficiencies and greater range of goods that a nation can achieve that people establish governments. The common assumption in all governments that are more than self-serving oligarchies is that those who operate the government have by their election or employment entered into a kind of "contractual" relationship with the whole society to do their jobs fairly and objectively. Practice, of course, frequently falls short of this ideal, but we constantly find that there are plenty of critics who hark back to it.

It is because these assumptions are made about the purpose of government and the attitude of those who serve in it that society finds it wrong for politicians and government employees to allow private, personal interests to dominate the "contractual" obligation to act fairly and objectively, i.e., not to solicit bribes from, or to make extortionate demands on, business interests, nor to accept proffered bribes from those interests to bias their behavior. No matter what justification is offered for making political payments, it is always in conflict with this generally accepted ideal.

Adverse Economic Effects of Bribery and Extortion

In addition to violating a basic principle of democratic government, bribery and extortion, even legal political payments, can impair the efficiency of the competitive market economy. Markets work most efficiently and the economy of a country develops best when the price and merits of products and services are the criteria that determine buying and selling—not secret payments to well-placed politicians and government employees. Since our form of economy generally gives an advantage to those who can put into operation the most efficient equipment and techniques, any factor that serves to distort the natural competitive advantage of those who make "a better mousetrap" must be rejected as undesirable.

And it is clear that at least some bribery has the effect of putting less efficient equipment into use. The company that is attempting to sell less efficient equipment to a government, and thereby is in danger of losing an order, is particularly tempted to offer a politician or government employee a payment to guarantee the selection of such equipment. Of course, the price of the equipment is raised to cover the cost of the bribe. Thus, there is frequently a double loss to the government purchasing the equipment—first it provides the additional funds that go to pay its own corrupt official his bribe; and then it pays the extra costs during the life of the equipment that stem from its lesser efficiency. This diversion of public funds, originally intended for the public good, into private pockets hurts the economy of the purchasing country relative to what was possible to it by purchasing the most efficient product.

The Arguments Against Political Payments from the Standpoint of Business

It is probably fair to assume that, given a free choice, businesses would prefer not to make political payments, much less to engage in bribery or extortion. The reasons for this are not hard to find—a political payment of whatever sort means a reduction in the profits of the company or an increase in the price of its product.

On the other hand, if a payment is seen as needed in order to compete, if business is likely to go to another firm, or if property is likely to be expropriated (resulting in large losses) if payments are not made, then such payments become similar to many other expenses that are necessary for competitive and survival reasons. Because of this, some businessmen prefer to classify such payments as "a cost of doing business." But still this does not dispense with the fact that a business would prefer not to make them if possible, as with any other cost of doing business.

And there is the matter of the public reputation of the company when it becomes public knowledge that it has been involved in the payment of bribes. Earlier we noted that such knowledge does not appear to have a strong influence on the stock-market prices of the shares of such companies. Here, however, we call attention to some less easily determinable costs that such public knowledge may have—perhaps a falling off in sales to the public, perhaps a loss of self-respect among the employees of a company resulting in a somewhat heightened sense of discontent with company work, perhaps difficulties in hiring the quality of employee that the company might prefer. These are, of course, rather subjective matters and no one knows quantitatively what these effects are—but just their possibility makes for a certain feeling of discomfort about the company involved. Thus, in general, we are probably safe in saying that no company rationally seeks to make political payments.

The Arguments for Political Payments

Although the arguments against governmental extortion and business bribery are strong, we are forced to recognize a myriad of factors that muddy the purity of our judgment in this matter. In many parts of the world, bribery and extortion are established social and economic ways of payment for services that would not—given historical expectations—be rendered otherwise. Short of the reformation of a country's laws and morals, bribery and extortion are a datum for businesses in many countries. Some companies, of course, resist successfully—perhaps the manifestation of an unusually strong personality running a business—but most cannot. And those few who resist for some special reason are usually not strong enough to reform the system—they simply exist in a tension with the mainstream. And those who, because of their high position in business or the government, *could* reform the system, are, frequently, disinclined to do so because they are the main beneficiaries. Let us look then at some of the main reasons for making political payments.

When in Rome

The most traditional argument for practicing bribery and responding to extortionate demands and solicitations for bribes in other countries is best expressed in the old maxim that stems from advice St. Augustine received from St. Ambrose when he noted that Christians in Milan did not fast on Saturday as they did in Rome: "When you are at Rome," St. Ambrose advised, "live in the Roman style; when you are elsewhere, live as they live elsewhere." Unfortunately, this old maxim, "when in Rome, do as the Romans do," has an ambiguity if taken as a serious principle for action. For St. Ambrose and St. Augustine, it was clear *which* Romans' customs were to be followed: the Christian Romans. But for us, the maxim, in itself, does not make clear whether we are to follow the customs of the most virtuous, the most conventional, or the most corrupt in a country.

Putting this ambiguity aside, the maxim has, of course, for the most part been taken as a counsel to follow the *prevailing* local custom, however it may sit with one's own views. It has, by and large, been taken to be a counsel of ethical relativism, implying that the good is relative to man, and that, since there are many groups of men, goods are relative to each group. Such a counsel of relative values may or may not be the ultimate truth of ethics, but it does seem to be a plausible rule in view of the situation confronted by businessmen operating in foreign countries.

It is surely true that host countries admit foreign investors and businessmen on the assumption that they will carry on business according to local practices. Indeed, if a company does not, host countries will punish or expel the recalcitrant firm. You are not required to do business here, they would argue, but if you do, then you do so with an implicit commitment to live by local standards. Indeed, American multinational companies are often critized for *failing* to conform to the customs and traditions of host countries. And Americans must remember how disturbed we are by foreigners, even naturalized citizens, who are not willing to live according to *our* lights.

186

The Relative Smallness of the Payments

It is often argued that foreign political payments are permissible because they are *de minimis*, i.e., very small relative to the total amount of business involved. This has been true overall, though, in some cases, the payments have been relatively large, as in some military aircraft deals in the Middle East. In general, however, the payments, particularly those made to high government officials, are frequently large as compared to the salaries that these officials receive from their government posts.

While businessmen tend to emphasize the point that payments are small relative to the total amount of business involved, those more sensitive to moral matters might point to the corrupting effect on individuals, some highly placed in a society, that follows from bribes that are untaxed and many times larger than regular salaries. While a fraction of one percent of a company's budget can be passed off as almost incidental to a large multinational company, payments of $1 million or even $100,000 to an individual can make the recipient forget all the principles of right conduct he ever learned. This corrupting effect on individuals, especially top political figures with great power and socially important decisions to make for a country, is a considerably more important matter than the fact that political payments have been a relatively small part of the cost of doing business. In this perspective, the *de minimis* argument would appear to lack the force that has frequently been assigned to it.

Rejection of Cultural and Moral Imperialism

The current rejection of what we may call the doctrine of cultural and moral imperialism, once grandly called the White Man's Burden, makes many of us now look askance at efforts to try once again to export our morality to other countries. Since so many of our efforts to impress our nation's views on others have fallen so short of our expectations in the last hundred years, many now feel that we must learn to tolerate the historical, indigenous practices of other countries, even those that are, by our standards, corrupt. Politically, we have learned even to give aid to tyrannies for our own protection. While doing this has not come easily and quite a few still reject it, many now accept it. In any case, the doubt about our imposing our own value systems on other peoples serves to weaken our conviction that we must insist that other peoples change their traditional ways to accord with our own. Later we will discuss at greater length the arguments for and against exporting our own morality abroad.

Most Foreign Political Payments are Extortions or Solicited Bribes

The clarity of our moral judgments about this subject is further clouded when we attend to the distinction between extortion and bribery. The media have tended to emphasize the notion that it is the American company that initiates the bribe, without laying any emphasis on the fact that around the world, for hundreds of years, companies from other countries have been making payments and paying bribes, and that usually the reason they have done so is that they have been solicited or extorted by politicians and government employees. To point this out is not to negate the blame for making the payments and paying the bribes, but simply to make it clear that in many, if not most, cases the payments are made under duress. All other things being equal, an American business manager would rather avoid the costs of bribes.

The Corruption of Political Leaders Distinguished from the Lubrication of Government Employees

In a significant amount of the public discussion of foreign political payments by American multinational companies, the distinction between the large payoffs to high political figures and relatively small "lubricating" or "facilitating" payments to middle- and low-level civil service government employees has frequently been made. The distinction has seemed so important that there have been proposals to require the reporting of political payments only of a certain size and larger. Facilitating payments of $1,000 or less, for instance, have been seen by some to require neither criminalization nor disclosure. But why the distinction? Are not secret payments to individuals to bias their judgment and actions equally odious whether they are large or small? Let us examine the background of this distinction more closely.

Political leaders are involved where the goal of a company is the initial establishment of a business with the investment of millions of dollars, or its continued presence in a country. Politicians are also involved with the formulation of the laws and regulations that affect a company's operations and profitability. Often, in many countries, the leading political figures are involved, and they make it clear that business can only be begun or continued successfully in their country if a payment is made to them.

This gross sale of public trust by the leading politicians of foreign countries troubles Americans deeply because we assume that public office is a public trust. But to what degree is this notion even a norm in other countries? Granted, it would appear to be moderately well observed in the Western European and the large communist countries, although there are some significant exceptions. But outside of these, it is apparent that, despite pious claims, in many places the basic

189

purpose of political leaders is to guarantee control by, and rewards to, themselves. No especial pretense is made to the contrary, and the masses in most of the countries of the world cynically accept the facts of life. Even in a rather nominal way, equal justice is not the goal. The system is simply used by those in power to reward themselves economically.

When a foreign company is allowed to enter a country's economy, it is compelled by the nature of the situation to compete with other established economic interests in the country for labor, perhaps for raw materials, perhaps for local markets, and perhaps for a portion of the disposable income of the people of the country. These interests are frequently represented in the country's government, and they are always alert to protect themselves. Making payments to the leading political and economic interests of a country can be seen as a way of smoothing out some of the economic dislocation that is bound to follow from the entrance of the subsidiary of a highly sophisticated, well-managed American multinational corporation. And, indeed, entering a country's economy means conforming to all sorts of other conditions as well as making political payments. But very specifically, however, it does not mean attempting to reform the society it is entering, or, in particular, trying to change the system of bribe making. It is simply understood that the entering company will join in the process of helping the politicians and economic interests then in power to stay in power.

In the case of the so-called facilitating payments to government bureaucrats or employees, we are dealing with a somewhat different situation with a somewhat different moral complexion to it. Civil service employees in many nations are underpaid exactly in the expectation that they will receive bribes. They are burdened with work (or so they frequently allege), so that it is a matter of discretion as to when they get to a particular item. Further, such employees are frequently given a considerable amount of personal discretion in the way in which they dispose of a particular matter. In both cases, a company that wants some request acted on—replacement parts cleared through customs or a construction variance approved—is compelled to pay some government employee to do his job and do it in a way favorable to the company.

Where this tradition of demands by governmental employees for payments to expedite the handling of requests from businesses and the payment by companies of bribes to government employees exists, it is usually deeply ingrained in a whole society and involves thousands of such employees as opposed to a few politicians who can receive the large bribes. While it is true that not everyone in such a country will agree that this is the best way to run the government's "civil service," by and large one has to conclude that a system of petty extortion and bribery has become entrenched over time simply because the country and its people have decided that they want it that way.

And the system is not totally irrational. It does maintain an element of competition by rewarding the company that is strong enough to pay the tribute. As it turns out, the demands are not so high that many companies cannot pay them; on the other hand, they are high enough to eliminate those companies that are so weak financially that they cannot afford them. While this is probably not a very efficient way to run an economy and is no doubt counter-productive in many instances, it has held on just because it has some strong survival characteristics built in to it.

If then an American company sees a government apparatus and a civil service designed to operate on a system of low- and medium-level bribery and extortion, and if it sees that such system has been tacitly approved by the people and the ruling elites for many decades or centuries, the American company may well puzzle over the question of whether it is called on to attempt to reform the country in which it proposes to invest.

191

The source of difficulty in this matter for many Westerners is the assumption that governments are established and operated to treat all citizens (and corporations) with an even hand. We assume that one of the purposes of government is to carry out public functions justly and fairly to all. This is a deeply ingrained conviction in Western societies, even where actual performance falls way short of the ideal. It causes Americans great difficulties to be compelled—if we are to do business at all in these countries—to adapt to a system in which fairness to all is not even the guiding principle, far less the practice.

No Bribe—No Business

There is a still deeper issue that further weakens our conviction that every foreign political payment is immoral. During the recent discussion of these payments, some have said that if American companies do not make the required payments or pay the required bribes in their business activity abroad, they simply will not do business abroad. Either the business will not be done at all (because only the American company could do it) or companies from other countries, lacking our scruples or legal restrictions, will make the payments to get the business.

It is, obviously, hard to know the merit of this reason for continuing with the practice of paying bribes prior to any test of a policy to restrict or completely cease payments and bribes. Some may feel that the risks involved are too great to take, that we simply cannot afford even to test such a cutoff. Others would hold that we should proceed incrementally, cutting off the worst of the political payments abroad first, so that if there are to be economic penalties we will experience them slowly and can adjust to their effect.

Various estimates have been published as to what the likely

effect of a cutoff of political payments would be. In its *Report*, relying on the remarks of the first group of reporting companies, the SEC concluded that the cessation of these payments "will not seriously affect the ability of American business to compete in world business."[6] Other estimates have set the possible loss of business at 10 percent. A report in February of 1977 indicated that losses thus far, as a result of the investigations up till then, had not been serious, but noted that it would take some years for the full effect of a payments cutoff to be felt.[7]

Economic Activity and Growth Are More Important Than Avoiding Corruption

Deeper, perhaps, is the question of whether the drive toward increased economic activity and growth in the world—in which multinational corporate investment has played a central role—should weigh more heavily than moral considerations about the corruption of public officials. This is a perplexing question, extremely difficult to resolve.

In ultimate terms, the issue, regarding both payments to politicians to secure and protect investments and payments to government employees to move papers through administrative channels expeditiously and sympathetically, is whether the benefits of economic activity (the expansion of American business, products for Americans and others, as well as jobs and products for those in the host—or other—countries, and all that economic activity implies about the survival of peoples as well as their well-being and luxury) outweigh the moral imperative not to perform actions that violate the public trust of politicians and government employees in other countries.

Economic development usually means that more people have the minimum conditions for a decent human life. If

American corporations abroad bring economic development in their wake, then one might be willing to tolerate some official corruption on the grounds that the aggregate evil of the corruption was small relative to the good that economic development could bring to millions.

Where one could show that the merit of a foreign investment for the real needs of people was high enough, then, and only in that case, a stipulated amount of bribery might be permissible in a kind of moral trade-off. Particularly, we might be willing to take this position if there were a strong showing that it was really next to impossible to change the social and economic habits of those who insisted on the receipt of bribes.

Historically, as far as American business has been concerned, the overwhelming answer has been that it was more important to do business and try to make a profit, even if corruption was involved. Indeed, it is hard to think of an American businessman (or public official) who ever spoke out against the system of bribery and extortion that U.S. corporations faced in foreign economic life, prior to the Watergate and the SEC investigations.

But this historical response by the American businessman has not resolved the matter—as we have found out. Some argue that this involvement in political and governmental corruption around the world has given the communists and other critics of capitalism further ammunition. It has, it is argued, strengthened the position that we are an immoral force, interested only in our own profit, even if we must corrupt local politicians and government employees. Sometimes the argument is added that there is vast, if unarticulated, popular unhappiness with these age-old systems of corruption and that there would be more vocal popular opposition if anyone would champion their demise—and this the communists and others propose to do, since we do not.

The Ethical Ambiguity of the Issue

After this review of the factors bearing on the ethics of making foreign political payments and bribes, it is clear that any hope for an easy way out of the dilemma has vanished. Thus, when in other countries of the world, whose business ethics do we follow? The payments are small for a corporation, but they are large for individuals, and, after all, it is individuals who make the decisions in this world. We have rejected cultural imperialism, but are we thereby required to agree to anything? We want to continue to expand our economic activity abroad, but perhaps we should simply pass up involvement in certain kinds of business in those areas of the world where the corruption is too great. Thus it is clear that we confront a serious conflict between a number of different economic, social, and ethical values. How we decide to balance the demands of these values will have long-term consequences for the development of world business.

As we approach the debate over these values, traditional American moral attitudes will, in any case, continue to exert a strong influence on policy formation. The strength of these attitudes raises the very serious question of the degree to which we can expect other peoples to follow our lead in these matters. In other words, should we by the passage of laws in this country or even by the establishment of norms with less than legal sanctions attempt in any way to modify the customs and traditions of other nations with respect to their practices of bribery and extortion in the economic field? Should we, in short, attempt to "export morality" to other countries?

The Pros and Cons of Exporting Morality

The "exportation of morality" is really part of a much larger subject that might be defined as the transference of any form of thought from one human group to another. World history can be seen, in one perspective, as an account of the ways in which ideas, values, and emotions have been transferred from one nation or society to another. The development and transference of moral, aesthetic, religious, and scientific ideas, attitudes, and beliefs has been viewed by some as the slow and unpredictable emergence of a world consciousness or soul; or it can be interpreted as no more than the haphazard jumping of ideas, imperatives, and feelings over borders and boundaries.

Historically the "exportation of morality" is by no means a new phenomenon. However carried out, there have always been nations and societies that have tried to impress their moral attitudes on others. American attitudes on this matter have been developing all through the history of the nation. This history is useful to look at as we try to evaluate approaches to the problem of bribery and extortion in world business.

The Puritanical Origins of American Moral Attitudes

Washington's farewell address, in which he counseled the nation to avoid "permanent alliances," derived from a native aversion to the Europe that early Americans were glad to have left. They were not, in general, the sons of its aristocracy, so they had little if any vested interest in their original homeland. Those who left were mainly from the working masses, and they had accumulated many reasons for wanting a change in their social, political, religious, and economic environment. The settlement of America provided the historically appropriate opportunity. There was at first, therefore, a strong sentiment not to get involved with the rest of the world, however aware Americans were that the whole world was watching their experiment in nationhood. Since the end

196

of the nineteenth century, this attitude of detachment has undergone a radical change.

Current American attitudes on many subjects, including corporate political payments abroad, reflect the variety of conflicting values and attitudes that have accumulated during the history of America. They strongly reflect in particular the Puritan point of view, which did so much to shape the culture of New England and subsequently of the nation. The Puritans brought to the New World a complex set of beliefs, which, as the country developed, became the dominant formulations of the nation's goals and attitudes. New Englanders, like the ancient Jews on whom they modeled themselves, were raised in the belief that man could communicate directly with God without the benefit of priestly intermediaries. This individualism and independence made each citizen personally responsible for his conduct. Coupled with this belief was the preoccupation with the doctrine of predestination: the essentially gloomy belief that most men were inherently sinful and that only a few would be saved.

The Puritans brought to America a vigorous belief in what has come to be known as the "Protestant work ethic." One's job was not merely something that one did to earn a living; it was a calling to which one was summoned by God. Therefore, it behooved man to make the maximum possible effort to succeed in (God's) work; and, indeed, success in business came to be equated in many minds with proof of divine favor and perhaps predestination for salvation.

The American tendency to equate economic efficiency with moral virtue has deep roots in our history. It helps to explain why Americans so widely embraced the ideology of Adam Smith, whose *Wealth of Nations* was published in the same year as the Declaration of Independence. Competition in open markets was seen as the most efficient way to allocate limited human resources and to maximize the satisfaction of human wants. Interference with market processes by government officials—whether lawful or illicit—was interpreted as not only inefficient but immoral.

Finally, and even more important, the Puritans shared with the ancient Jews the belief that they, too, had been summoned by God to a new and favored land of milk and honey, which He had given them by virtue of their special relationship to Him. Because of this, their duty was to erect a temple to His worship, and to create (in and around Boston), "a new Jerusalem," or as they frequently wrote, "a City on a Hill." This City on a Hill, from the very fact of its dominant position, was supposed to be a beacon and model of perfection, which would serve as a light to the rest of the world, and a means by which it could transform its own sinful institutions into the more perfect ones that the Puritans proposed to establish in this country. We find reiterated in Puritan writings the statement that the whole world was watching and that thus they must set a high example for others. Such views explain the spiritual depression they experienced when reality did not live up to their ideals—as sensible people should have known in advance.

This belief in American moral leadership and in our national destiny to provide the world with a shining standard of conduct has been a persistent theme in American history. One has only to examine the speeches made during the 1976 political campaign, and the public reactions to the revelations of deceit and corruption involved in the Watergate affair, to be convinced that this form of ethnocentrism is still very much with us.

The Evolution of American Idealism

As the American experiment began to succeed, there was the temptation to hold up our achievements to the rest of the world to admire and to follow. And writers like de Tocqueville and Bryce helped to make the American experiment interesting and attractive to peoples around the world.

During the nineteenth century, there were waves of religious enthusiasm that were manifested in the sending of missionaries around the world. While the announced purpose of these missionaries was religious, they could not help but carry with them the elements of the whole American culture. Indeed, what foreign peoples have permanently accepted, it now appears, was more the social and political idealism of the American experiment than its religious content. In any case, the Christianity that was so vigorously exported in the nineteenth century was not destined to remain the major force it had been; and the twentieth century has seen its influence decline steadily. But the American experiment has inspired one social and political revolution after another.

By the beginning of the twentieth century, with the Civil War behind us and great economic strength developing, American idealism could no longer contain itself. After World War I, Woodrow Wilson, the idealistic protagonist of the American experiment, turned his energies to tired, war-ridden Europe. His effort to create the League of Nations was American idealism grown strong in its own soil and then broadcast to the whole world. This most striking American missionary effort was received with skepticism by the other leaders of the world, but it was so strongly advanced by Wilson that the world acquiesced. Despite its setback at home, the League of Nations was launched—surely our greatest effort to export morality to the world.

Subsequently, Americans assumed vast economic and political obligations to the rest of the world. Missionaries of many kinds went forth. We sent Herbert Hoover to postwar Europe to organize an effort to save people from starvation. After World War II, we sent engineers and management experts to every nook and cranny of the world to advise people on how to organize and operate their own societies. We gave, spent, and lent over $100 billion in economic aid to other lands. We were the main force behind the creation of the United Nations; and for many years we were its main supporter. The headquarters of the United Nations stands on land purchased with funds from the fortune begun by that great exponent of Baptist ethics and capitalist economics, John D. Rockefeller. We sent out the Peace Corps and the International Executive Service Corps to assist in the saving of mankind. Our research fomented the Green Revolution, unlocking the secrets to increased food production for the rest of the world.

We raised a whole generation of Americans who were going to "make the world safe for democracy." That our efforts have not been conspicuously successful, or that they have frequently done little more than change the nature of the problems, has by no means discouraged us. Possessed of the true faith, on fire with inspiration, willing to spend billions to make the rest of the world love its new Messiah, we have by now a long history of exporting morality. Indeed, we will not only export our moral values; we will even lend others the money to make the adoption of American values as painless as possible! Hence, when the American public became aware that U.S. companies made political payments abroad, it was not surprising that they wanted at once to push other peoples to change their behavior. This explains the vigorous— and ethnocentric—reactions of the U.S. Congress and the federal bureaucracy described in chapter 2.

Coerciveness in the Exportation of Morality

Whenever any thought or idea or moral imperative is transferred from one society to another an important question is whether that which is transferred is freely sought by the recipient or is, to one degree or another, forced down his throat. Does the transference occur freely through reading or the reports of visitors to other lands, i.e., does it occur as a voluntary importation by one society of what another has developed or found, or does it occur through the coercion of the bayonet or propaganda?

Sometimes, of course, one group of people will consciously *import* what they find of value in another society. Thus, many Americans desire to appropriate the skills of the French in cooking. This could properly be called an importation by Americans, and the French are quite willing to export their knowledge of fine cooking. Nothing is forced on the Americans by the French, nor taken from them unwillingly. And we are glad to import what they export.

But not all exportation of morality is eagerly imported. Indeed, by the phrase, the "exportation of morality," we mean mainly those situations in which one culture, society, or nation makes specific efforts to impress its views about what is good, proper, and desirable on other societies and nations. And obviously a whole spectrum of degrees of coerciveness can be attached to the process of getting other societies to accept a nation's view of what is good, proper, and desirable. The most coercive case is that which follows a war, where the victor forces the vanquished to adopt his point of view or mode of behavior. And there are many variations of this. In the most extreme case, the vanquished is made a slave, brainwashed with the ideas of the victor, and threatened with death for the failure to adopt his attitudes. Even here, some slaves, at least in the first generation, can resist, but usually after a generation or two, assuming the victor remains in control, the process of transference of the victor's ideology will be moderately successful. The American slavery experience is an example. Successful resistance to the victor's views is, perhaps, best exemplified by the Greek intellectuals who became slaves of the Romans. They not only resisted

Roman mores, but, to a considerable degree, they imposed their own on their masters.

Somewhat less coercive has been the experience of peoples in the Eastern European nations, who have been required to adopt a socialist outlook and scale of values impressed on them by the Soviet Union. Descending further on the scale of coerciveness, we find the religious proselytizing of Christian missionaries in the non-Western world. Certainly, this phenomenon has covered a wide range of coerciveness, from the most gentle to the most forceful. The efforts of government leaders and diplomats to persuade other nations to adopt their countries' points of view, which frequently have a moral or ethical aspect, likewise span a large range from mild persuasion to the threats of war.

History confirms that peoples and nations have little if any objection to the *voluntary* importation of ideas and values from other societies. It is the coercive exportation—the efforts at imposition—of foreign values that are resented. Indeed, such impositions are often in time rejected, even after centuries. The history of Mexico has been punctuated with the efforts of the Mexican people to eliminate this or that aspect of the Spanish influence that was so long imposed. Indians have made efforts to expunge various aspects of the British culture that was imposed on them. Such efforts are not always successful, but the hostility against the original exporter of customs and morality remains.

It appears now that our efforts to impose our views concerning political payments on other nations will involve mild forms of persuasion or coerciveness. This will be particularly true if we simply pass our own laws prohibiting American subsidiaries abroad from following local customs of which we disapprove as opposed to negotiating international treaties to which all can agree. The happier result would seem to follow from the multilateral process of negotiation rather than from an effort to export our views of right and wrong to others.

The Need for U.S. Moral Leadership

A brief review of arguments for and against a U.S. effort to export its business ethics to the rest of the world leads to a qualified conclusion. Although our assessment of the probable success of such an effort is not optimistic, neither is it a counsel of despair.

The United States operates the leading competitive market economy of the world. Our country cannot avoid a role of leadership in setting a pattern for business-government relationships in market economies everywhere. By virtue of its dominant size, the U.S. does possess influence over the behavior of world business, albeit a limited influence. It should exert its influence in ways that enhance the efficiency of international trade and investment, while elevating its ethical behavior. This must necessarily involve an effort to reduce the amount of improper political payments made in conducting world business.

Experience has taught that a great power must always act with deliberation and restraint in pursuing its national interests, even when they coincide with the long-run global interest. U.S. efforts to reduce corruption in the business-government relationship throughout the world should be undertaken patiently and persistently, with an understanding of the problems confronting the governments of other nations, and without unrealistic expectations of speedy results. It would be a mistake unilaterally to impose penalties on U.S.-based corporations that would handicap them in competition with companies based in other industrialized nations. *The wise course is one of U.S. leadership in bringing about international cooperation to reduce political payments by the multinational enterprises of all nations.* The world does not need a U.S. moral gendarmerie; it needs U.S. leadership in a movement to bring global business-government behavior into closer conformity with universally acceptable standards of probity.

PART **III**

What Should Be Done

7

A Critique of Reform Proposals

Proposals to deal with overseas political payments by U.S.-based multinational corporations run the gamut from individual company codes, to federal legislation, to a proposed international treaty. Although the executive and legislative branches of the U.S. government were divided during the Ford presidency on how to curb the making of political payments by U.S. companies abroad, the United States—alone among the industrialized nations—sought to treat with the issue through legislation outlawing these practices. The methods and philosophies embodied in the various proposals that have been put forth are analyzed here.

Corporate Codes of Conduct— Strengths and Weaknesses

One result of the widespread publicity given to corporate payoffs abroad was a movement among multinational firms to adopt—or to tighten up—policies regulating the making of political payments by their employees. Such corporate codes of conduct often went to extreme lengths. Some corporate chief executives sought to repair the media's image of the U.S. multinational corporation as a wholesale purveyor of bribes by mea culpa breast-beating. Garbed in sackcloth and ashes, these executives have, to borrow the language of Gaylord Freeman, Honorary Chairman of the First National Bank of Chicago, embraced "codes of conduct so self-righteous as to make a monk's vow of poverty seem greedy by comparison."[1] A number of companies required their executives and employees to sign annual statements that they had adhered to the rules prescribed in the company's published code of conduct and had not participated in the payment of cash or gifts to foreign government officials. In some companies, strict adherence to published guidelines of conduct was made a condition of continued employment.

Some companies segregated their small lubrication payments from those that contravened government regulations or which were illegal under local laws, sanctioning the former but forbidding the latter. Other companies treated, case-by-case, with each type of overseas political payment. Some firms ran special audits to detect potential sources of unrecorded funds that could be manipulated by foreign law firms, bankers, suppliers, or public relations firms with which they dealt. Still others required their outside law firms to furnish certificates stipulating that they had not been conduits for political contributions or other payments to foreign government officials. And other companies scrutinized abnormally large agents' and consultants' fees, which might serve to disguise the payment of bribes and kickbacks.

But the American business community has not at all been unanimous in desiring to proscribe overseas political payments. For example, the Conference Board, a nonprofit business-supported research group, reported in 1976 that only slightly more than 50 percent of a panel of senior executives, representing a wide variety of industries doing business in both industrialized and less-developed countries, were opposed to the practice of making such payments abroad.[2] And a 1975 survey by the Opinion Research Corporation showed that nearly half (48 percent) of a sample of businessmen believed payments *should* be made, if the practice was prevalent in a foreign country.[3]

It seems unlikely that unilateral rules of business conduct for American corporations will, by themselves, eradicate the underlying conditions that make for corruption in business-government relations in most Third World countries. In consequence, a vow of eternal righteousness may be difficult, if not impossible, to keep in those national environments in which the payoff is traditional and inescapable.

Moreover, a company code of conduct has little or no impact on the judgments of the multinational corporation's critics and antagonists at home and abroad. They are likely to see in such codes only a confirmation of their off-expressed suspicions of misbehavior by multinational corporations. Nor will corporate codes of conduct induce those Third World governments who regard the multinational corporation as an object of economic and political warfare to change their attitudes. Regimes that are hostile to the international corporation are far more apt to be influenced by a denial of investment and technology than by the mere publication of a company's rules of ethical conduct.

As Leonard Silk has observed:

> Despite all the headlines in the last two years over corporate bribery of foreign government officials, little has been done to deal with the problem. This . . . is chiefly a result of the complexity of . . . how to prevent, or punish, corrupt relationships between business and government that lie beyond the reach of national sovereignty.[4]

In the discussion that follows, we examine the approaches taken to this complex problem by two prominent U.S. Senators and by the Ford Administration. And in Chapter 8 we describe actions that, in our opinion, will be practical and effective in dealing with this problem.

Legislating Disclosure of Foreign Political Payments—the Church Bill

Early in May 1976, Senators Frank Church, Dick Clark, and James B. Pearson submitted S. 3379 to the Senate Committees on Foreign Relations and Banking, Housing and Urban Affairs. The proposed legislation began with a declaration of the "findings" of the Congress, which were asserted to have been a consequence of an "extensive examination of facts presented in public hearings, by the Securities and Exchange Commission, and in public statements made by major United States companies and foreign governments."

Among other "findings" purported to have been made as a result of these hearings, S. 3379 concluded that overseas payments by U.S. corporations "create substantial foreign policy problems for the United States." We pointed out in chapter 2 that Senator Church's panel itself had created more foreign relations "problems" than had any actions by the companies investigated. As former Under Secretary of State Robert S. Ingersoll pointedly remarked before a Congressional committee,

> I wish to state for the record that grievous damage has been done to the foreign relations of the United States by recent disclosures of unsubstantiated allegations against foreign officials. . . . it is a fact that public discussion in this country of the alleged misdeeds of officials of foreign governments cannot fail to damage our relations with these governments.[5]

Another "finding" was that "contributions, payments, and gifts . . . can create and foster an anti-American sentiment in individual countries." According to the Church bill, the U.S.

Congress found that "certain contributions, payments, and gifts . . . have an adverse impact on the long- and short-term operations of United States business abroad" by generating economic reprisals. It would have been more to the point if the report of the Subcommittee had confessed that the wholesale dissemination to the press of confidential memoranda taken from corporate files by the Subcommittee's investigators, the flagrant breach of the confidentiality of information disclosed by corporate witnesses in private hearings with members of the panel and counsel, and the disclosures of payments required by the SEC had led some foreign governments to wonder whether they could any longer afford the risk of doing business with U.S. companies!

The main substantive proposal of the Church bill was to require the *disclosure of overseas payments* by U.S. firms or their agents. A maximum fine of $25,000 and imprisonment up to two years would be imposed for failure to comply. A foreign agent retained by a U.S. company would be obligated to keep *in the United States* copies of his books and records—or make them available to his principal—for a period of five years! The idea that a responsible and well-known commercial agent who is a citizen and resident of a foreign nation would place his private books of account on file in this country, where they would be available to any U.S. Congressman and the media, is naïve to say the least.

Under the Church bill, the Secretary of State would have been required to make annual reports to the House and Senate Committees on Foreign Relations, showing each country in which U.S. firms had made payments, and describing the foreign policy implications for the United States of each such payment. And to determine whether the Department of State was an "accomplice" to illicit transactions, the Secretary of State would be enjoined to state whether he "was aware of such contributions, payments, and gifts prior to their making. . . ."

Senator Church's bill would have required companies to furnish shareholders with annual reports describing payments made to foreign government officials and contributions to political parties and candidates. Shareholders would be authorized to bring suits against managements for making such payments (presumably even where they were permitted by host country laws to contribute to political parties and candidates), or for failing to comply with disclosure requirements. To cap it off, companies who claimed to have been damaged by payments made by a competitor would be allowed to sue the offender for triple damages.

Senator Church's bill would also have established the requirement that business corporations must have "at least one-third," or a "minimum of three," outside directors on their boards. Audit committees would have to consist entirely of outside directors. Reports by such audit committees of the incidence of foreign payments would "in their discretion" be submitted to the SEC (which already has such a requirement) and to "other relevant bodies."

Neither the Foreign Relations Committee nor the Committee on Banking, Housing and Urban Affairs of the U.S. Senate held hearings on the Church bill during 1976. Senator Charles Percy may have voiced the views of his colleagues in describing this legislative proposal for wholesale reporting and disclosure of the details of foreign political payments as "overkill." It is to be hoped that such an ill-conceived approach to the problem of foreign political payments, holding such potentially damaging consequences to U.S. multinational companies and the nation, will not be revived.

Criminalizing Foreign Bribery—the Proxmire Bill

Senator William H. Proxmire of Wisconsin proposed a different legislative approach to corporate political payments abroad. In its original version his bill was numbered S. 3133 and its purpose was to *prohibit bribery overseas* by U.S. corporations. "If we permit bribery to become a regular policy of U.S. corporations doing business abroad," the Senator said, "it will only be a matter of time before these same corrupt practices afflict our domestic economic system."[6]

Senator Proxmire sought to accomplish his objective through several amendments to the Securities Exchange Act of 1934. Corporate issuers of securities registered under this act would be required to (1) *maintain* accurate records of overseas political payments, (2) *disclose* the names of recipients of all such payments over $1,000 to officials of foreign governments, and (3) *report* the name of any agent hired to obtain or maintain business with a foreign government or to influence its decisions. The bill would make it a criminal offense under U.S. law for American business executives to make overseas payments to foreign government officials for the purpose of obtaining or maintaining business— whether or not the payment was sanctioned under foreign law. In passing, it should be noted that Senator Proxmire's bill did not mention the *extortion* of money from U.S. companies by foreign officials or politicians, thus perpetuating the myth that *all* political payments made by U.S. companies are bribes.

In the course of hearings on the bill by the Committee on Banking, Housing and Urban Affairs, the SEC took exception to both its disclosure and criminalization features. Although supporting the measure's underlying philosophy, particularly the mandate for maintaining accurate corporate records of overseas payoffs, the SEC objected to the requirement that corporations subject to its jurisdiction should disclose foreign political payments starting with an amount as low as $1,000. The SEC was attracted to the idea of having specific levels of payments that should be disclosed, but it was fearful of becoming overwhelmed with paper work relating to picayune payments of the lubrication variety. The Commission also objected to the provision in the bill that calls for naming the person to whom a payment had been made. "In some cases, disclosure of the identity of the person receiving such payments may be important to an investor's understanding of the transaction," the Commission said, but "more frequently the identity of a particular government employee who received a payment may have little or no significance to the investor."[7] In general, the SEC believed its existing statutory authority to be adequate to obtain disclosure of "questionable or illegal" payments and related practices.

Individual SEC commissioners who appeared before the Banking Committee had even stronger objections to the section of the Proxmire bill that would have required the SEC to enforce the criminal aspects of the statute. Chairman Hills commented that the SEC lacked the manpower to police such a law, adding that " 'the legal profession has enough business without going to all parts of the world to spell out what is right and wrong.' "[8] Subsequently, Mr. Hills warned it would be difficult for his agency to judge whether foreign payments actually represented bribes. " 'We ought not to be in the position of deciding whether the law has been violated or not,' " he said.[9]

To obtain the SEC's support, Senator Proxmire offered to drop the disclosure requirement from his bill. The Banking Committee eliminated this requirement, but retained the criminalization provisions.[10] The new bill bore the number S. 3664. In its final form, the Committee's legislation created a dual system of enforcement. The SEC would police the companies whose securities are listed on the stock exchange, and the Department of Justice would monitor the behavior of all other companies, numbering some 30,000 in all.[11] The Committee's bill also incorporated the SEC's proposal that companies over whom it exercised supervision should be required to keep accurate records and books relating to overseas political payments, along with a controversial provision making it unlawful for a corporate executive or employee to mislead outside auditors.[12]

Just prior to the October 1976 adjournment of the 94th Congress, the Senate voted 86 to 0 to approve the amended Proxmire bill. The House of Representatives, however, took no action on a companion bill, H.R. 15481. It would be a mistake to assume that the lopsided vote in the Senate signified that every voting Senator really favored the Proxmire philosophy. When a complex economic-social-political issue is simplistically reduced to an apparent choice between good and evil, as is the case with the Proxmire bill, apparently no American politician will expose himself to a charge by his political opponents that he supports corruption and immorality—which is how a vote *against* the Proxmire bill would have been construed.

Flaws in the Criminalization of Foreign Bribery

Many observers contend that there is "no merit in the criminalization approach" to foreign bribery. Criminalization, they say, will not add "significantly to the deterrent effect of existing law and will impair the ability of the U.S. to negotiate effective international arrangements" for curbing overseas political payments.[13] Former Secretary of Commerce Richardson observed that the problem with a criminalization bill, such as Senator Proxmire's, is that "we would be making criminal under U.S. law an act that takes place in another country and that would create problems of investigation and enforcement."[14] With commendable candor, the SEC also pointed out two critical constitutional and foreign policy deficiencies in the Proxmire legislation:

> ... the question whether there should be a general statutory prohibition against the making of certain kinds of foreign payments presents a broad issue of national policy with important

implications for international trade and commerce, *the appropriateness of application of United States law to transactions by United States citizens in foreign countries, and the possible impact of such legislation upon the foreign relations of the United States.*"[15] (emphasis added)

Let us consider these arguments.

First, we strongly question whether, in view of the criminal and civil sanctions in existing U.S. laws, a new criminal statute is necessary. In chapter 2, we examined an emerging trend to utilize existing laws for the censorship of U.S. companies that have made overseas political payments. We noted that this was a departure from the traditional regulatory role of government. It needs to be emphasized that there now exists a wide array of criminal and civil sanctions for coping with such payments by U.S. companies. These sanctions can be summarized as follows:

CURRENT CIVIL AND CRIMINAL SANCTIONS AGAINST FOREIGN POLITICAL PAYMENTS

1.	Securities Act of 1933	Mandatory and voluntary disclosure of payments
2.	Securities & Exchange Act of 1934	Mandatory and voluntary disclosure of payments
3.	Internal Revenue Code	Prohibition against the deduction of political payments as business expenses
4.	Tax Reform Act of 1976	"Bribe-produced income" taxable to U.S. parent
5.	Sherman Act	Monopolization of foreign markets prohibited
6.	Federal Trade Commission Act	Unfair methods of competition prohibited
7.	Clayton Act	Unfair methods of competition prohibited
8.	Fraud and False Statements Act	False and fraudulent statements to government agencies and departments (particularly relevant in transactions with AID and Export-Import Bank) prohibited

9. International Security and Assistance and Arms Export Control Act of 1976	Agents' fees to be disclosed
10. Armed Services Procurement Regulation (ASPR)	Disclosure requirement on agents' fees
11. Bank Secrecy and Reporting Act of 1970.	Disclosure of sums in excess of $5,000 leaving or entering the United States. Banks required to report any unusual transfers of funds in excess of $10,000.

In addition to this wide spectrum of existing statutory law, there is the recently formed "Mutual Cooperation Pact" between the Department of Justice and ten other nations for the exchange of information on political payments made by U.S. companies. There is also the Department of Justice–SEC Joint Task Force to determine whether U.S. firms involved in overseas political payments have committed prosecutable offenses under any U.S. statute. And, finally, there is the right of shareholders to bring class action or derivative suits against managements and directors.

Given this framework of statutory law and prosecutorial authority available to U.S. government agencies, opponents of criminalization plausibly contend that the

> prime need is not for new Federal law, but for international agreements to protect U.S. business against extortion, to subject competitors of U.S. companies to the same constraints as those properly imposed on U.S. business, and to assure impartial law enforcement by foreign governments.[16]

Second, one must question the appropriateness of applying a U.S. law to transactions by U.S. citizens in foreign countries. As Secretary Richardson pointed out in his letter to Senator Proxmire, the defect in a criminalization statute lies in its presumption that a U.S. law can reach out and punish as a crime a bribe conceived, offered, and accepted in a foreign country.[17] "Successful prosecution of [such an offense] would typically depend on witnesses and information beyond the reach of U.S. judicial process," the Secretary declared. U.S. law enforcement officials have considerable difficulty in obtaining proof of official bribery in the United States. Securing such proof in a foreign country would be practically impossible. In order to obtain judicially admissible evidence, U.S. investigators would have to obtain proof that (1) a payment was intended for a foreign official, (2) it was made with a corrupt intent, and (3) it was made for a prohibited purpose. Collecting such evidence would necessitate the cooperation of foreign governments. Whether foreign governments would allow U.S. investigators to implicate one of their own nationals in a criminal offense *under U.S. law* is doubtful. Bribery is now an offense under the laws of virtually all nations. It would be regarded as an intrusion into the domestic affairs of other sovereign nations for the United States to attempt to investigate an illicit transaction involving the bribery of a foreign official by a U.S. citizen in the foreign national's *own country*.

Moreover, a U.S. citizen accused of foreign bribery would be denied due process of law under the U.S. Constitution unless he could produce foreign witnesses and documents in his own defense. These essential components of a fair defense would not be available to a defendant, as they are beyond the compulsory judicial process of U.S. federal courts.

As William F. Kennedy, Co-Chairman of a Special Committee on Foreign Payments, Association of the Bar of the City of New York, testified before a House Subcommittee, ". . . one should ask whether criminalization will deter foreign officials and foreign politicians from soliciting bribes and from engaging in extortion. It is plain on the face of it that an official or politician determined to violate the law of his own country will not be restrained by concern that the U.S. company making the payment may be violating U.S. law."[18]

Third, criminalization would have an adverse impact on the foreign relations of the United States. If the United States seriously intended to enforce a criminal statute outlawing foreign political payments, it would need to establish a massive surveillance of the foreign activities of U.S. citizens as well as of foreign politicians and government officials. U.S. embassy staffs would have to be vastly enlarged. U.S. agents would need to swarm over foreign countries in which U.S. multinational corporations operated and in markets in which U.S. exporters traded. The presence of a horde of undercover agents would be resented. And, with considerable justification, the United States would be accused of "moral imperialism." These implications of the enforcement of such a statute make one wonder whether the U.S. Senate really intended that the law it had passed should be implemented!

Thus, Americans were understandably hostile to the presence of foreign agents, when it was revealed in 1976 that the Republic of South Korea's CIA had systematically engaged in surveillance of Korean nationals residing in the United States; and that a South Korean businessman, apparently acting in behalf of his government, had distributed between $.5 million and $1 million annually during the past two years in cash, expensive gifts, and campaign contributions to members of the U.S. Congress.

The past efforts of the U.S. government to enforce extraterritorial laws have involved unpleasant controversies with host governments. An example was the effort of the U.S. government to enforce the Trading with the Enemy Act to prevent the sale of goods by U.S. subsidiaries abroad to the People's Republic of China.[19] The overzealous attempt by U.S. District Courts to extend the Sherman antitrust concepts into foreign jurisdictions led to diplomatic protests by Britain, Canada, and Switzerland.

More recently, the Argentine government declared that, if the Argentine subsidiaries of General Motors, Ford, and Chrysler were prevented from selling cars and trucks to Cuba by the United States embargo against trade with the Castro regime, they would be nationalized. When Litton Industries ordered its Canadian subsidiary to cancel a contract for the sale of office furniture to the Cuban government, after learning that the transaction was in violation of U.S. embargo policy, Litton's action was denounced by Alistair Gillespie, Canadian Minister of Trade, who said, "I consider this action an intolerable interference and a form of corporate colonialism."[20]

To sum up: the arguments are overwhelming *against* passage of a U.S. statute that would make the payment of a bribe by U.S. corporate executives to a foreign government official a criminal act. Other solutions to the problem of corruption in business-government relations, free of the serious flaws in a criminalization statute, must be found.

Disclosure Proposals of the Ford Administration

Congressional attempts to legislate a solution to the problem of overseas political payments by American corporations were matched by an executive initiative. On March 31, 1976, President Ford announced the creation of a Cabinet-level Task Force on Questionable Corporate Payments Abroad under the chairmanship of Elliot L. Richardson, Secretary of Commerce. The Task Force was asked to consider the implications of such payments for U.S. foreign policy, antitrust enforcement, corporate disclosure, military sales and assistance, and the reporting of taxes. The major product of the Task Force was a proposed "Foreign Payments Disclosure Act," which was transmitted to the Congress by President Ford on August 3, 1976. The President described the bill as "a measured but effective approach to the problem of questionable payments abroad," which would help to deter improper payments, reverse the trend toward impugning the integrity of American business, deter would-be foreign extorters, and "allow the United States to set a forceful example to our trading partners and competitors regarding the imperative need to end improper business practices."[21]

The Ford Administration proposal to curb overseas payments by U.S. firms rested exclusively on a system of disclosure. It rejected the criminalization approach as unenforceable and therefore impracticable. Secretary Richardson, however, did mention in his letter to Senator Proxmire that the President's Task Force had considered "one criminalization scheme" in which a U.S. law against overseas bribery

> would be applied to improper payments made abroad, *provided* the country in which such payments were made had entered into a mutual enforcement assistance agreement with the United States and had enacted its own criminal prohibitions against bribery.

As with domestic legal standards for the determination of bribery, such multilateral agreements "would entail the drawing of very difficult distinctions between criminal payments on the one hand and proper fees or political contributions on the other." For these reasons, the Task Force had rejected this approach.

A strong argument for the adoption of a disclosure statute, the Task Force believed, was the relative ease of obtaining proof of violation. A prosecutor need only prove the making of a payment and the failure to report it. In a criminalization case, on the other hand, he must prove that a government official was the ultimate recipient of the payment, and that there was a corrupt motive, and a prohibited purpose. As we have already seen, this proof is difficult, if not impossible, to establish when the evidence is in a foreign country.

In requesting legislation by Congress, President Ford stipulated that *all* companies be required to report the making of overseas political payments to the Department of Commerce. Fines of $100,000 and, in the case of a deliberate omission to file a report, jail terms up to three years would be imposed.

Although the Administration's proposal did not specifically outlaw political payments to foreign officials, information regarding such payments would be sent, at the option of the Departments of State and Justice, to governments whose officials were reported to have received such payments. Prosecution of the foreign government official named could then be undertaken by the designated country under its own laws, if it chose to do so.

Reports filed with the Department of Commerce would be made available to other appropriate agencies as well as to committees of the Congress. After a delay of one year, the reports would be disclosed to the public, unless the Secretary of State or the Attorney General requested they be kept secret for reasons of foreign policy or because disclosure would prejudice an investigation by the Department of Justice.

The Administration's legislative proposal was characterized by Senator Proxmire as a " 'bureaucratic cop-out.' " It is " 'a tacit admission,' " he said, " 'that . . . (bribes) may be necessary,' " and " 'involves the U.S. government as a co-conspirator.' "[22] Proxmire's condemnation was unjustified. The proposed law was, as President Ford described it, a "measured and effective" legislative approach to the problem of corporate political payments abroad. A requirement that U.S. companies disclose such payments to appropriate U.S. government authorities is reasonable, especially if foreign nations simultaneously require their disclosure abroad. However, like the Church and Proxmire bills, the legislation failed to pass the 94th Congress during its 1976 sessions.

A United Nations Agreement on Overseas Political Payments

The cornerstone of the Ford Administration's program for curbing overseas payments by U.S. firms was, however, its proposal for a multilateral agreement by the member states of the United Nations.[23] The proposed treaty embodied the following principles:

A. It would apply equally to those who offered to make improper payments and to those who solicited them (i.e., bribery *and* extortion).

B. Foreign governments would agree to establish clear guidelines with respect to the use of agents employed in connection with their procurement and other transactions.

C. All governments would cooperate in the exchange of information to help eradicate corruption.

D. Uniform requirements would be agreed upon for the disclosure by enterprises, agents, and officials of payments, gifts, and political contributions made in connection with stipulated transactions.

An international treaty was the "ultimate legal basis," the President's Task Force believed, for adequately addressing the problem of overseas political payments. With adherence to a treaty, by the industrialized nations as well as those of the Third World, would come the assurance that "all nations, and the competing firms of differing nations, are treated on the same basis."

Secretary Richardson, however, was not optimistic that the member states of the United Nations would agree to such an international treaty. In his letter to Senator Proxmire he wrote:

A realistic assessment of prospects for international action would have to suggest that it is probable the desired international agreement may—in spite of our best efforts—take a considerable amount of time to achieve. *International prospects are, in any case, highly uncertain.*[24] (emphasis added)

This evaluation reinforced a similar pessimistic judgment, made in another context, by then Secretary of State Henry Kissinger. In an address before the American Bar Association in Montreal, Canada, on August 11, 1975, Dr. Kissinger declared: "A multilateral treaty establishing binding rules for multinational enterprises does not seem possible in the near future." One must regretfully conclude that these opinions are amply supported by historical experience.

The Voluntary Guidelines of the OECD

In June 1976, the Paris-based Organization for Economic Cooperation and Development (OECD), consisting of the twenty-four industrialized nations of Western Europe, Japan, and the United States and embracing the world area in which 70 percent of U.S. overseas investment is concentrated, adopted a series of *voluntary guidelines* for the conduct of private and state-owned multinational enterprises as well as a complementary codification of governmental responsibilities.

The guidelines covered antitrust, taxation, financing, competition, employment, and industrial relations, as well as admonitions with respect to the making of political payments. Multinational corporations "should not render—and they should not be solicited or expected to render—any bribe or improper benefit, direct or indirect, to any public servant or holder of public office." A related provision abjured corporate contributions to candidates for office or to political parties, unless such contributions were legally permissible and were disclosed. Finally, multinational corporations were urged to "abstain from any improper involvement in local political activities."

The United States and a majority of the OECD members had opposed *mandatory* guidelines, which Sweden and the European Social Democratic trade unions had sought, in the belief that an international body should not attempt to impose standards of business conduct. The majority agreed that each multinational enterprise should, within a broad admonitory framework, institute its own rules of ethical behavior.[25]

Some American businessmen are skeptical that the multinational enterprises based in other nations will adhere to the OECD guidelines, particularly with respect to disclosure. They predicate this skepticism on the fact that many European firms are organized as private liability companies. Under European company laws, private liability companies are not required to reveal detailed information concerning their activities. Such information as they must disclose is not even remotely comparable in scope to that required of registered U.S. companies. Many large European companies—the Michelin firm is an example—are privately owned. Traditionally, they have been accustomed to conducting their affairs in virtual secrecy.

Other American executives believe that, if the OECD guidelines are widely disregarded, there will be a reverse "domino effect." Strong political pressures for "more restrictive and *mandatory* rules for the multinationals" will arise.[26] These rules, they fear, would be imposed by the United Nations Commission on Transnational Corporations, a body controlled by the Third World members of the U.N. A code of conduct for multinational enterprises drafted under the imprimatur of this group, they contend, would be one-sided. Multinational corporations from the industrialized nations would be placed under strict rules of conduct, but no similar restraints would be imposed on the governments of Third World nations. U.S. executives who participated in the formulation of the OECD's voluntary guidelines believe that compliance with them by all multinational enterprises will stave off politically inspired, mandatory restrictions emanating from the U.N.

Because U.N. member states are unlikely soon to accede to an international treaty, according to U.S. official assessments, the solution proposed by the OECD, in our view, makes sense.

Companies should determine for themselves how best to function in the sovereignties in which they operate, subject to the OECD guidelines. The OECD's declaration of policy tacitly recognizes that the multinational enterprise should not serve as an instrumentality of any one nation's laws or moral precepts. Because the U.S. international corporation operates in a myriad of cultures under diverse environmental constraints—cultural, economic, sociological, legal, and political —it must fit itself into "the prevailing legal and moral beliefs of the political sovereignty in the country in which it operates."[27]

The Code of Conduct Proposed by European Parliamentarians and Members of the U.S. Congress

Paralleling the OECD effort, a group of fourteen members of the European Parliament, the assembly of the nine-nation European Economic Community, and a number of U.S. Congressmen endeavored to forge a *binding* code of conduct for the activities of international corporations. A section of this code, entitled "Pernicious Political Activities," included language virtually identical to that of the OECD guidelines. It stated

> Multinational enterprises shall not make, or be solicited to make, payments in money or other items of value to host government officials other than for manifest public purposes. Multinational enterprises shall not contribute to political parties or candidates in any way unless such contributions are lawful and details on the amounts and beneficiaries are disclosed in a timely manner.

An "explanatory note" to this caveat states: "This provision is aimed at preventing multinational enterprises from attempting to exercise undue influence over political processes in host countries." Like the OECD's declaration of principles,

226

the joint parliamentary-congressional code also prescribed rules of conduct for multinational corporations in their relations with national governments.

At a joint meeting of the group in Washington, D.C., during September 1976, the Belgian delegate is said to have questioned the need for another code of business conduct in the light of the promulgation of the OECD's voluntary guidelines.[28] After three years' work, it was announced by the group's chairman that a final draft of a code had been postponed for another year.[29]

The Moral of the Story

Several years of conferring, investigating, and drafting of laws, codes, and treaties, mainly in the United States but also by international bodies acting under U.S. stimulus, have failed to produce any satisfactory solution to the problem of curbing foreign political payments by multinational companies. The lack of progress results from the fact that most of this activity has been carried on by the legislative and executive organs of *governments,* whose standard approach to problems is to enact laws—when *legislation is not the answer.* We have noted before that bribery and extortion involving public officials *already* are crimes in nearly every nation in the world. Another U.S. law would be redundant.

Our critique of the reform proposals advanced by governments and international bodies indicates that we must look in another direction for a solution. It is time to inquire into new policies and actions by governments—not the enactment of new legislation—that could help to curb corruption in the business-government relationship. At the same time, we should investigate ways in which multinational corporations could organize and manage themselves so as to minimize the incidence of foreign payoffs. To these topics we now turn.

8

Some Proposals for Action

Our inquiry has shown that the problem of foreign political payments by multinational corporations is extremely complex. Such payments have a multiplicity of causes, take many forms, and are interwoven with the cultures of societies. In reducing the corruption that infects business-and-government relations, there is no single culprit to be punished, no one institution to be blamed. Nor can any single action—corporate or governmental—eliminate these practices.

We have shown that many well-meaning reforms proposed to solve this problem are naïve and simplistic. They raise false hopes and invite disillusionment. Some could even backfire. Like the American "noble experiment" with prohibition during the years from 1919 to 1933, they might serve to drive these practices still further underground and to generate more wrongdoing than they suppress. The problem of corruption in the business-government relationship requires a multi-faceted attack, mounted on many fronts. Moreover, the prescriptions for improvement offered by governments of nations in the less-developed Third World differ from those of the governments of the industrialized nations. Even with determined effort success can be expected to come slowly and in small increments.

Why Political Payments Should Be Reduced

The authors of this book share with most Americans the belief that bribery, extortion, and other political payments are a regrettable and unnecessary burden on international trade and investment. However one views the morality of such payments, *their economics are wrong.* Because of their surreptitious and uncertain character, they interfere with the workings of efficient markets. The world's business would be carried on more efficiently and its resources would be allocated more productively, if all multinational transactions were open, aboveboard, and conformed to established laws and regulations. For economic reasons alone, it is important to reduce the volume of political payments by representatives of business corporations to government officials and political organizations of all kinds.

Although the case for reducing political payments in world business is compelling on purely economic grounds, such actions can also be supported on legal grounds. It is a fact that *virtually all nations formally outlaw bribery and extortion,* even though these laws are widely violated. And bribery and extortion violate the moral standards of societies all around the world. Nations differ considerably more in the degree to which actual business-government relationships deviate from their announced moral and legal standards than in the standards themselves. While these standards differ somewhat, much progress would be made if government officials and businessmen would make their behavior conform more and more to them. Such changes in behavior would be good in themselves, even if they lacked any economic benefits. In fact they would yield both economic and moral benefits.

Political payments in world business can be reduced significantly over a period of time, if multinational corporations, the U.S. government, foreign governments, and international organizations all take actions toward that end. Each must play its part if the goal is to be achieved.

The reduction of corruption calls more urgently for actions by governments than for reforms in corporate behavior. Governments set the framework and make the rules for multinational business. As fashioners of the sociopolitical environment of business, governments exert more influence on the quality of business-government relationships than do enterprises. But business enterprises are not merely passive reactors to their environments; they are also active forces in shaping them. Hence, we begin our discussion of steps to reduce political payments by proposing policies that multinational corporations should adopt, as well as the organizational structures needed for carrying out those policies.

Steps to Be Taken by Multinational Corporations

Every multinational company should adopt written policies —and the organizational procedures for carrying them out— that will minimize unlawful foreign political payments. The disclosures made to the SEC during 1975 and 1976 showed that many American companies had—at the least—been negligent in these matters. Policy statements have been non-existent, or vague and full of loopholes. Firms had been slipshod in their accounting controls over the managers of their foreign affiliates. Many had been careless in selecting and monitoring their foreign consultants and sales agents. As a result, corrupt payments were made by such agents, usually without the knowledge of the boards of directors or of top corporate managements. What is the *substance* of policies that will help to reduce such misbehavior?

Internal Corporate Policies

The board of directors of a multinational company should formally adopt *written policies* to govern all officers and employees with respect to foreign political payments. These policies should be explicit and should prescribe penalties to be imposed on violators.

Formulating such policies is not an easy task. It is not enough merely to lay down broad principles of good behavior. These platitudes may sound impressive, but they will fail to provide practical guidance to foreign managers who confront complex, cross-cutting values in difficult situations in alien societies. Nor is it possible to lay down a detailed code of conduct that will cover every possible set of circumstances that may arise. Written policies should state the general rule *and* illustrate it with examples, avoiding the problem of being too general *or* too particular. They should set forth guidelines that resolve the majority of questions. The written policies should make it clear that cases not resolved by these guidelines should be referred to senior corporate management. Exceptions to the general policies of the company—and they are bound to occur—should be made only by the board of directors or its executive committee, for they bear the company's ultimate responsibility to society and to its shareholders. Although the policies of individual companies may be expected to differ according to their respective organizations, industry, and the foreign countries in which they operate, some should be common to all:

1. Obedience to Foreign Laws. The *general policy* of a company and its foreign affiliates should be to conduct business in strict accordance with the laws of each country in which business is done, when the law is clear and unambiguous. An (American) multinational company should not practice, or condone, clear violations of law. Where the foreign law is ambiguous, the company should follow the commercial customs of native enterprises in the host country. Where the law is very general in its terms, leaves administrators wide discretion in its applications, or is being applied arbitrarily or improperly, the company should seek the advice of reputable local counsel and be guided by that advice. We believe that these rules constitute a guide to corporate behavior that is both ethical and practical.

2. No Payments (Except Small Facilitating Payments) to Government Officials or Employees. The *general policy* of a company should be to *prohibit* any payment to or for the benefit of any officer or official of a foreign government, or of a corporation wholly or partly owned by a foreign government, for services specially rendered to it. An *exception* may be made to this rule where the employment of a foreign government official is lawful under the laws of his country, the board of directors of the company and the foreign government have determined that the services rendered to the company do not conflict with the employee's duties to his government, and the payment is approved by the board of directors or its executive committee. (Such exceptions will be comparatively rare.) Also, an *exception* should be made of small facilitating payments to minor government employees in those countries in which such payments are customary.

3. No Payments to Foreign Political Organizations. The *general policy* of the multinational company should be *not* to intervene in the internal political affairs of any foreign nation in which it does business, nor to make contributions to any foreign political candidate or political organization. Being

232

basically an economic and not a political institution, the foreign-based company should normally maintain a low political profile abroad. However, *exceptions* may be made to this rule in countries where corporate political contributions are lawful and customary, where they appear to be necessary to conform to local customs or to protect the property of the company against adverse political action, and where they are specifically approved by the board of directors or its executive committee.

4. *Monitor Foreign Business Representatives.* A multinational company may properly retain persons who are *not* officials or employees of a foreign government as its agents, representatives, or consultants to assist it in penetrating markets in a foreign country where this is the commercial custom. The *general policy* of the company should be (a) to pay foreign representatives such compensation as is consistent with commercial practice and with the value of the services performed, and (b) to take such actions as are within its power to assure that fees or commissions paid to such agents are *not* improperly channeled by them to officials or employees of foreign governments. Specifically, the company should:

A. *Conduct an investigation* prior to its appointment of a foreign agent, and annually thereafter, to determine that he has a good character and reputation in the country in which he does business and has no official connection with a foreign government;
B. Ascertain that the amount of the *fee or commission paid the agent falls within the range of commercial practice* and is reasonably related to the value of services performed by him;
C. *Be alert to any information of improper conduct by its foreign agent*, and if such information is received, promptly terminate his service; and
D. *Pay all compensation to its foreign representatives openly through normal channels*, and refrain from making any

233

deposits for their benefit into numbered bank accounts not identified by their names.

5. *Maintain Accurate and Complete Accounts.* The *general policy* of the company should be to maintain accounts and records that meet high standards of completeness, accuracy and consistency, and to prohibit all deceptive, concealing or misleading practices. Specifically, officers and employees should—

A. *Not establish or use any secret corporate entity,* whose true purposes are not disclosed to, and approved by, the board of directors;
B. *Not establish or maintain any off-the-books fund or account;*
C. *Not knowingly make any false or misleading or incomplete entry in any account;* or
D. *Not knowingly provide any false or misleading information to the company's auditors.*

Multinational companies have been most culpable—and the SEC has been most justified in its criticism—of secrecy, subterfuge, and the distortion of books and records to cover up questionable foreign payments. The integrity of the corporate accounting system is absolutely essential to the efficient investment and use of resources. It should never be compromised. The corporate motto should be: "Pay if you must, but don't conceal."

6. *Support Studies of Business Ethics at Home and Abroad.* A multinational company should give ongoing support to studies of business ethics at academic institutions both in the United States and in foreign countries. The broad purpose of such studies should be to clarify the ethical dilemmas, the conflicts of values, and the likely consequences of different courses of action for business executives and political leaders. Out of such studies would come, initially, a greater awareness and understanding of the depth of these conflicts. Later, it may be expected that increased understanding would lead to a reduction in those conflicts.

Implementation of Corporate Policies

Even the best corporate policies are not self-executing. To be effective, they must be understood and accepted by a company's employees. Management controls are needed to detect any violators. Penalties must be imposed on them to deter wrongdoing. The chairman and the president of the multinational company must, as its leaders, stand forth as personal examples of integrity and ethical business behavior. Beyond this, *the board of directors should be so constituted as to be an independent monitor of corporate management.* And the board should establish watchdog agencies over the ethical as well as the economic performance of the company. In a well-organized enterprise, such agencies will include the audit committee of the board, the internal audit staff, and the independent external auditors. Let us look at each of these proposals.

A Majority of Outside Directors

As the governing authority of the corporation, the board of directors can powerfully influence the ethical behavior of its employees. The multinational company—indeed all publicly owned business corporations—should have a board the majority of whose members are "outsiders"—not salaried managers. No management can audit itself objectively. Only an outsider-controlled board can perform the essential board function of auditing the performance of the management. Not being preoccupied with day-to-day administration (and operations), outside directors can also provide an important perspective on the firm's relationships to society, including its ethical behavior.[1] It is possible that such companies as Gulf Oil might have avoided impropriety and public censure if their boards had been less dominated by management.

An Audit Committee of Outside Directors

The board of every multinational company should establish an audit committee whose members are outside directors. Its duties should be to conduct an ongoing review of the company's performance, its accounting and reporting practices, and the obedience of management to company policies. The audit committee should meet at least quarterly, in order to maintain close contact with events and to see that its recommendations to management are being carried out. It should meet *privately* with both the director of the internal audit staff of the company and the company's external public accountants. In this way, the internal and external auditors can discuss their findings with complete candor, uninhibited by the presence of management. The audit committee should give both the internal and external auditors of the company standing instructions to be alert to questionable payments and to report them when found. The committee should study these reports, make remedial recommendations to management, and follow up on them. Needless to say, these are time-consuming responsibilities for which outside directors should be paid adequately.

An Internal Audit Staff Reporting Directly to the Audit Committee

The multinational corporation needs an internal audit staff whose function is to make financial and managerial field audits of all company operations. Customarily, the internal audit staff reports to the company's controller. It should also report directly to the audit committee, to whose members its written reports and recommendations should routinely be sent for study and comment. The staff should possess enough manpower to be able to audit *all* of the operations of the company at least once every two years.

A Vigilant External Public Auditor Reporting Directly to the Audit Committee

Finally, the multinational company requires a vigilant external public accounting firm to audit its accounts and to help it to devise accounting controls that will make violations of company policy more difficult and their detection easier. The external auditors should meet at least quarterly with the audit committee, without the presence of any corporate managers, in order to foster candid discussion. American public accounting firms have come under attack in recent years, by the SEC and by frustrated investors, for approving allegedly false or incomplete accounts of their corporate clients. This has led them to use more rigorous auditing procedures.

The independent auditor has a responsibility for detecting "irregularities" (i.e., intentional distortions) in a company's financial statements that result from misrepresentation, omission, manipulation, or falsification of records, the recording of transactions without substance, or the intentional misapplication of accounting principles or misappropriation of assets. However, his responsibility is limited. The independent auditor need merely search for irregularities that would have a "material effect" on the financial statements, and exercise "due skill and care" in the conduct of his examination. He must examine the company's internal accounting controls and test samples of the data being examined. But he does not, and cannot, thereby *assure* that all irregularities will be detected. Nor can he *guarantee* that management will not override internal controls, engage in collusion for personal gain, forge documents, fail to record transactions, or misinform him. If the auditor finds that irregularities are present and that they may materially affect the company's financial statements, his responsibility is limited to qualifying or declining to express an opinion on the financial statements or, in extreme cases, withdrawing from his engagement as auditor.[2] The basic responsibility for the integrity of a company's accounts and financial statements rests, in the end, with the board of directors.

Steps to Be Taken by the U.S. Government

A multinational company that has adopted the policies, the organization, and the procedures just described will surely reduce the number of its questionable and improper political payments to foreign government employees. It will not, however, have thereby reduced foreign *political risks* and the payments made to avert them. These include the risks of loss through war, revolution, civil insurrection, expropriation without adequate compensation, inconvertibility of currency, or punitive regulation and taxation. As we have seen, some of the largest foreign political payments by U.S. multinationals have been made for the purpose of reducing these risks. Of course, *foreign* governments can and should reduce these risks by changing their behavior. But we are concerned here with actions that the U.S. government should take to reduce them, thereby diminishing the need for payments by multinational companies.

One approach to this problem might be for the U.S. government to offer multinational companies broad-coverage investment insurance. The U.S. government could offer to insure its multinational corporations against losses on account of a *broad spectrum* of political risks *in all nations* in which they make foreign investments. And we have some experience with this approach. Since 1961 the Overseas Private Investment Corporation (OPIC), a U.S. government corporation, has offered insurance against loss due to currency inconvertibility, expropriation, and war, on long-term investments made in friendly less-developed countries. Why not extend such insurance to cover *all* political risks in *all* countries? The answer is that the experience of OPIC with its limited program discourages the expansion of the programs.

The weaknesses in OPIC have proved to be (1) an adverse selection of high-risk investments in its insured portfolio, and (2) an adverse influence on the behavior of foreign governments. Not unexpectedly, companies have tended to insure with OPIC their high-risk foreign investments, and have chosen to carry on their own the lower political risks of their other eligible investments. Thus OPIC has accumulated a high-risk portfolio of insurance liabilities, and has had to pay out more in claims than it has collected in premiums. Equally important, knowledge by the governments of foreign countries that multinational companies had insured their investments with OPIC has tended to make them *less* responsible in their treatment of foreign investors. They reasoned that, if Uncle Sam would bail out the American company, why should they respect its property rights? For these reasons, a different approach to the problem of reducing foreign political risks has become necessary.

U.S. Economic Sanctions against Governments Violating Investment Agreements or International Law

We propose that the federal government of the United States should resume its historical role of protecting the persons and property of American citizens abroad. The trenchant language of the commercial arbitration tribunal in the case of ITT versus OPIC should be recalled:

> It has long been regarded as a legitimate function of the United States, as a government, to assist its nationals in the protection of their persons and property abroad. The Supreme Court has expressly recognized this function of the State Department. Following an expropriation of any significance, the Executive engages in diplomacy aimed to assure that United States citizens who are harmed are compensated fairly. Representing all claimants of this country, it will often be able, either by bilateral or multilateral talks, by submission to the United Nations, or by the employment of economic and political sanctions, to achieve some degree of general redress.[3]

Despite its responsibility to act, the U.S. government has during recent years adopted a hands-off attitude toward violations of investment agreements and international law by foreign governments. Thus it has encouraged even more flagrant violations. The absence of effective diplomatic protection has thus made it necessary for American companies to make political payments in foreign countries to buy the protection that should have been provided by the U.S. government. In the interests of international economic order, not to mention justice to American investors, this policy should change.

To be sure, a return to gunboat diplomacy is neither feasible nor desirable in the last quarter of the twentieth century. However, diplomatic overtures can be made by the U.S. Department of State to an offending government. If these fail, strong *economic* sanctions can be invoked by the United States against foreign regimes that flout international law. The U.S. government, preferably in concert with other countries in the OECD, could veto an offending nation's access to the International Monetary Fund or to the World Bank. It could freeze foreign deposits in its banks. As the knowledge spread that the United States would promptly intervene to protect the property of its citizens abroad from depredation, foreign nations would become more responsible in their behavior. The need for intervention by U.S.-based corporations in the political affairs of foreign countries would diminish.

Open intervention for this purpose by the U.S. Department of State would have another beneficial effect. It would reduce the pressure for *covert* intervention by the Central Intelligence Agency to protect U.S. business investments abroad or for U.S. firms to make political payments to friendly politicians overseas at the behest of the CIA.[4]

U.S. Diplomatic Action Against Attempted Extortion or Bribery

The U.S. Department of State should make it known around the world, through its ambassadors and consular officials, that the shield of American diplomacy will protect U.S. firms that are subjected to extortionate demands by foreign government officials. Similarly, it should make it clear that it will not support any U.S. company that initiates a foreign bribe. It should bring to the attention of foreign governments any instances of improper demands by their officials and seek their cooperation in ending such demands.

Former U.S. Ambassador to Saudi Arabia, James Akins, set the right pattern for action. In testimony to the Senate Subcommittee on Multinational Corporations, he said that he had taken up the matter of bribery with every top Saudi official:

> They all told me that they would [protect American firms from extortionate demands], and if ever an instance came up . . . I should take it up with them and they would take it up with the King. . . . I told American companies from the very beginning that they should not pay bribes, that they would get no

support from me or the embassy if they did, and if they were touched for bribes, I would support them all the way to the King.[5]

Ambassador Akins's intercession undoubtedly did deter the making of some improper payments, and it should be emulated by American diplomats in other countries. Nevertheless, such a *unilateral* anti-corruption policy of the United States is subject to limitations that should be recognized. Our country has a plurality of national interests, many of them more important than the reduction of corruption in world business. An example is an assured supply of foreign oil. The single-minded pursuit of one aim may damage the ability to realize other equally important objectives. American economic and political leverage is limited in many nations. Hence its power to obtain the full cooperation of other governments in an anti-corruption policy is restricted. Moreover, even if a foreign government does cooperate wholeheartedly with the U.S. government, it may *not* cooperate with the governments of other nations. As a result, American companies could lose business to less scrupulous competitors based in European countries or Japan.

The optimum solution would be a *multilateral* diplomatic anti-corruption policy and effort on the part of *all* nations in the OECD group. Manifestly, such an objective will not be easily achieved. In the interim, however, unilateral diplomatic action by the United States certainly can help to improve the ethical behavior of those involved in world business.

Steps to Be Taken by Foreign Governments

Foreign governments, especially those of Third World nations, have an even larger opportunity than does the U.S. government to take actions that will reduce the incidence of political bribery and extortion. In the economic analysis of foreign political payments contained in chapter 4, reference has already been made to the nature of the needed reforms.

Adhere to a Code of Direct Investment Behavior

Any government that seeks active and sustained direct investment by foreign companies in the development of its economy will be wise to behave in ways that will augment the flow and reduce the cost of such investment. A code of investment behavior should, of course, contain commitments by multinational companies to operate in ways consistent with host country objectives, as well as state the obligations of governments to maintain an equitable and predictable environment for foreign companies.[6] The obligations of the host country government should include the following:

1. To make explicit the national developmental priorities and to maintain them through time with reasonable consistency;
2. To tax and regulate affiliates of foreign-based companies equally with home-based enterprises, neither offering foreign firms special inducements nor imposing on them special burdens;
3. To respect investment agreements with foreign companies and not to make unilateral or retroactive changes in such agreements;
4. To pay prompt and adequate compensation to a foreign company whose local properties it has expropriated or nationalized, as required by international law;
5. To allow reasonable payments of dividends by a local affiliate to its foreign parent and to permit reasonable repatriation of capital to the foreign parent;
6. To agree to arbitrate disputes over investment agreements with foreign companies through the International Center for the Settlement of Investment Disputes or the International Chamber of Commerce (Paris), to abide by such agreements, and not to withdraw from the jurisdiction of the arbitral body once a dispute has arisen.

Countries that abide by these rules will benefit from a progressive improvement of the terms on which they can attract and retain foreign direct investment. Equally important, in a more stable and hospitable environment, multinational companies will find it less necessary to make payments to reduce political risks.

Expand Market and Reduce Bureaucratic Regulation

A nation that expands the role of competitive markets and restricts the amount of governmental regulation of its private sector will thereby diminish the opportunities for political bribery and extortion. As a general rule, the most dirigiste societies are the most corrupt. Governments that closely regulate their business enterprises by granting to public officials the authority to determine prices, wages, products, production methods, employment, investment, imports, exports, and a hundred other details enormously increase the scope for corruption. To the maximum extent, business decisions should be guided by the impersonal forces of market competition. Such a policy will not only elevate the moral plane of business-government relations, but it will also pay off in enhanced productivity and efficiency as well. In view of the socialistic ideology that prevails in many of the world's governments, however, and the personal interest of many political leaders in maintaining the status quo, we are not sanguine that this recommendation will be accepted widely.

Make Laws Explicit and Reduce
Administrative Discretion

Governments can diminish improper payments to politicians and public officials by enacting laws that are clear and unambiguous, and that minimize the discretionary authority granted to the officials who administer them. Vague and ambiguous laws invite bribery and extortion. The wider the scope of authority conferred on public officials to make decisions affecting the profits and losses of enterprises, the greater the potential for corruption. Negotiation of tax liabilities by local tax officials is a prime example. Vagueness and ambiguity exist partly because legislative bodies fail to do their homework and leave to administrative agencies the task of statutory clarification. They may also result from conscious efforts to create opportunities for payoffs of public officials. Whatever the cause, this road to impropriety should be closed.

An important example of official discretion in many countries concerns the awarding of government contracts for the purchase of services and supplies or of concessions to develop natural resources. Where a single public official has the power to make such decisions by private negotiation, payoffs are encouraged. National laws governing public procurement or the awarding of concessions should require that competing businesses submit sealed bids, to be opened publicly by a committee of public officials with *collective* authority to act. This simple change would greatly reduce the opportunity for misbehavior.

Adequately Compensate Public Officials

Governments that desire to minimize corruption in their relationships with business should compensate their public officials sufficiently to attract and retain competent personnel. Civil servants should be able to support their families decently without having to resort to shakedowns of multinational firms. The history of the United States bears testimony to the inverse correlation between the salaries of public employees and the volume of corruption. Only during the last quarter-century has compensation in the public sector become equal to that in the private sector; and this change appears to have been accompanied by a sharp reduction in official corruption. Although a policy of adequate pay to public officials will add to government expenditures and to taxes, it will not expand, and will probably diminish, *social costs*. Open public expenditures and taxation will displace an equal or greater amount of surreptitious "taxation" of the private sector by public officials.[7] The economy will gain in efficiency, and the society will benefit.

Enforce Existing Laws Against Corrupt Acts by Public Officials

As has been noted, nearly all nations have enacted laws making the solicitation or taking of bribes by public officials a crime punishable by severe penalties. And public employees are generally aware of these laws. Unfortunately, they are very loosely enforced. Although the public condemns official corruption, it widely condones it, or at least is not sufficiently aroused by it to demand the prosecution of violators. Strengthening the enforcement of existing laws would, by itself, reduce the number of unlawful political payments made by local as well as by multinational enterprises. New laws are unnecessary. Indeed, they would be a mockery until laws long on the books are enforced.

The list of actions that governments—especially those of Third World nations—could take to reduce unlawful political payments could be extended. We have noted, for example, that political instability is in many lands a prime cause of the insecurity felt by public officials, and hence of their venality. Corruption could be reduced in many countries by expansion of the democratic basis of government, thereby enhancing its stability. However, it is unrealistic to believe that political stability can soon be achieved in an unstable country. The political milieu of any nation is too heavily determined by its culture and its history to be susceptible to rapid change. So it is with other reforms we have proposed, such as heavier reliance upon market regulation of business or higher salaries for public officials; reforms will come slowly and in increments, with many setbacks along the way.

Steps to Be Taken by International Organizations

We have already set forth reasons for skepticism about the effectiveness of international treaties on corporate ethics in reducing business bribery and extortion around the globe. As the voluntary guidelines proposed by the OECD demonstrate, international codes express the least common denominator of agreement among nations with different histories, cultures, legal systems, and commercial customs. They end up as innocuous statements that fail to give much practical guidance to the managers of multinational companies. They are so general as to be little more than admonitions to obey the law!

As former Secretary of State Henry Kissinger has observed, the probability is small that, in today's world, any meaningful international compact on the subject of multinational corporations will soon be made. The industrialized nations are at a historic watershed in their relations with the Third World, especially the raw-material-producing nations. Third World extremists seek to "legislate" through the United Nations a redistribution of the world's wealth by establishing a New International Economic Order. In their thinking, the multinational corporation is assigned "duties" and the Third World governments "rights," with little regard to the reciprocal relationships between the two. Most Third World political leaders do not share the moral sanctimoniousness of American Congressmen in seeking to outlaw bribery and extortion. This is not because they are less moral than American politicians, but because their minds are conditioned by cultures having different moral assumptions than ours.

An International Agreement for Mutual Assistance in the Enforcement of Anti-Corruption Laws

There is only a faint hope of establishing a global code of ethics in business-government relationships via an international treaty. However, there is a good prospect of *improving the enforcement of existing national laws* against official bribery and extortion by an international agreement. Such an agreement would merely require each signatory government to call upon enterprises within their respective jurisdictions to *disclose* payments made to government employees for services rendered. It would oblige each government to *exchange information* with other governments that would be helpful in law enforcement. And it would commit each government to *cooperate in judicial proceedings* begun by another government against suspected violators of its own anti-corruption laws. The chances of obtaining support for an international agreement would be much improved by limiting its scope to these minimum provisions.

Efforts to Harmonize National Laws on Business Regulation

International organizations, such as the United Nations and the OECD, can also reduce the amount of improper political payments in world business by efforts to harmonize national laws affecting multinational companies. Many improper political payments have their origin in disparities among, and ambiguities in, national laws dealing with financial accounting, taxation, competition, labor practices, and other aspects of business regulation. The harmonization of national laws on these subjects would create a more uniform and certain business environment that would be both more efficient and freer from corruption.

The removal of conflict and ambiguity from the apparatus of governmental regulation of world business should be a primary aim of international organizations. As progress is made toward this goal, the behavior of world business will assuredly improve as a by-product.

The formulation of international standards of financial accounting and reporting would be a good starting subject. As Robert I. Jones, Chairman of Arthur Anderson & Company, has pointed out, "international accounting and business ethics go hand in hand."[8] General adherence by governments to a uniform set of standards would greatly reduce frictions and disagreements between governments and multinational companies, the scope for corrupt business practices, and opportunities for shakedowns of foreign companies by unscrupulous government officials. Similarly, the development of uniform concepts and standards of business taxation, of fair competition, of industrial relations, and of other aspects of business operation would also contribute to a reduction in bribery and extortion.

It is reassuring that the Commission on Transnational Corporations of the United Nations has begun to address this task. Similar bodies within the European Economic Community and in the more broadly based OECD are also grappling with the problems of standardizing business accounting and reporting requirements, taxation, and the rules of competition. Out of these efforts, it is to be hoped, there will eventually emerge a clearer and less diverse pattern of corporate regulation. This, in turn, will reduce subterfuge, deception, influence peddling, bribery, and extortion by employees of

249

multinational companies and the governmental employees with whom they deal.

We have no illusions about the difficulty of achieving international standards of business regulation, nor about the time required to attain significant results. Yet the great importance of the goal justifies a maximum effort. The multinational company is, as former U.S. Ambassador to the United Nations Daniel Moynihan remarked, perhaps the most important institutional creation of the twentieth century. The United Nations has described it as a "powerful engine of world development." *We must make the political world fit for global business.*

Subduing the Many-Headed Hydra

The reasons for foreign political payments by American multinational companies are complex and profound. We hope that this inquiry will serve to dissipate the cultural taboo that has existed against open discussion of the subject. No society is immune from such transactions. *The reduction of foreign political payments requires reform of the policies and actions of governments more than it calls for changes in the behavior of American businessmen.* No American executive *wants* to make foreign payoffs. His entire motivation and experience leads him to minimize expense, to conserve resources, and to operate efficiently. He pays off because he believes—rightly or wrongly—that circumstances make it the least bad course of action. He simply adapts to a foreign environment, which he can do little to change. It is mainly the responsibility of governments, which *do* control the environments of business, to create conditions under which bribes will not be offered nor extortions sought.

Although governments—including the U.S. government— must be the primary institutions whose attitudes and policies need reform, the multinational company shares in the responsibility to change the environment of world business. It is not simply a passive agent; it can help to shape the milieu in which it operates. We have described policies and procedures by which it can discharge this responsibility.

Reducing corruption in the business-government relationship in any society is like reducing crime, or liquidating the subcultures that sustain professional criminals. The many-headed hydra must be attacked simultaneously at many points. Despite its stubborn recuperative powers, it can be subdued in time by persistent action based on understanding. In this book we have sought to contribute to that understanding and to propose steps that will help to resolve some of the ethical dilemmas of the multinational corporation.

As we begin to take those steps, we could do no better than to be guided by the principle wisely stated (about supporting human rights around the world, but equally applicable here) by Secretary of State Cyrus R. Vance at the Law Day ceremonies of the University of Georgia on April 30, 1977:

> We must always keep in mind the limits of our power and of our wisdom. A sure formula for defeat of our goals would be a rigid, hubristic attempt to impose our values on others.

Notes

Introduction

1.   See Irving Kristol, "Morality, Liberalism and Foreign Policy," in the *Wall Street Journal*, November 19, 1976. See also Leonard Silk and David Vogel, *Ethics and Profits: The Crisis of Confidence in American Business* (New York: Simon and Schuster, 1976).

2.   See the *New York Times*, February 23, 1977.

Chapter 1: Political Payments Around the World

1.   The failure of a number of well-known U.S. companies—Raytheon, Celanese, Rheem, Union Carbide—in Sicily in the mid-1960s was largely a consequence of management's inability to cope with the Sicilian environment, whose culture, social attitudes, and politics are different even from the cultural outlook prevailing on the Italian mainland, particularly in the industrial North. See Douglas F. Lamont, *Managing Foreign Investment in Southern Italy* (New York: Frederick A. Praeger, 1973).

Japanese–American joint ventures on occasion turn sour when the American partner seeks to transfer U.S. management practices and principles into a business and cultural environment in which they are not accepted, where there are different approaches to employment, labor-management relations, and to

253

middle management participation in the formulation of basic company policies. Accustomed to the tradition in which government and business are perennial adversaries, U.S. executives have not always understood that in Japan they are closely related and that the Japanese business executive expects to be "guided" by his bureaucracy—a practice the American executive regards with something resembling horror.

2. *Wall Street Journal,* April 27, 1976. IBM reported to the SEC that it had, over a period of seven years, made foreign political payments amounting to $53,000.

3. *Wall Street Journal,* August 27, 1976, p. 4. In a speech before the Commonwealth Club in San Francisco, Lockheed's chairman, Robert W. Haack, confirmed the written request by Prince Bernhard for $4 million. See the *Los Angeles Times,* February 5, 1977, pt. 3, p. 8.

4. A handbook of statecraft written by an eighteenth-century Ottoman official gives much attention to bribery and sheds light on the degradation of the Sultan's government. The official wrote: "It is essential to be on guard against giving office through bribery to the unfit and to tyrannical oppressors. For the giving of office to such as these because of bribes means the giving of permission to plunder the property of the subject people. An equivalent for the bribe which is given must be had. In addition to what is given as bribe, he must make a profit for himself and his followers. Bribery is the beginning and root of all illegality and tyranny, the source and fountain of every sort of disturbance and sedition, the most vast of evils, and greatest of calamities. It is the mine of corruption than which there is nothing whatever more calamitous to the people of Islam or more destructive to the foundations of religion and government." Quoted in David M. Miller and Clark D. Moore, eds., *The Middle East Yesterday and Today* (New York: Frederick A. Praeger, 1970), pp. 123–24.

5. The distinguished French scholar Fernand Braudel reminds us that corrupt conduct by state officials in the Ottoman empire was widespread in the sixteenth century. See Fernand Braudel, *The Mediterranean and the Mediterranean World in the Age of Philip II* (New York: Harper & Row, 1973), vol. 2, p. 693. See, also, Sydney Nettleton Fisher, *The Middle East* (New York: Alfred A. Knopf, 1967), pp. 237–38.

6. See, for example, Manfred Halpern, *The Politics of Social Change in the Middle East and North Africa* (Princeton, N.J.: Princeton University Press, 1963), p. 237.

7. For a discussion of this point, see Halpern, *The Politics of Social Change in the Middle East and North Africa,* pp. 46–49.

Although Israel has produced a middle class capable of challenging the regime in power, this class—or some of its members—appears to have become a participant in business-government corruption. For example, the United Press International news service reported on September 23, 1976, that Israeli military police had arrested two senior army officers on charges of taking bribes from an American firm. The two officers, who face a court-martial, had been assigned to the Israeli Defense Ministry mission in New York, which handles the bulk of the procurement of U.S. military supplies. This incident followed an earlier bribery episode in which civilian personnel and an air force officer in the Defense Ministry were implicated with executives of an Israeli engineering firm in corrupt practices. See the *Los Angeles Times,* November 13, 1975, p. 1.

That irregularities within Israel's military establishment are not isolated occurrences is suggested by the dramatic courtroom confession of Asher Yadlin, a once powerful political and financial figure, who said he took kickbacks at the behest of the long-ruling Labor Party. His confession followed the death in January 1977, of Abraham Ofer, the minister of housing, who shot himself after having been linked to illegal real estate deals. See the *Los Angeles Times,* February 15, 1977, p. 1.

8.   Braudel, *The Mediterranean and the Mediterranean World in the Age of Philip II,* n. 5, p. 693.

9.   See Halpern, *The Politics of Social Change in the Middle East and North Africa.* Halpern cites the corruption and incompetence of civil regimes as one of the principal reasons for the frequency of the military coup d'etat in the Middle East. See pp. 251–80.

By general agreement, corruption is widespread in Egypt's government. Cairo's government-owned newspapers, while avoiding direct criticism of President Sadat, published numerous reports during 1976 of corruption by government officials and managers of state-owned corporations. Ordinary people in Cairo call these irregularities "kusa" (squash), which is their expression for corruption in high places.

In addition to pervasive internal corruption, there is external corruption in business-government relations. The public prosecutor early in January 1977 announced that a former deputy prime minister and a former director of civil aviation were under investigation on suspicion of taking political payments in connection with the sale of Boeing jets to the national airline, Egyptair. See the *Los Angeles Times,* January 23, 1977, p. 1. The state prosecutor subsequently announced that a former consultant to

Egypt's national airline, Hilmay Shams, was jailed on charges of receiving kickbacks from the Boeing Corporation to arrange the airline's purchase, "at inflated prices," of four 707 jets "that it did not need." Two former cabinet ministers have been named as suspects in the case but not arrested. According to the prosecutor, Shams admitted receiving $150,000 from Boeing for his part in transaction. See the *Los Angeles Times*, January 25, 1977, p. 2.

10. U.S., Congress, Senate, Committee on Foreign Relations, Subcommittee on Multinational Corporations, *Multinational Corporations and United States Foreign Policy*, Hearings on Political Contributions to Foreign Governments, pt. 12, 94th Cong., 1st sess., June 9–10, 1975, pp. 180–86.

11. While there is no reason to doubt the Shah of Iran's sincerity in desiring to eliminate the middleman in arms procurement, the hydra-headed "corruption factor" has appeared in other aspects of Iranian government relations with U.S. businesses. According to confidential documents from the U.S. embassy at Tehran to the CIA in Washington, leaked to the *Washington Post*, recently retired Ambassador and former CIA Director Richard Helms is reputed to have said he was "washing his hands" of the $500 million Rockwell International surveillance system because it was shot through with corruption. See the *Washington Post*, January 2, 1977, p. 1.

12. Saudi Arabia and Kuwait have legal requirements making the employment of local agents mandatory for *all* transactions with the governments of the two countries. Among the seven desert sheikdoms on the Persian Gulf–Arabian Peninsula (formerly known as the Trucial States), a foreign company for all practical purposes will be unable to do business with any of these regimes unless it retains one of the Middle East's wealthiest and most influential middlemen, Mehdi al-Tajir. On the role and function of the Middle East's intermediaries, see Peter Nehemkis, "Business Payoffs Abroad: Rhetoric and Reality," *California Management Review* 18, no. 2 (Winter 1975): 16–17.

13. President Kaunda has dealt forthrightly with corruption among his high-ranking political leaders. In 1966, he fired his Minister of Labor and Social Services and Minister of Trade and Industry for being involved in a company that had received substantial loans from the government. And, in 1970, in a much publicized purge, Kaunda suspended four ministers and a number of high-ranking civil servants for misappropriating government funds. Two of the suspended individuals stood trial; the others were cleared of the charge of corruption, which, in turn, raised the charge of tribalism in Zambia's judicial system. Part

of Kaunda's success in dealing with corrupt officials, according to *The Weekly Review*, May 12, 1975, published in Kenya, "lies in his own personal Christian convictions about the moral needs of Zambia. He has been striving to set up a system of government in which what he calls humanism is the highest value, and in his humanistic society he finds no room for corruption."

In President Nyerere's socialist society, Tanzania's political leaders are not expected to enrich themselves at the expense of the people or to live ostentatiously. Nyerere himself lives modestly in a small home on the outskirts of Dar es Salaam. And unlike other African leaders, Nyerere has been free of corruption and nepotism. In commenting on Tanzania's socialist egalitarian experiment, however, *The Weekly Review* observed that only lip service was paid to Nyerere's socialist ideals by his ministers and high-ranking civil servants. These civil servants and politicians, the *Review* claimed, had made fortunes through government contracts and had otherwise abused their public trust. "The leadership code," the *Review* asserted, "has precipitated corrupt practices beyond imaginable proportions."

14.   See Frantz Fanon, *The Wretched of the Earth* (New York: Grove Press, 1966), p. 126 and *passim*.

15.   The ruby mine incident described in the text is based on a report filed from Nairobi by the *Washington Post*'s correspondent, David B. Ottaway, and reprinted in the *Los Angeles Times*, October 2, 1974, pt. 1-A, p. 6. A special issue of the influential *Weekly Review*, on May 12, 1975, featured several articles on corruption in Kenya. P. S. Mbolu wrote: "Corruption cannot be dismissed as 'one of those things'; it is an evil which challenges the very bedrock on which our juridical independence stands."

16.   For an extended discussion of Nigeria's dash system, see Ronald Wraith and Edgar Simpkins, *Corruption in Developing Countries* (New York: W. W. Norton, 1964), pp. 11–52.

17.   General Telephone & Electronics refused to pay dash in connection with the award of a telephone contract for $1.8 billion. The initial government decision gave the entire contract to the two competitors, ITT and Siemens of West Germany. However, that decision "proved embarrassing even before it was announced and is being reconsidered. The competition is being restored to save everyone's face." *Forbes*, December 1, 1976, pp. 51–52.

18.   Quoted from Levi A. Nwachuku, "Nigeria's Uncertain Future," *Current History* 71, no. 421 (November 1976): 165.

19.   Nwachuku, "Nigeria's Uncertain Future."

20.   Gunnar Myrdal, *Asian Drama: An Inquiry into the Pov-*

erty of Nations (New York: Random House, 1968), vol. 3, chap. 20, p. 937 ff.

21. Richard Butwell, "The Burmese Way of Change," *Current History* 71, no. 422 (December 1976): 208. Professor Butwell writes: "Ironically, Ne Win's 'Burmese way to socialism' stimulated his countrymen to the most free-wheeling capitalist enterprise that the nation has ever known. Black markets do not usually enjoy good relations, but Burma's contemporary version deserves recognition; it has literally saved the country from economic collapse and rescued the Burmese people from even more depressed living conditions. In Burma an incompetently conceived and soldier-run socialist system has worked so feebly that it has provoked an antithetical free enterprise system that is more illegal than evil. A primitive or rudimentary capitalist economy has come to Burma."

It was in this economic climate that President Ne Win, early in 1974, asked the World Bank to establish an aid consortium to assist his country. An account of the development is reported in the *New York Times*, August 23, 1976, and by Butwell, "The Burmese Way of Change." Burmese leaders now appear eager for foreign aid as a means for rescuing the country from its devastating socialist experiment. See the *Wall Street Journal*, December 27, 1976, p. 6.

22. Butwell, "The Burmese Way of Change," n. 21.

23. *Wall Street Journal*, August 3, 1976, p. 1.

24. *Wall Street Journal*, August 3, 1976, p. 1.

25. Myrdal, *Asian Drama*, p. 943.

26. Quoted in Myrdal, *Asian Drama*, p. 943.

27. See Garth Alexander, *The Invisible China: The Overseas Chinese and the Politics of Southeast Asia* (New York: Macmillan, 1973), p. 221.

28. *Los Angeles Times*, October 24, 1973, pt. 1-A, p. 1. Godber had casually left behind $50,000 in a local bank account, while $40,000 in bills was found in the trunk of his car. The latter sum, detectives calculated, was about one week's take.

29. See the *New York Times*, January 25, 1977, p. 1.

30. *New York Times*, January 25, 1977, p. 1.

31. See the *Wall Street Journal*, February 3, 1977, p. 4, and the *Los Angeles Times*, February 3, 1977, pt. 3, p. 13.

32. *Wall Street Journal*, February 3, 1977, p. 4.

33. Alexander, *The Invisible China*, p. 61.

34. In addition to exacting tribute from vassal states, the Chinese exacted tribute from those who sought to trade with them. The owners and sailing masters of the clipper ships that sailed

from the Eastern seaboard to China in the 1780s were the earliest American traders to encounter the Oriental tradition of official "squeeze." As the American sailing vessels anchored in the Pearl River, preparatory to trading with the merchants of Canton, Chinese officials boarded them and left with the captains a detailed itemization of the specific amounts payable to the various officials. These money payments were shared among the mandarinate all the way back to Peking. "There was scarcely an official in Canton who did not make an illicit profit out of the *Fan-qui,* the 'foreign devils.' " Christopher Hibbert, *The Dragon Wakes: China and the West, 1793–1911* (New York: Harper & Row, 1970), pp. 5–6.

Even the Emperor's financial representative was deeply involved. He held his appointment for three years, having paid a great deal of money for it, and it was expected that he would submit part of his take to Peking and supply mandarins at the imperial court with generous gifts. It was the rare Hoppo—a British corruption of the Chinese name for Board of Revenue—who did not realize a fortune from his share of the rake-off. Customs officials, interpreters, pilots, and compradors, who acted as agents in buying supplies for the European and American business houses, all pocketed as customary tribute their appropriate share of the extortions and illicit commissions.

35.   Alexander, *The Invisible China,* p. 61.

36.   The reader who cares to pursue this Latin American attribute is referred to the late Frank Tannenbaum's *Ten Keys to Latin America* (New York: Alfred Knopf, 1962) and to Peter Nehemkis, *Latin America: Myth and Reality* (New York: Alfred Knopf, 1964).

37.   See Charles T. Goodsell, *American Corporations and Peruvian Politics* (Cambridge: Harvard University Press, 1974), p. 98 and *passim.*

38.   Goodsell, *American Corporations.*

39.   The one day strike on November 24, 1976, by Mexican industry and commerce, which paralyzed business activity outside the capital, although directed against the government's seizure of 243,000 acres of land in the state of Sonora for distribution among *campesinos,* was also a protest against the leftist policies of the then president, Luis Echeverría Alvarez. See the *Los Angeles Times,* November 25, 1976, p. 1. Following two devaluations of the peso, a floodtide of hundreds of millions of dollars, estimated to have been as high as $400 million a week, was carried by apprehensive middle class and well-to-do Mexicans over the border for deposit in Texas banks, dramatizing a wide-

spread loss of confidence in the government of outgoing President Echeverría. See the *Los Angeles Herald-Examiner*, November 26, 1976, p. 1, and *Business Week*, December 6, 1976, p. 33.

40. *Wall Street Journal*, June 16, 1976, p. 6. See also the *Wall Street Journal*, January 28, 1977, p. 2.

41. *Wall Street Journal*, May 9, 1975, p. 1.

42. *Business Week*, March 8, 1976, p. 41.

43. *Wall Street Journal*, September 22, 1976, p. 3.

44. *Wall Street Journal*, December 28, 1976, p. 2.

45. *Wall Street Journal*, December 30, 1976, p. 5.

46. *Wall Street Journal*, December 27, 1976, p. 2.

47. *Wall Street Journal*, December 30, 1976, p. 5.

48. *Wall Street Journal*, December 27, 1976, p. 2.

49. *Wall Street Journal*, December 27, 1976, p. 2.

50. *Wall Street Journal*, December 27, 1976, p. 2.

51. *Wall Street Journal*, August 11, 1975, p. 2.

52. *New York Times*, February 24, 1976, p. 55. See also the *Wall Street Journal*, February 24, 1976, p. 4.

53. *Los Angeles Times*, July 25, 1976, pt. 7, p. 9.

54. Letter to the Editor, *New York Times*, September 14, 1975.

55. See the *Los Angeles Times*, November 27, 1976, pt. 1, p. 2.

56. Luigi Barzini, *The Italians* (New York: Grosset & Dunlap, 1964), pp. 108–09.

57. Tax evasion in Italy during 1975—mostly by big and small industrialists, commercial enterprises, and the self-employed—has been estimated at the equivalent of about $12 billion, equal to the state's deficit for that year. Although the Rome government has not disclosed any official figures on tax evasion, it acknowledges that the practice is Italy's paramount economic problem and has placed tax collection at the top of the "obligatory priorities" in order for Italy to avoid financial collapse. Some Italians justify tax evasion on the grounds that they pay so much *bustarella* there seems little reason to pay the right amount of taxes. See the *Los Angeles Times*, December 16, 1976, pt. 8, p. 4.

58. Hedrick Smith, *The Russians* (New York: Ballantine Books, 1976, paperback ed.), p. 113.

59. Smith, *The Russians*, p. 113.

60. See the *Los Angeles Times*, December 8, 1976, pt. 1-B, p. 10.

61. The textual material is based on Seymour Freiden's dispatch in the *Los Angeles Herald-Examiner*, June 12, 1975, p. A-3.

62. *Business Week,* June 2, 1975, p. 28.

63. *Wall Street Journal,* July 29, 1976, p. 20.

64. *Los Angeles Herald-Examiner,* June 12, 1975, p. A-3.

65. *Business Week,* April 19, 1976, p. 41. A Conference Board report states that during 1975 reports were published of trials of trade officials and state trade corporation officials, in Czechoslovakia, Romania, Bulgaria, Poland, and the Soviet Union, for accepting and soliciting political payments from Western firms. See James R. Basche, Jr., *Unusual Foreign Payments: A Survey of the Policies and Practices of U.S. Companies* (New York: The Conference Board, 1976), p. 4.

66. *Wall Street Journal,* March 22, 1976, p. 4.

67. Nathan Miller, *The Foundling Finaglers* (New York: David McKay, 1976). In the same vein, see Walter Goodman, *All Honorable Men: Corruption and Compromise in American Life* (Boston: Little, Brown and Co., 1963). See also, Joseph Borkin, *The Corrupt Judge: An Inquiry into Bribery and Other High Crimes and Misdemeanors in the Federal Courts* (New York: Clarkson N. Potter, 1962).

68. A United Press dispatch published in the *Evening Outlook* (Santa Monica, Cal.), December 24, 1975. The Federal Trade Commission has launched an investigation to determine whether kickbacks by aerospace companies had occurred in violation of federal laws prohibiting unfair competition. See the *Los Angeles Times,* August 24, 1976, pt. 3, p. 7.

69. See, for example, John Hutchinson, *The Imperfect Union: A History of Corruption in American Trade Unions* (New York: E. P. Dutton, 1970), pp. 25–61. New York City's multibillion dollar construction industry is said to pay at least $25 million yearly in bribes to city building inspectors, highway officials, policemen, state safety inspectors, agents of the Federal Housing Administration, clerks in various city agencies, and union representatives. *Los Angeles Herald-Examiner,* June 26, 1972, p. A-3 (from the *New York Times News Service*). A two-year investigation by officials of New York City uncovered "a multimillion dollar bribe-taking scheme involving city employees and the contruction industry," according to Mayor Abraham D. Beame; see the *Los Angeles Times,* November 8, 1974, pt. 1, p. 5.

70. These conclusions are supported by two eminent scholars with extensive first-hand experience in observing corruption in business-government relations in developing countries. See Ronald Wraith and Edgar Simpkins, *Corruption in Developing Countries* (New York: W. W. Norton, 1964), pp. 11–52.

Chapter 2: The Emerging Censorship of
Foreign Political Payments

1. U.S., Securities and Exchange Commission, *Report on Questionable and Illegal Corporate Payments and Practices*, Submitted to the Committee on Banking, Housing and Urban Affairs, United States Senate, May 12, 1976, 94th Cong., 2nd sess., p. 2; hereafter, SEC *Report*.

2. SEC *Report*, p. 4.

3. Quoted in Frank Freidel, *Franklin D. Roosevelt: Launching the New Deal* (Boston: Little, Brown and Co., 1973), vol. 4, p. 344.

4. Louis D. Brandeis, *Other People's Money* (New York: Frederick A. Stokes, 1914), p. 92.

5. Freidel, *Franklin D. Roosevelt*.

6. See William O. Douglas, *Go East Young Man* (New York: Random House, 1974), pp. 272. Mr. Justice Douglas served as an SEC commissioner and chairman from 1936 to 1939.

7. At the request of Raymond Moley, a member of the original "brain(s) trust," the initial draft of the securities legislation was prepared by Samuel Untermeyer, a noted New York lawyer who had served as counsel to the celebrated Pujo Committee, which publicized J. P. Morgan and the "money trust," and paved the way for the creation of the Federal Reserve System during the Wilson administration. Unbeknown to Moley or Untermeyer, President Roosevelt had asked his Secretary of Commerce, Daniel Roper, to draft a bill. Roosevelt also enlisted Huston Thompson, a former chairman of the Federal Trade Commission, to help shape the legislation. Untermeyer's version placed reliance on the Post Office Department for policing the securities markets; Huston's on the FTC. Sam Rayburn, then Chairman of the House Interstate Commerce Committee, informed Moley that Thompson's bill was confusing and flawed; "It'll have to be thrown out," he told Moley. "I want you to get me a draftsman who knows this stuff to write a new bill under my direction. And you've got to persuade the Chief that this Thompson bill won't do." Moley telephoned the then Professor Felix Frankfurter for help. He produced three young protégés—James M. Landis (professor of legislation at the Harvard Law School), Thomas Corcoran (who was to become famous as "Tommy the Cork" and chief of the New Deal's legal janissary), and Benjamin V. Cohen (a gentle and wise counsellor). Both Corcoran and Cohen had worked in New York law offices as specialists in corporate reor-

ganization. Their draft was based on the English Companies Act
and became the Securities Act of 1933. See Freidel, *Franklin D.
Roosevelt*, pp. 344–46.

8.   See Mira Wilkens, *The Maturing of Multinational Enterprise: American Business Abroad from 1914 to 1970* (Cambridge: Harvard University Press, 1974).

9.   See the SEC *Report*, pp. 18–19.

10.   SEC Rule 405 (1), 17 C.F.R., Section 230. 45(1) (1975).

11.   A. A. Sommer, Jr., "The Slippery Slope of Materiality," delivered before the Practicing Law Institute, New York, December 8, 1975.

12.   See Walter Guzzardi, Jr., "An Unscandalized View of Those 'Bribes' Abroad," *Fortune*, July 1976, p. 120.

13.   Walter Guzzardi, Jr., *Fortune*, p. 120.

14.   Paul A. Griffin, "Disclosure Policy and the Securities Market: The Impact of the 1975–76 Sensitive Payment Disclosures." Summary of a research report prepared at the request of the SEC Advisory Committee on Corporate Disclosure (Washington, D.C.: November 1976). Reported in the *New York Times*, November 12, 1976.

15.   See *Yale Law Report* 23, no. 1 (Fall 1976): 4–5.

16.   See William Beaver, "What Should be the FASB's Objectives?," the *Journal of Accountancy*, August 1973, pp. 49–55. See also Joseph M. Burns, *Accounting Standards and International Finance with Special Reference to Multinationals* (Washington, D.C.: American Enterprise Institute for Public Policy Research, September 1976), pp. 14–16.

17.   "Although participation in the voluntary program does not insulate a company from Commission enforcement action, it does diminish the possibility that the Commission will, in its discretion, institute an action." SEC *Report*, p. 8, n. 7.

18.   See SEC *Report*, pp. 8–9.

19.   *Wall Street Journal*, May 13, 1976, p. 2.

20.   See discussion of Senator Proxmire's bill, chap. 7.

21.   SEC *Report*, p. 13.

22.   SEC *Report*, p. 29.

23.   SEC *Report*, p. 27.

24.   See Theodore C. Sorenson, "Improper Payments Abroad: Perspectives and Proposals," *Foreign Affairs* 54, no. 4 (July 1976): 723–4, wherein the author provides seven illustrations involving "family connections" in which "a fair-minded investigator or judge would be hard-put to determine whether a particular

payment is a legitimate and permissible business activity or a means of improper influence."

25. SEC *Report,* p. 28.

26. SEC *Report.*

27. SEC *Report,* p. 26.

28. SEC *Report,* p. 27. See chap. 1 for a discussion of the "lubrication" payoff.

29. SEC *Report,* p. 27.

30. See *Wall Street Journal,* July 16, 1976, p. 2, on the part played by a former (now deceased) U.S. ambassador in importuning Aluminum Company of America to make payments to a nonexistent educational foundation, which in reality were intended for Jamaican politicians and their parties—payments that were made against a backdrop of the possible nationalization of U.S. companies' bauxite mining and processing facilities.

31. Ray Garrett, speech before the American Society of Corporate Secretaries, June 27, 1975.

32. Elliot L. Richardson, Secretary of Commerce, letter to Senator William Proxmire, Chairman, Committee on Banking, Housing and Urban Affairs, June 11, 1976, pp. 16–17.

33. Secretary Richardson's remarks were taken as a criticism of the SEC. Chairman Hills countered that Richardson's allegations were "unfounded, inappropriate and ill-timed." Secretary Richardson tendered his apologies. See Louis M. Kohlmeir, "The Bribe Busters," the *New York Times Magazine,* September 26, 1976, p. 58.

34. See Milton V. Freeman, "The Legality of the SEC's Management Fraud Program," the *Business Lawyer,* vol. 31 (March 1976), pp. 1295–1303.

35. Securities Act Release No. 5627, October 14, 1975, p. 46.

36. Securities Act Release No. 5627, October 14, 1975, pp. 45–46, n. 72.

37. Garrett, speech to the American Society of Corporate Secretaries.

38. See the *Los Angeles Times,* July 8, 1976, pt. 3, p. 11.

39. *Los Angeles Times,* July 8, 1976, pt. 3, p. 11.

40. See *Business Week,* October 11, 1976, p. 70.

41. *Business Week,* October 11, 1976, p. 70.

42. See, for example, Chairman Hills' address to a *New York Law Journal* gathering in New York City, June 30, 1976, p. 16, where he stated: "Bribery is not a material factor in the capacity of American business to compete abroad."

43. Hills, address to *New York Law Journal* meeting.

44. See the *Los Angeles Times,* September 14, 1976, pt. 3,

p. 13. A correspondent for the *Los Angeles Times* who attended Chairman Hills' press conference wrote that his proposals were "designed to reassure the business community."

45. *Wall Street Journal,* December 10, 1976. On March 29, 1977, an IRS official testified before the House Subcommittee on Government Operations that: "In a Group of over 800 large case examinations, there have been approximately 280 with indications of slush funds or illegal activity," and that more than 50 were under criminal investigation. The *Los Angeles Times,* March 30, 1977.

A Federal District judge has ruled that the IRS has gone too far in its efforts to investigate corporate bribery, slush funds, and kickbacks. U.S. District Court Judge R. Merhige, ruling on a case involving Fidelity Corporation, an Atlanta insurance holding company, said, "The IRS must limit its investigation of corporate wrongdoing to its effects on tax payments by the corporation." In his decision, Judge Merhige ruled that the eleven questions asked of the former chairman of Fidelity Corporation related to ". . . potentially illegal payments, not deductions made by . . ." Fidelity. "If the corporation had made such illegal payments, but had not utilized such payments to affect its tax liability in any way, such payments would be beyond the scope of the present investigation," the court held. See the *Wall Street Journal,* April 20, 1977, p. 29.

46. See the *Los Angeles Times,* August 24, 1976, pt. 3, p. 7. Rockwell International has challenged the authority of the Federal Trade Commission to investigate overseas payments as a form of unfair competition. See the *Wall Street Journal,* December 24, 1976, p. 5.

47. See, for example, *United States* v. *Imperial Chemical Industries, Limited, et al.,* 100 F. Suppl. 504 (S.D.N.Y., 1951).

48. U.S., Congress, Senate, Committee on Foreign Relations, Subcommittee on Multinational Corporations, *Multinational Corporations and United States Foreign Policy,* Hearings on Political Contributions to Foreign Governments, pt. 12, 94th Cong., 1st sess., June 9–10, 1975.

49. *Multinational Corporations and United States Foreign Policy,* p. 2.

50. *Multinational Corporations and United States Foreign Policy,* p. 2.

51. See Samuel P. Huntington, "The Democratic Distemper," *Public Interest,* no. 41 (Fall 1975): pp. 9–38.

52. That the media *are* generally hostile to the business community has been demonstrated by opinion surveys. The distin-

guished sociologist Seymour Martin Lipset has written: "The impression that the core of the intellectual and the communications world is hostile to the managerial components of society has been sustained by a variety of opinion surveys. These show that among those employed in such work, the more socially critical, the ones who most strongly reject the status quo, are most likely to come from the most successful. . . . The more prestigious the newspaper or broadcast medium, the more socially critical its editors, culture critics and reporters. A survey of the opinions of 500 leaders of American life conducted in 1971–72 found that those in the media—publishers, editors, television executives and columnists—were the most 'anti-establishmentarian' of all groups interviewed." Seymour Martin Lipset, *Commentary*, July 1975, p. 59.

53. See the *Wall Street Journal*, February 28, 1977, p. 1.

Chapter 3: Classes and Cases of Foreign Political Payments

1. John J. McCloy, "Improper Payments and the Responsibility of the Board of Directors," the *Conference Board Record* 13, no. 8 (August 1976): 10 (from remarks made before the Board's conference on Preventing Illegal Corporate Payments at the Waldorf-Astoria on June 10, 1976).

2. *Black's Law Dictionary*, 3rd ed. (St. Paul, Minn.: West, 1968), p. 250.

3. *Black's Law Dictionary*, p. 731.

4. At the date of writing, neither man had been convicted of these charges. Tanaka was indicted, on August 16, 1976, of accepting a bribe from Lockheed and of violating Japan's foreign exchange control laws by receiving the money directly rather than through approved channels. Bernhard was accused of taking a bribe, but denied the charge. An investigating commission of the Dutch Parliament reported, on August 21, 1976, that it had "failed to prove or disprove the allegation." However, the Commission reported that Bernhard had shown himself "open to dishonorable favors and offers" and had "harmed the interests of the state." Bernhard thereupon resigned as Inspector General of The Netherlands armed forces and from all other public offices. The *Los Angeles Times*, August 17, August 21, and August 25, 1976.

5. See *Report of the Special Review Committee of the Board of Directors of Gulf Oil Corporation,* filed as Form 8-K with the Securities and Exchange Commission, Washington, D.C., December 30, 1975; hereafter, *Gulf Oil Report.*

6. Underbilling can also be employed to conceal a questionable payment. The Gardner-Denver Company, a machinery manufacturer, reported that it marketed its products in foreign countries through distributors, who were paid commissions based on the amount of sales. In many countries, local law required that the amount of the commission be shown, either on the invoice to the customer or on a supplier's certificate delivered to the customer. In several countries, at the request of distributors, the company admitted that it had shown on the invoice or supplier's certificate a commission that was *smaller* than the one actually paid. Presumably, this was in connivance with its local distributors to help them escape taxes or exchange controls. The company reported that it had discontinued this obviously improper practice. *Current Report pursuant to Section 13 or 15 (d) of the Securities Exchange Act of 1934 to the Securities and Exchange Commission* for the month of February 1976, by the Gardner-Denver Company, Dallas, Texas.

7. Former U.S. Ambassador Edward M. Korry charged on CBS's *60 Minutes,* January 9, 1977, that U.S. multinational corporations operating in Chile during his ambassadorship had made political payments directly to the late Salvador Allende to stay his seizure of their properties, and that the former president of Chile had demanded $1 million as "protection money" to desist from the expropriation of U.S.-owned assets. Commenting on Ambassador Korry's testimony before the Senate subcommittee on intelligence activities, presided over by Senator Church, the *Wall Street Journal* said in an editorial on January 12, 1977: "Allende and his government were corrupt in the most ordinary, garden-variety sense. They took bribes, and from the same multinational corporations for which they expressed such hatred and contempt."

8. U.S., Congress, Senate, Committee on Foreign Relations, Subcommittee on Multinational Corporations, *The International Telephone and Telegraph Company and Chile, 1970–71,* Report to the Committee by the Subcommittee, June 21, 1973. A popular and hostile account of this episode is given in Anthony Sampson's *The Sovereign State of ITT* (Greenwich, Conn.: Fawcett Publications, 1973), chap. 11.

9. See *In the Matter of the Arbitration between ITT, Sud*

America and the Overseas Private Investment Corporation. Case No. 16 100038 73 (1973).

10. "How United Brands Survived the Banana War," *Fortune,* July 1976, p. 146.

11. *Wall Street Journal,* December 13, 1976.

12. Cited in *Gulf Oil Report,* p. 99.

13. *Gulf Oil Report,* p. 101–03.

14. *Gulf Oil Report,* p. 103.

15. *Wall Street Journal,* February 2, 1976.

16. Italian judicial police claim to have found evidence that some of the payments may have been bribes to politicians in return for specific government favors. However, the police did not file charges, and no proof of bribery was established.

17. Shell's payments averaged $925,000 annually from 1969 to 1973, when its Italian subsidiary, Shell Italiana, was sold to an Italian state entity. British Petroleum's payments to the political parties of the coalition government totaled $1.5 million from 1969 to 1973, when it withdrew from the Italian market after posting large deficits throughout the period. See the *Wall Street Journal,* April 14, 1976.

18. Exxon's auditors descended on the Rome offices of Esso Italiana in 1972. They found that the secret bank accounts had been swollen with funds from political contributions that weren't actually made, kickbacks from engineering consultants for work paid for but never done, and rebates on Esso Italiana overpayments for crude oil. The money in these accounts vanished mysteriously. Cazzaniga was fired. Exxon had to make good the deficit. See *Wall Street Journal,* May 24, 1976, p. 26.

19. See *Report on the Investigation Conducted by the Finance and Audit Committee of the Board of Directors of Castle and Cooke, Inc., with Respect to Payments to Foreign Governments and Officials,* Castle and Cooke, Inc., P. O. Box 2990. Honolulu, H.I., July 28, 1976, p. 4.

20. U.S. Securities and Exchange Commission, *Report on Questionable and Illegal Corporate Payments and Practices,* Submitted to the Committee on Banking, Housing and Urban Affairs, United States Senate, May 12, 1976, 94th Cong., 2d sess., Exhibit A; hereafter SEC *Report.*

21. *Wall Street Journal,* September 12, 1975.

22. *Wall Street Journal,* March 18, 1976.

23. It was reported that TWA paid an agent commissions totalling $20.1 million or 11 percent on the sale to the government of Iran of nine used Boeing 747 "jumbo" jets during 1975. See the *Wall Street Journal,* March 31, 1976.

24. *Wall Street Journal,* September 12, 1975.
25. *Wall Street Journal,* June 15, 1976.
26. *Wall Street Journal,* December 9, 1976.
27. *Wall Street Journal,* December 16, 1976.
28. SEC *Report.*
29. SEC *Report,* p. a.
30. A United Nations study listed 2,468 U.S.-based multi-national companies in 1968–69. See *Multinational Corporations in World Development* (New York: Department of Economic and Social Affairs, United Nations, 1973).
31. SEC *Report,* p. 54.

Chapter 4: The Economics of Political Payments

1. This point is made cogently by Arthur M. Okun in his *Equality and Efficiency: The Big Tradeoff* (Washington, D.C.: The Brookings Institution, 1975).
2. See the *Wall Street Journal,* August 11, 1976.
3. Anthony Downs, "An Economic Theory of Political Action in a Democracy," *Journal of Political Economy* 65, no. 1 (February 1957): 135–50.
4. See Edward C. Banfield, "Corruption as a Feature of Government Organization," the *Journal of Law and Economics* 18, no. 3 (December 1975): 591–605).
5. See the *New York Times,* April 27, 1976.
6. Murray L. Weidenbaum, *A New Approach to Business-Government Relations,* Publication 10, Center for the Study of American Business (St. Louis: Washington University Press, May 1976), p. 2.
7. U.S., Securities and Exchange Commission, *Report on Questionable and Illegal Payments and Practices,* Submitted to the Committee on Banking, Housing and Urban Affairs, United States Senate, May 12, 1976, 94th Cong., 2d sess., p. 1.
8. Economists generally agree that the existence of dishonesty or fraud in a market is socially inefficient in comparison with a world in which the costs of making transactions are lesser because of the absence of corruption. See, for example, Michael R. Darby and Edi Karni, "Free Competition and the Optimal Amount of Fraud," the *Journal of Law and Economics* 16, no. 1 (April 1973): 67–87.

Chapter 5: The Politics of Corruption in Business-Government Relations

1. The authors are greatly indebted to Professor James C. Scott of the University of Wisconsin for the point of view expressed in this chapter. See his *Comparative Political Corruption* (Englewood Cliffs, N.J.: Prentice-Hall, 1972).

2. Scott, *Comparative Political Corruption*, p. 3.

3. See Edward C. Banfield, "Corruption as a Feature of Government Organization," *Journal of Law and Economics* 18, no. 3 (December 1975): 591–605.

4. See, for example, Joseph J. Senturia, "Corruption, Political," *Encyclopedia of the Social Sciences*, vol. 4, p. 499: "Any analysis of its prevalence must therefore regard corruption as a phenomenon of group psychology, conditioned by the entire cultural setting of the group; and no remedial program can be successful if it limits itself atomistically to prosecution of individual offenders or even to administrative reorganization."

5. Gunnar Myrdal, *Asian Drama—An Inquiry into the Poverty of Nations* (New York: Random House, 1968), vol. 2, p. 957.

6. Carl J. Friedrich, *The Pathology of Politics* (New York: Harper & Row, 1972), pp. 134–35.

7. See Nathan Miller, *The Founding Finaglers* (New York: David McKay, 1976), p. 48.

8. Friedrich, *The Pathology of Politics*, p. 135.

9. The UPI wire service reported on August 6, 1976, that Assistant Attorney General Richard Thornburgh of the Criminal Division of the Justice Department told Chicago's Better Government Association that federal prosecutors had won convictions of an estimated 1,000 federal, state, and local officials for corruption in office since 1970. On October 15, 1976, the UPI reported a *Washington Post* story of the same date that a federal grand jury was investigating charges that 22 present and former Congressmen have received cash and gifts from an emissary of the government of South Korea. The report quoted the *Post* as saying this inquiry "involved the most sweeping allegations of congressional corruption ever investigated by the federal government."

10. See Scott, *Comparative Political Corruption*, p. 10; and Marcel Mauss, *The Gift: Forms and Functions of Exchange in Archaic Societies* (New York: The Free Press, 1954). See, also, Melville J. Herskovits, *The Economic Life of Primitive People* (New York: Alfred A. Knopf, 1940), pp. 138–54.

11.   Louis Kraar, "Japan is Opening up for *Gaijin* Who Know How," *Fortune*, March 1974, pp. 148–49.

12.   Scott, *Comparative Political Corruption*, p. 11.

13.   Miller, *The Founding Finaglers*, p. 4. Richard Ollard in his *Pepys: A Biography* (New York: Holt, Rinehart & Winston, 1974) describes the prevalence of the "sale of places," as it was called, and the handsome gifts and sums received by officials of seventeenth-century Restoration England for each appointment they made. Pepys, in conformity with the custom of the time, was not above using his official post to line his pockets. See, especially, pp. 120–21.

14.   Scott, p. 35.

15.   See the *Los Angeles Times*, October 9, 1976, pt. 1, p. 20.

16.   Levi A. Nwachuku, "Nigeria's Uncertain Future," *Current History* 71, no. 421 (November 1976): 165.

17.   Nwachuku, "Nigeria's Uncertain Future."

18.   *Wall Street Journal*, November 9, 1976, p. 24.

19.   Edwin Lieuwin, *Arms and Politics in Latin America* (New York: Frederick A. Praeger, 1960), pp. 149–50.

20.   See the *Los Angeles Times*, October 17, 1976, p. 1. Sra. Perón claimed that a government ministry check for 700,000 pesos bearing her signature had "mistakenly" been deposited to her account. She also allegedly misappropriated one billion pesos that had been raised for flood victims. Although the Argentine Congress subsequently dropped the charges against the former president, it was widely believed that she was guilty of transferring over half a million dollars from public charity funds to her personal account. The Peronist tolerance of corruption, which penetrated every class of society in addition to the highest echelons of government, was unacceptable to the Argentine armed forces and contributed to the coup which deposed Sra. Perón. See David C. Jordon, "Argentina's Military Government," *Current History* 72, no. 424 (February 1977): 59.

21.   See Garth Alexander, *The Invisible Chinese: The Overseas Chinese and the Politics of Southeast Asia* (New York: Macmillan, 1973), p. 61.

22.   U.S., Securities and Exchange Commission, *Report on Questionable and Illegal Payments and Practices*, Submitted to the Committee on Banking, Housing and Urban Affairs, United States Senate, May 12, 1976, 94th Cong., 2d sess., Exhibit A.

23.   Of the eleven reporting companies, Exxon Corporation's total contributions of $46,031,000 constituted 97.6 percent of the total. If Standard Oil Company of Indiana's contributions are added to those of Exxon's these two oil companies accounted for

97.7 percent of the total contributed by the eleven reporting companies. Oil companies and pharmaceutical companies appear to be the most important contributors to foreign political parties and candidates. Both industries are closely regulated.

24. U.S., Congress, Senate, Committee on Foreign Relations, Subcommittee on Multinational Corporations, *Multinational Corporations and United States Foreign Policy*, Hearings on Political Contributions to Foreign Governments, pt. 12, 94th Cong., 1st sess., May 16, 1975, p. 35.

25. *Wall Street Journal*, February 27, 1976, p. 8.

26. See A. Carl Kotchian, *Lockheed Sales Mission: Seventy Days in Tokyo*, unpublished English manuscript. Published in Japanese by *Asahi Shimbun*, Tokyo, Japan, 1976.

27. See the *Los Angeles Times*, September 29, 1976, pt. 1, p. 2.

28. For a discussion of the effect of the Lockheed payments in Japanese politics, see Hans H. Baerwald, "Lockheed and Japanese Politics," *Asian Survey* 16, no. 9 (September 1976): 817–29.

29. *Wall Street Journal*, December 28, 1976, p. 5.

30. *Wall Street Journal*, December 8, 1976, p. 24. That the so-called "Lockheed scandal" was only a partial factor in the poor showing of the ruling party is also confirmed by the Toyko bureau of the *Los Angeles Times*, December 12, 1976, pt. 8, p. 1. Writing in the *Los Angeles Times*, January 16, 1977, pt. 5, p. 2, Edwin Reischauer, former U.S. Ambassador to Japan and Asian scholar, said: "The eventual loss of the Liberal Democratic majority has long been predictable, because the vote for the party has been declining during the whole period by a steady 1% per year as the population moved to areas—the cities—and into organizations—such as labor unions—where it was more likely to vote for the opposition parties than the conservatives."

31. *Wall Street Journal*, December 7, 1976, p. 1.

32. *Los Angeles Herald-Examiner*, December 18, 1976, A-4.

33. *Wall Street Journal*, December 24, 1976, p. 18.

34. See *Multinational Corporations and United States Foreign Policy*, pt. 12, p. 316.

35. See *Multinational Corporation and United States Foreign Policy*, pt. 12, p. 251.

36. See Norman Kogan, *The Government of Italy* (New York: Thomas Y. Crowell, 1962), p. 66.

37. See Michael Ledeen and Claire Sterling, "Italy's Russian Sugar Daddies," *The New Republic*, April 3, 1976, pp. 16–21.

38.　See *Multinational Corporations and United States Foreign Policy*, pt. 12, p. 318 ff.

39.　See, for example, Theodore C. Sorenson, "Improper Payments Abroad: Perspectives and Proposals," *Foreign Affairs* 54, no. 4 (July 1976); 719–33. As legal counsel to President Kennedy with the vantage point of the White House, Mr. Sorenson may be expected to know whereof he speaks.

40.　See *Multinational Corporations and United States Foreign Policy*, pt. 12, p. 265.

Chapter 6: Ethical Perspectives on Foreign Political Payments

1.　One highly placed officer of a multinational corporation told one of the authors that he had resigned his position abroad and returned to the United States to avoid the moral strains placed on him by the demands for political payoffs.

2.　John J. McCloy, "Improper Payments and the Responsibility of the Board of Directors," the *Conference Board Record* 13, no. 8 (August 1976): 9 (from remarks made before the Conference Board meeting on Preventing Illegal Corporate Payments at the Waldorf-Astoria on June 10, 1976).

3.　*Black's Law Dictionary*, 3rd ed. (St. Paul, Minn: West Publishing Company), p. 250.

4.　Here it should be noted that there are certain countries, particularly those in the Arabian peninsula, which operate not on the basis of written, but rather customary, law. This law, in turn, is based on the Koran and it is obvious that any seventh-century document is bound to become somewhat incoherent when applied to modern forms of skulduggery that have been invented in the interval. As it turns out, the Koran does have prohibitions against the bribing of officials to participate in acts of oppression or injustice. Interestingly, gifts to officials and judges are permitted, and there is a fine line to be drawn for Moslems between what is a gift and what is intended to sway judgment as a bribe. Insofar as this affects our interests here, the important consideration is that the Koran does not seem to place any limitation on the way Moslems can treat nonbelievers. Hence, from a religious and legal point of view, Moslems, especially Moslem defense ministers and oil sheiks, are not prohibited from extorting as much as they can from the officers of foreign multinational corporations. It is said that, since the ruling family of Saudi Arabia is conservative and religious, if such a restriction were to be found in the Koran, they would enforce it—but none is to be found, so they do not.

5.   Edward C. Banfield, "Corruption as a Feature of Governmental Organization," *Journal of Law and Economics* 18, no. 3 (December 1975): 591–605.

6.   SEC *Report,* p. 42–3.

7.   *Wall Street Journal,* February 28, 1977, p. 1.

Chapter 7: A Critique of Reform Proposals

1.   Gaylord Freeman, "A Code of Conduct for Transnational Corporations," Comments before the Chicago World Trade Conference, Chicago, Ill., April 22, 1976.

2.   James R. Basche, Jr., *Unusual Foreign Payments: A Survey of the Policies and Practices of U.S. Companies* (New York: The Conference Board, 1976).

3.   *Executive Attitudes Toward Morality in Business* (Princeton, N.J.: Caravan Surveys, Opinion Research Corporation, July 1975).

4.   Leonard Silk, the *New York Times,* October 26, 1976, p. 41.

5.   Robert S. Ingersoll, Statement before the Subcommittee on Priorities and Economy in Government of the Joint Economic Committee, U.S. Congress, March 5, 1976.

6.   *Business Week,* May 17, 1976, p. 162.

7.   U.S., Securities and Exchange Commission, *Report on Questionable and Illegal Payments and Practices,* Submitted to the Committee on Banking, Housing and Urban Affairs, United States Senate, May 12, 1976, 94th Cong., 2d sess., p. 60. Hereafter, SEC *Report.*

8.   *Wall Street Journal,* May 19, 1976, p. 5.

9.   *Wall Street Journal,* June 23, 1976, p. 2.

10.   *Wall Street Journal,* May 19, 1976, p. 5. S. 305, approved by the U.S. Senate on May 5, 1977, contains substantially the same criminal provisions as S. 3664.

11.   *Wall Street Journal,* June 23, 1976, p. 2. For a listing of the 100 largest, privately owned corporations, see *Forbes,* November 1, 1976, p. 38.

12.   For a statement of critical objections to this proposal, see Statement of William F. Kennedy, Esq., Co-Chairman, Special

Committee on Foreign Payments, Association of the Bar of the City of New York, before the Subcommittee on Consumer Protection and Finance of the Committee on Interstate and Foreign Commerce, House of Representatives, September 22, 1976.

13. Kennedy, statement cited.

14. Letter from the Secretary of Commerce to the Honorable William Proxmire, Chairman, Committee on Banking, Housing and Urban Affairs, June 11, 1976.

15. SEC *Report*, pp. 61–62.

16. Kennedy, statement cited.

17. Senator Proxmire apparently acknowledged this defect in his proposed legislation. See *Los Angeles Times*, June 23, 1976, pt. 3, p. 11. He also conceded that the proposed law would not permit prosecution of a foreign national who, as an employee of an overseas U.S. subsidiary, was "acting entirely on his own initiative" in the payment of a bribe to a foreign official. See *Corrupt Overseas Payments by U.S. Business Enterprises*, 94th Cong., 2d sess., Report No. 94-1031 (to accompany S. 3664), p. 7.

18. Kennedy, statement cited.

19. For a discussion of the cases, see Peter Nehemkis, "Supranational Control of the International Corporation: A Dissenting View," *California Western Law Review* 10, no. 2: 291–92.

20. See the *Wall Street Journal*, December 26, 1974, p. 5, and the *Los Angeles Times*, December 25, 1974, pt. 1, p. 24.

21. Release of the White House Press Secretary, Washington, D.C., August 3, 1976.

22. *Los Angeles Times*, June 15, 1976, p. 2. President-elect Carter likewise regarded the Ford Administration's proposals as too lenient, calling them "permissive criminality." See *Wall Street Journal*, August 10, 1976, p. 5.

23. Robert S. Ingersoll, Statement before the Subcommittee on Priorities and Economy in Government of the Joint Economic Committee, U.S. Congress, March 5, 1976.

24. See Secretary Richardson's letter of June 11, 1976, to Senator Proxmire, cited above.

25. See Paul H. Boeker, Deputy Assistant Secretary of State for Economic and Business Affairs, "A Code for Multinationals," *Wall Street Journal*, May 28, 1976.

26. *Forbes*, August 1, 1976, p. 49.

27. Peter Drucker, *Management: Tasks, Responsibilities, Practices* (New York: Harper & Row, 1974), p. 360.

28. *Los Angeles Times*, September 26, 1976.

29. In conformity with the declared intention of the Ford Administration to enlist other international bodies to take action

on overseas political payments, U.S. Ambassador Frederick Dent —the U.S. negotiator—requested the General Agreement on Tariffs and Trade (GATT) to consider U.S. Senate Resolution 265, which calls for the American representative in the international trade negotiations to seek a multilateral agreement to curb "bribery, indirect payments, kickbacks, unethical political contributions and other such similar disreputable activities." However, the misgivings expressed by Richardson and Kissinger on obtaining an international treaty would appear to apply equally to this forum.

Chapter 8: Some Proposals for Action

1.   One of the authors has proposed that American corporation laws should *require* publicly owned corporations to have a majority of outside directors; they should also require committees on nominations, audit, and public affairs to have a majority of members who are not employees. See Neil H. Jacoby, *Corporate Power and Social Responsibility* (New York: Macmillan, 1973), pp. 179–80.

2.   See *Statements on Auditing Standards, Nos. 16 and 17* (New York: Auditing Standards Executive Committee of the American Institute of Certified Public Accountants, January 1977).

3.   Commercial Arbitration Tribunal in the matter of ITT and OPIC, Case Number 16100038 73. Citing the U.S. Supreme Court decision in *Banco Nacional de Cuba* v. *Sabbatino*, 367 U.S. 398,431.

4.   See the *Wall Street Journal*, March 1, 1977, p. 2.

5.   U.S., Congress, Senate, Committee on Foreign Relations, Subcommittee on Multinational Corporations, transcript (unpublished) of Hearings, Tuesday, May 4, 1976, pp. 11–14.

6.   See Neil H. Jacoby, "A Code of Direct International Investment," the *Center Magazine*, vol. 9, no. 2 (March–April, 1976).

7.   This point is forcefully made by Nathan Miller in *The Founding Finaglers* (New York: David McKay, 1976).

8.   Address at California State College at Northridge, September 9, 1976. See the *Los Angeles Times*, September 10, 1976.

Index

Index

Export-Import Bank, 84
expropriation, 102
  of ITT's Chilean property,
    103
extortion, xvii, xviii, 63, 69, 77,
    100, 112, 113, 142,
    185–86, 213, 229, 241,
    245; *see also* political
    payments
  defined, 90
  distinguished from bribery,
    90–92
  economic effects of, 183–84
  Filipino, 23–24
  meaning of, 175–77
  petty, entrenched, 191
  psychology of, 177–78
Exxon, 51, 54, 56, 75, 95, 119,
    120, 155, 161, 271
  Italian affiliate of, 165–67
  in Italy, 108–10
  support of Italian parties by,
    165–69

F

Fanon, Frantz, quoted on
    conditions in Kenya, 11
Federal Communications
    Commission, 129
Federal Power Commission, 129
Federal Trade Commission
    (FTC), 45, 49, 73, 76,
    129
Fiat, 165, 166
Finance Committee to Re-elect
    the President, xiv, xv
Firestone Tire & Rubber, 27
First Amendment, 78
Ford Administration, disclosure
    proposals of, 220–22
Ford Motor, 219

Foreign Military Sales (FMS),
    85
Foreign Payments Disclosure
    Act, proposed, 220–22
Foreign Relations Committee,
    212
Foremost-McKesson, 65
Form 8-K, 48, 59
Form 10-K, 48
Fortune, 114
  quoted on United Brands
    case, 105
Fowler, William, 34–35
France, 34–35, 160
Fraud and False Statements
    Act, Section 1001
  quoted, 83–84
Freeman, Gaylord, quoted, 208
Freeman, Milton V., 64
Friedrich, Carl J., quoted, 148
Fukuda, Takeo, 165
Fukunago, Kazuomi, 163
functionaries, 4–6, 232
  "grease" to, 93–94, 189–92

G

Garrett, Ray, quoted, 63, 64
General Motors, 26, 219
General Refractories, 41
General Telephone and
    Electronics, 20, 21,
    120, 257
General Tire & Rubber, 73, 120
gift-giving, 149–50
  of property and services,
    97–98
Gillespie, Alistair, 220
Godber, Peter Fitzroy, 18, 258
Goodrich, B. F., 120
Goodsell, Charles, cited, 25
Goodyear Tire & Rubber, 73,
    120

STUDIES OF THE MODERN CORPORATION
Graduate School of Business, Columbia University

The Program for Studies of the Modern Corporation is devoted to the advancement and dissemination of knowledge about the corporation. Its publications are designed to stimulate inquiry, research, criticism, and reflection. They fall into three categories: works by outstanding businessmen, scholars, and professional men from a variety of backgrounds and academic disciplines; annotated and edited selections of business literature; and business classics that merit republication. The studies are supported by outside grants from private business, professional, and philanthropic institutions interested in the program's objectives.

PUBLICATIONS

FRANCIS JOSEPH AGUILAR
  Scanning the Business Environment

MELVIN ANSHEN, *editor*
  Managing the Socially Responsible Corporation

HERMAN W. BEVIS
  Corporate Financial Reporting in a Competitive Economy

COURTNEY C. BROWN
  Putting the Corporate Board to Work

COURTNEY C. BROWN, *editor*
  World Business: Promise and Problems

CHARLES DE HOGHTON, *editor*
  The Company: Law, Structure, and Reform

RICHARD EELLS
  The Corpoation and the Arts

RICHARD EELLS and CLARENCE WALTON, *editors*
  Man in the City of the Future

JAMES C. EMERY
  Organizational Planning and Control Systems:
  Theory and Technology

ALBERT S. GLICKMAN, CLIFFORD P. HAHN, EDWIN A. FLEISHMAN, and BRENT BAXTER
Top Management Development and Succession: An Exploratory Study

NEIL H. JACOBY, PETER NEHEMKIS, and RICHARD EELLS
Bribery and Extortion in World Business: A Study of Corporate Political Payments Abroad

NEIL H. JACOBY
Corporate Power and Social Responsibility

NEIL H. JACOBY
Multinational Oil: A Study in Industrial Dynamics

JAY W. LORSCH
Product Innovation and Organization

KENNETH G. PATRICK
Perpetual Jeopardy—The Texas Gulf Sulphur Affair: A Chronicle of Achievement and Misadventure

KENNETH G. PATRICK and RICHARD EELLS
Education and the Business Dollar

IRVING PFEFFER, *editor*
The Financing of Small Business: A Current Assessment

STANLEY SALMEN
Duties of Administrators in Higher Education

GEORGE A. STEINER
Top Management Planning

GEORGE A. STEINER and WARREN M. CANNON, *editors*
Multinational Corporate Planning

GEORGE A. STEINER and WILLIAM G. RYAN
Industrial Project Management

GUS TYLER
The Political Imperative: The Corporate Character of Unions

CLARENCE WALTON and RICHARD EELLS, *editors*
The Business System: Readings in Ideas and Concepts

About the Authors

NEIL H. JACOBY, Professor of Business Economics at the Graduate School of Management of UCLA, of which he was the founding dean, has combined the careers of scholar, administrator, and corporate director. Born in Canada, he holds the Ph.D. in economics from the University of Chicago, where he was later Professor of Finance and Vice President. He served on the President's Council of Economic Advisers between 1953 and 1955, and was U.S. Representative to the U.N. Economic and Social Council in 1957. He has been president of the American Finance Association and is a director of one of the largest multinational corporations. Author or co-author of more than fifteen books, including *Corporate Power and Social Responsibility* and *Multinational Oil*, he is an Associate of the Center for the Study of Democratic Institutions.

PETER NEHEMKIS, a member of the faculty of the UCLA Graduate School of Management, has had a career that has included government service, the practice of law, and business management. A graduate of the Yale Law School, he was an early staff member of the Securities and Exchange Commission. In 1960 he was a member of a study group that prepared for President-elect John F. Kennedy a report entitled "Alliance for Progress." A founding trustee of the Pan American Development Foundation, he is the author of *Latin America: Myth and Reality*. Author of numerous legal and business articles, he has lectured at the Foreign Service Institute, George Washington and American Universities, and has been a consultant to the Departments of State and Commerce, several foreign governments, and a number of U.S. companies.

RICHARD EELLS, Director of the Program for Studies of the Modern Corporation and Adjunct Professor of Business at the Graduate School of Business of Columbia University, has combined an interest in many business policy issues with an involvement in philanthropic and not-for-profit organizations. In 1949 and 1950, he held the Guggenheim Chair of Aeronautics at the Library of Congress, and, later, was Manager of Public Policy Research for the General Electric Company. He has received various scholarly awards, including research grants from the Alfred P. Sloan Foundation and the Rockefeller Foundation. He travels widely and lectures frequently in the United States and abroad; he is the author or co-author of ten books, including *Conceptual Foundations of Business*, *The Corporation and the Arts*, and *Global Corporations*.